create™

Annual Editions: Adolescent Psychology, 10/e
Claire N. Rubman

http://create.mheducation.com

ISBN-10: 1259929922   ISBN-13: 9781259929922

Contents

Detailed Table of Contents

New Foundations of Adolescent Learning, Laurence Steinberg, *Independent Schools*, 2015
Steinberg describes three phases of brain development during adolescence that combine our self-regulatory skills with our emotional control. This, he reports, transforms us from children. Looking more closely at our emotional development, Steinberg addresses issues such as why adolescents care so much about their peers' opinions, why they engage in such risky behavior, and why they are such sensation seekers. Read more about the emotional "highs" and "lows" of adolescence.

Unit 3: The Self

The Obesity Challenge, Kinga Adamaszwili, *IDM International Dairy Magazine*, 2016
There are more than 641 million people globally who are classified as obese. To what extent do food manufacturers bear any responsibility for our eating habits and subsequent weight gain? To what extent are we personally responsible for what we consume? Read about how weight impacts this and future generations of adolescents.

Anorexia Nervosa and the Adolescent Self, Wendy Jones, *Healthcare Counseling and Psychotherapy Journal*, 2016
Oftentimes, we do not know that we have a distorted "sense of self." Read about one example of this is where adolescents suffer from psychiatric illness that causes them to see their body in a distorted light. This can lead to extreme dieting, purging, and laxative use. Read about potential ways to help those with this distorted sense of self, for example, those with a pathological fear of gaining weight.

Separation and Stuckness, Jim Pye, *Therapy Today*, 2015
An important milestone in the development of an adolescent is "letting go." Read about the trials and tribulations of separation in the quest for self-identity through the fictitious lives of Steven and Eveline and their separation issues.

The Young and the Riskless, Kayt Sukel, *Discover*, 2016
Read about Johnathon, a "good kid," and his brush with adolescent risk taking and poor decision-making. He, like most adolescents, admits that he knows better than to engage in unprotected sex, drug use, skipping school, and getting into fights, so why does he?

Unit 4: Parenting and Educational Issues

How Helicopter Parents Cause Binge Drinking, Caitlin Flanagan, *Atlantic*, 2016
Would you describe your parents as "Get Real" parents or "Good" parents? Learn about these distinctions as defined by Caitlin Flanagan and learn about the long term consequences of trying to "over parent." Learn how "hovering" parents can lead to binge drinking.

Why Cool Parenting Doesn't Help, Marybeth Hicks, *Catholic Digest*, 2016
What is a "cool parent"? What type of parent(s) do you have? Do you wish yours were cooler? Read on to discover why the research suggests that "cool" is not ideal for parents. Think of your parents as your role models, your disciplinarians and your guides rather than your buddies. Read about the benefits of solid parenting practices.

Parenting Versus Teens' Digital Privacy, Marybeth Hicks, *Catholic Digest*, 2016
In this digital age, how do we allow our adolescents to use the Internet, monitor their usage, and yet respect their privacy? How do we keep our teens safe in virtual space?

First Do No Harm, Susan C. Roberts, *Independent School*, 2015
Read about the impact of stress on the developing brain. Think about grades and test scores and the anxiety that they cause. Think about how that success or failure translates into approval and love in an adolescent's mind. Follow Robert's plan to destress including acknowledging the stress, modifying expectations and removing judgment.

Unit 5: Sexuality

Teenagers in Love, Susan Moore, *Psychologist*, 2016
Read about the sexual desires of adolescents whose brains are maturing unevenly—emotional maturity, and impulse control sometimes lags behind physical development and puberty. What happens in the "dating world" when an adolescent's slow developing executive functioning allows for poor decision-making and risk-taking behavior? What happens when this is

compounded by an environment that is rife with online dating apps, sexting, and a plethora of other social media? How has the dating world changed for adolescents today?

It's Complicated, Stephen Gray Wallace, *Camping Magazine*, 2015
American teenagers are 15 times more likely to become pregnant than their Swiss counterparts. Since they are all adolescents, this begs the question; what is going on in American culture that is so different from Swiss or other cultures where teens are less likely to become pregnant?

A Second Puberty, Jessica Firger, *Newsweek Global*, 2016
Read about Jordan, one of the 700,000 transgender adolescents in our community. Read about the issues and concerns surrounding transgender students. When, for example, should adolescents like Jordan use hormones or surgery to reassign their gender?

Study: Heavy Viewers of "Teen Mom" and "16 and Pregnant" Have Unrealistic Views of Teen Pregnancy, Indiana University Communications Department, Indiana University Bloomington Newsroom, 2014
What do our teens "see" when they watch reality TV? Studies used to suggest that it put teens off motherhood and reduced the number of teen pregnancies but new research suggests otherwise. Does reality TV actually give adolescents a more realistic or a less realistic view of life? Read about the impact of shows based on pregnancy and teenage mothers on 14 to 18 year-old viewers. Read about how perceptions of teen pregnancy shows have changed.

Unit 6: The Context of Adolescence in Society

Training Teens to Drive, Garry Embree and Kimberly Embree, *Old Schoolhouse*, 2016
How do teenagers learn to drive? Two parents give tips on helping your adolescent through the process. They suggest that good driving lessons can begin much earlier in childhood, touting the benefits of Bandura's "Social Learning Theory" where parents serve as role models. They suggest that teens learn from their parents when they demonstrate good driving habits such as waiting patiently at stop signs or keeping the cell phone turned off while driving. Embree and Embree remind us that we can develop our pre drivers observational skills such as navigation from home to popular destinations.

Is It Fair to Pay Teens Less Than Adults? Bob Battles and Marilyn Watkins, *New York Times Upfront*, 2016
Is there a lack of jobs for teens? If they do have a job, are they paid a fair wage? Do teens earn the same as adults who engage in the same job? Would lowering teen pay address some of the issues associated with teen unemployment? Read about the staggering drop in teen employment since 2000. Learn about some of the issues surrounding adolescent jobs, for example, teens can't always find employment so lowering pay might create more opportunities in the work place. However, some teens have to find work to support their family or to pay their way through college, so lowering their pay might seriously impact their lives. Teen spending contributes $250 billion per year to the U.S. economy—how would that be impacted by teen unemployment or lower wages?

The Benefits and Limitations of Social Networking, Paris Strom and Robert Strom, *Education Digest*, 2012
Twenty percent of our teens text more than 120 messages per day. Read about the demographic that is most likely to text excessively and the behaviors that are associated with this including smoking, binge drinking, substance abuse, physical fighting, and multiple sexual partners.

Peggy Sue Got Sexted, Nina Burleigh, *Newsweek*, 2016
How do you "Grow up female online"? Read about what teenage girls are concerned about. Nancy Jo Sales interviewed over 200 teenage girls. She listed to their concerns about many issues including social networking. One pervasive concern was the over sexualization of women including provocative photos, "slut shaming," online porn, cyberbullying, and "slut pages."

Unit 7: Behaviors and Challenges Associated with Adolescence

#NODARETOOSTUPID, Jessica Firger, *Newsweek Global*, 2016
What should we blame when adolescents act in crazy ways? Is it the Internet's fault? Can we blame their hormones, specifically dopamine? What prompts a teen to participate in viral crazes such as setting themselves on fire? What drives them to attempt dangerous feats such as #EraserChallenge or #CinnamonChallenge? Dr. Jay Giedd attempts to explain why the developing adolescent brain is so susceptible to Internet dares and challenges.

Pharming: Pill Parties Can be Deadly for Teens, Susan Solecki and Renee Turchi, *Contemporary Pediatrics*, 2014
In a country that has seen prescription drug use quadruple between 1999 and 2010, it is no surprise that teens are finding easier access to pills. Around 14 percent of high schoolers have used these drugs for nonprescription uses such as "pill parties" or cramming for exams. Read more about the dangers of playing "pill roulette" and what can be done to address this growing epidemic.

What are They Looking For? Catherine Jackson, *Therapy Today*, 2015
Who is most likely to become radicalized – the rich or the poor, the old or the young? Read about surprising climates and cultures that are potential breeding grounds for radicalization. Learn more about the social, emotional and psychological motivators that might drive a person to such radical thoughts and behaviors.

How Prison Stints Replaced Study Hall, Jody Owens, *Politico*, 2015
Does a super predator lurk in our school hallways? Are our youth prone to such terrible transgressions in our schools that they belong in prison? Read about the criminalization of our children and the devastating effects that it can have on their future. Learn about school resource officers, the "taxi service" and the delinquency that has spurred these punitive policies in our schools.

Unit 8: Psychological Well-being

Getting Unstuck, David Flack, *Counselling Today*, 2016
Flack suggests five strategies to help adolescents with addiction and other disorders. He focuses on helping adolescents to overcome the rigidity in their thinking. This, in turn, allows teens to become "unstuck" and begin the process of moving forward. Read about the approach that Flack employs including, slowing down, identifying motivators, anticipating ambivalence, and creating "correctedness."

Problematic Technology Use During Adolescence: Why Don't Teenagers Seek Treatment? Mark D. Griffiths, *Education and Health*, 2015
Some teenagers struggle with addiction. One form of addiction in our society is "technological addiction." This is the overuse of phones, video games, social networking, or other technologies. It is classified as an addiction when usage negatively impacts other domains of an adolescent's life including relationships and education. Griffith suggests that a technological addiction may be a symptom of an underlying problem such as a dysfunctional relationship or depression. If so, treating the underlying problem may cure this symptom. Or is there really no such thing as a technological addiction? Is it possible that researchers may have overinflated concerns about this "non-issue"? Griffith explores the idea that even if it does exist, adolescents don't seek help because it may be short lived or resolve itself.

Can't Turn Off the Night, Roni Jacobson, *Newsweek*, 2014
Are nightmares indicative of a deeper underlying problem? Is it possible that nightmares and psychosis might be connected? Could it be that there is a third link, that stress in an adolescent's life could trigger nightmares and psychotic experiences? Read about the effects of violence, sexual abuse, and bullying on nightmares and psychotic diagnoses.

Self-injury: Why Teens Do It and How to Help, Claire M. Brickell and Michael S. Jellinek, *Contemporary Pediatrics*, 2014
One in six adolescents has engaged in self-harm at least once. This self-injurious behavior is usually mild but in 5 percent of adolescents it is serious. Referred to as "non-suicidal self-injury" (NOSI), adolescents engage in self-injury to ease either intolerable emotions or a lack of emotional response. It is not viewed as an attention seeking behavior, but it can inadvertently shape parental behaviors as they feel manipulated by their child. The pediatrician is often the first to notice the tell-tale signs from self-harming.

Unit 9: Emerging Adulthood

Learning to be Together Alone, Nick Luxmoore, *Therapy Today*, 2014
Learning to cope with being alone is an essential part of "emerging adulthood." As adolescents leave the security of their family home, they have to learn to feel comfortable with themselves. Read about this developing skill that adolescents sometimes experience trouble mastering. Read from the perspective of a counselor and a psychotherapist.

Bumped Off, Natasha Vianna, *Kids These Days*, 2016
Perhaps teen mothers are "irresponsible and undeserving of respect" or perhaps that is how society portrays them and treats them. Read about the struggle to attain adult values and respect from the perspective of a teenage mother.

Preface

Is an adolescent just a teenager? Why do they care so much about what their friends think? Why do they constantly seek out greater and greater thrills and engage in dangerous behaviors?

Through this collection of articles, we will tease apart this unique period of development that is significantly different from childhood and yet quite unlike adulthood. We will discuss this time of enormous cognitive, social, and emotional growth that can be so deeply affected by insecurity or self-doubt.

Some of the topics that we will discuss in this collection of articles include why teens today are referred to as the "Ritalin generation," why they respond to viral dares such as the "#firespraychallenge" or why adolescents cut or engage in self-harm. Socially, we will debate issues such as social networking, "skittle" or pill parties and sexting. From an emotional perspective, we will discuss topic that include transgender adolescents, pregnant teens, and radicalization.

We will ask difficult questions such as:

- How young is too young for gender reassignment surgery?
- How do you teach adolescents about the dangers of pharming or robo-tripping?
- Do phthalates interfere with puberty?
- Would you know if your teenager is contemplating suicide or self-harming?
- Which personality type is more susceptible to radicalization propaganda and recruitment?
- What are "emerging adults" and are they lazy, over indulged and narcissistic?

We will look at the neural development that occurs in the adolescent brain and assess how this contributes to the social and emotional development of our adolescent. Read about what Perkins-Gough (2015) did to her two adolescent sons as she tried to figure out why one was preoccupied with his physical appearance while the other was engaged in poor decision-making and risky behavior! Read her research findings about a "slow to develop" limbic system and her conclusions about how it accounts for a lack of emotional stability in adolescence and an increase in teenage sex drive. Follow her arguments as she lashes out at the Internet for negatively impacting development by contributing to an adolescent's social isolation and by contributing to our "hypercompetitive culture."

Many of these adolescent issues are exacerbated the "sleep debt," according to Amos and D'Andrea (2012) in their article "Waking Up to the Unique Sleep Needs of Adolescents." We will explore what happens to the adolescent sleep cycle—why adolescents can't seem to go to bed and certainly experience difficulty waking up in the morning!

Read more about the pervasive problems associated with sleep, or a lack thereof, in Richter's article titled "Go to Bed" (2015). Richter suggests that that adolescent sleep deprivation or "social jet lag" has reached epidemic proportions, negatively impacting weight, learning, driving, mental health, and risk taking behavior.

In an attempt to nurture adolescent development, Steinberg (2015) focuses on the developing adolescent brain. Learn about the interplay between newly developing regions in the brain and how this can lessen the impact of peer pressure, sensation seeking, and risky behavior.

The adolescent preoccupation with "the self" is explored in Unit 3 as we discuss obesity, eating disorders, and body image. Read about the impact of social media on adolescent self-esteem. Adamaszwili (2016), Jones (2016), and Stanley (2016) tackle these issues through the lens of a developing adolescent brain that perceives the world differently than either adults or children.

Given the complexity of the developing adolescent brain, we turn our attention to parenting—how should you parent an adolescent? Some parents try to befriend their teens while others obsessively overparent or "helicopter" their every move. Learn from Flanagan (2016) and Hicks (2016) why neither approach leads to successful outcomes. Perhaps it is the complex issues that adolescents face that complicates the parent–child relationship even more. How do parents of adolescents talk with their children about teenage pregnancy, first loves, homosexuality, or gender reassignment?

While parents grapple with these issues, they also have to contend with their child's developing sense of autonomy in other domains such as learning to drive or working part-time. The same adolescent that can now legally work and drive may also be grappling with other behavioral issues such as prescription medication abuse or internet dares such as "#CinnamonChallenge." How do parents keep their adolescents safe while simultaneously allowing them to grow up? This is the great contradiction of adolescence. Teens who perceive that eating an entire teaspoon of cinnamon or ingesting a handful of unknown, random pills are the same adolescents that are sharing our roads and trolling the internet. Read about their reckless behavior in "#No Dare Too Stupid" by Jessica Firger (2016) or in "Pharming: Pill Parties can be deadly for teens" by Solecki & Turichi (2014). What are these teenagers thinking? Are they thinking? Compare their behavior and thought processes as Miller (2015) and Steinberg (2015) explain how the adolescent brain learns and grows. Learn about the development of the prefrontal cortex and the amygdala, learn about the executive functioning of the brain, and learn to think as an adolescent thinks.

As this erratic behavior and inconsistent thinking that is the hallmark of the adolescent paradox continues, how do we maintain our teenagers' psychological well-being? How do we help them to reduce their dependency on drugs or alcohol for cheap sensation-seeking thrills? Read about the psychology behind self-harm (Jellinek, 2014) or the potential for cognitive growth and change as adolescents mature (Sanders, 2015).

Our final unit in this collection of readings takes our adolescents to the brink of adulthood or "emerging adulthood." Read about how to motivate our adolescents as they leave home or seek out their first full-time job (Arnett, 2015). Read about the trial and tribulations of learning to live alone, away from their family home in Luxmoore's "Learning to be Together Alone." Read about the thrill of independence that is tempered by the realities of adult life.

Claire N. Rubman
Suffolk County Community College

Editor of This Volume

Dr. Rubman is a cognitive, developmental psychologist. She has numerous publications and radio interviews to her credit. She is frequently requested to present guest lectures, keynote addresses, and workshop presentation both within the United States and internationally.

Uniquely qualified to talk and write about adolescent development, Dr. Rubman has a refreshingly novel approach that appeals to students, teachers, parents, and experts in the field. Her conference presentations include titles such as:

- The 21st Century Brain and Other Stories.
- Neuropsychology and Cognition in the Classroom.
- Pixels in the Classroom.
- Time Out Doesn't Work!

Disruptive Students—A Cognitive, Developmental Perspective.

Magazine articles include such titles as:

- Read-iculous: The Challenges of Reading Through the Eyes of a Child.
- The Big Fat Question of Obesity.
- How Much Technology is Too Much?

Dr. Rubman is a professor at Suffolk County Community College in New York where she has taught for the past 18 years. She has also spent time in the classroom as a kindergarten teacher in London, England, and California, USA.

Born and raised in Glasgow, Scotland, she earned her PhD and MA degrees in cognitive, developmental psychology from the State University of New York in Stony Brook. She holds a BA degree from Glasgow University and she also earned her Fellowship and Licentiateship (Teacher's Diploma) from the London College of Music in London, England, where she currently serves as an external examiner.

Dr. Rubman can be contacted through her website "Education and Parenting Matters" at www.clairerubman.com.

Academic Advisory Board Members

Members of the Academic Advisory Board are instrumental in the final selection of articles for each edition of Annual Editions. Their review of the articles for content, level, and appropriateness provides critical direction to the editors and staff. We think that you will find their careful consideration well reflected in this volume.

Fredalene Barletta Bowers
Indiana University of Pennsylvania

Kimberly Brown
Ball State University

Leilani M. Brown
University of Hawaii, Manoa

Christy Buchanan
Wake Forest University

Maria Carla Chiarella
University of North Carolina, Charlotte

Deborah G. Conway
Community College of Allegheny

John S. Dacey
Boston College

Florence L. Denmark
Pace University

Ric Ferraro
University of North Dakota

Kathleen E. Fite
Texas State University, San Marcos

Suzanne Freedman
University of Northern Iowa

Wyndol Furman
University of Denver

Donald Gatchell
Ohio University, Chillicothe

Sally A. Gillman
South Dakota State University

William M. Gray
University of Toledo

William M. Grya
University of Toledo

Deborah Harris-Sims
University of Phoenix and Strayer University

Lisa Hill
Hampton University

Glenda Hotton
Masters College

Emily J. Johnson
University of Wisconsin, La Crosse

Maureen E. Kenny
Boston College

Steven Kaatz
Bethel University

Paul Klaczynski
University of Northern Colorado

Natalie Kozelka
Northeast Iowa Community College

Daniel K. Lapsley
Ball State University

Michael Martinsen
Edgewood College

Tai McMiller
York Technical College

Dean Meenach
Mineral Area College

Kenneth Mills
Florida Int'L University-Biscayne

John J. Mitchell
Okanagan University College

Michelle Morris
Northwestern State University

William A. Mosier
Wright State University

George Muugi
Kutztown University

Elizabeth B. Newell
California State University, Fresno

Bernadette Nwafor
Claflin University

David Opalewski
Central Michigan University

Jessie Panko
Saint Xavier University

Linda Pincham
Roosevelt University

Sarah Rankin
Lewis and Clark Community College

Mary Eva Repass
University of Virginia

Grant J. Rich
University of Alaska Southeast

Thomas R. Scheira
Buffalo State College

Stephen T. Schroth
Knox College

Laurence Segall
Housatonic Community College

Michael Shaughnessy
Eastern New Mexico University

Diana Shepherd
California State University, Chico

Linda A. Sidoti
The College of Saint Rose

Margaret B. Spencer
University of Pennsylvania

Robert Stennett
University of North Georgia, Gainesville

Julia Anne Thomas
National Louis University, Elgin

Sandra M. Todaro
Bossier Parish Community College

Lois J. Willoughby
Miami-Dade College

Paul Wills
Kilgore College and Troy University

Unit 1

UNIT

Prepared by: Claire N. Rubman, *Suffolk County Community College*

Perspectives on Adolescent Psychology

Consider adolescence as a unique stage of development that is entirely different from childhood and adulthood. While the onset of puberty marks its clearly defined start, the end of adolescence is less straightforward. Adolescence is purported to end with the attainment of adult responsibilities but what, in reality, does that really mean?

Our first article, by Rhodes (2015) looks at the cultural implications of adolescence. Rhodes compares adolescent behaviors in the animal kingdom with that of humans. She discusses adolescent rats that also experience peer pressure—adolescent rats actually drink more alcohol when they are among their rat peer group! Rhodes discusses the changes in the maturing adolescent brain that lead to notorious adolescent behavior such as impulsivity, sensation seeking, and risk taking.

Read about contrasting perspectives in adolescence. Learn about how a sophisticated country such as the United States of America "outlawed" adolescence (Ripley, 2016). Learn about the history of school and state laws that aggressively punished benign acts such as flirting, chewing gum, or having cell phones in school. In Texas, for example, read about how over 275,000 children were charged under the "disrupting class" laws. Read about one case in particular that was in the news recently regarding a student with a cell phone in class. Read about the fallout from that case. If the event had not been recorded by a classmate, think about what the potential outcome could have been . . . .

Think, as you read, about your behavior when you were in high school, or college. How do you think such disciplinary measures should be handled?

Thinking from an adolescent's perspective is the focus of "Making the Bad Times Good" by Morrison, (2015). Read about cyberbullying, self-harm, and suicide prevention among a myriad of other adolescent issues. Read about Morrison's surprising revelations and her career choices.

Pause for a moment to consider what adolescence must be like for those whose childhood did not follow the normal course of development. Walk in Ani's shoes as she passes through adolescence. Experience Ani's social isolation as her cognitive disabilities interfere with her communication skills, her ability to socially interact, and her ability to form lasting friendships. Take time to consider how we can make the lives of disabled adolescents just a little bit brighter.

Our last article in this unit on differing perspectives focuses on precocious puberty—6 and 7 year olds who enter puberty at such a young age. How is their childhood interrupted by the abrupt arrival of body hair, breast buds, and body odor? Some experts suggest that obesity is a contributing factor while others look to environmental chemicals in our daily lives. Whether it is the phthalates in our plastics or those excess pounds on our hips, think about the effects of puberty on a single digit child. Depression, for example, is a major symptom of early maturing girls (Steinberg, 2014). They are also more likely to smoke or have eating disorders. These issues are explored in "Childhood Lost" by Susan Scutti (2015). Ask yourself what you would do if you saw signs of early puberty in your child. Would you pay the $15,000+ a year in medical expenses for hormone therapy to stave off precocious puberty?

Article   Prepared by: Claire N. Rubman, *Suffolk County Community College*

Beyond the Average Adolescent

ELLA RHODES

Learning Outcomes

After reading this article, you will be able to:

- Describe a research study that demonstrates how peers influence adolescent behavior.

- Use "Theory of Mind" research to describe two specific changes in the adolescent brain.

Some look back on their teenage years with a sense of pride, at their rebellious nature, others cringe at the thought. Although we have our own personal experience of passing through that stage, teens are so often misunderstood and regarded with considerable wariness. Shakespeare once wrote: "I would there were no age between sixteen and three-and-twenty, or that youth would sleep out the rest; for there is nothing in the between but getting wenches with child, wronging the ancientry, stealing, fighting." In opening, the British Psychological Society's Annual Conference Sarah-Jayne Blakemore (University College London) sought to provide a more tolerant and evidence-based perspective on adolescent development, looking to the teenage brain to partially explain this age group's risky behaviour.

Professor Blakemore told the gathered audience how she became interested in teen brain development—through working with people with schizophrenia. Testing patients in a hospital outside Versailles during a postdoc, Blakemore realized that all of them reported onset of the condition at the end of adolescence. Why should this devastating and floral illness remain almost dormant during childhood and the teenage years? Unlike other developmental disorders such as autism and ADHD, "schizophrenia waits, and shows itself at the end of adolescence." But it's not alone in that: Blakemore showed that 75 percent of adult mental disorder has the onset before the age of 24, and mostly during adolescence. Blakemore thought the answers might lie in the typical development of the teenage brain.

Although often adolescence is described as starting with puberty and ending when a person gains a stable independent role in society, there are massive cultural differences in when this may occur. In some cultures, people marry and start having children very young, whereas in the West, many people continue to live with their parents and study until their 20s or 30s. But Blakemore argues that adolescence is, in fact, a distinct biological period that presents itself across cultures and in every one of us. Typical adolescent behaviors, including heightened risk-taking, peer influence, impulsivity, and self-consciousness, can be seen across cultures and even across species. Adolescent rats show increased risk-taking and increased exploration, during this period, and even drink more alcohol when in the company of other adolescent rats!

On a more sombre note, Blakemore pointed out that adolescent risk-taking has a real effect on teenage mortality rates, with accidents related to risky behaviors being the leading cause of death of people in that period of life. But why do adolescents generally take more risks? And in what circumstances? Blakemore outlined Larry Steinberg's research, which took three age groups, 13–16, 17–24, and 25 and over, and asked them to play a driving video game. Somewhat surprisingly, the adolescents took around the same number of risks—jumping lights, speeding, etc.—as the adults and young adults. So in optimal circumstances, where the adolescents can concentrate on the task in hand, the stereotypical view is not borne out by the research. However, when the groups were watched doing the task by a couple of friends, the number of risks that adolescents took tripled and the number of risks the young adults took doubled. The adults were unaffected. "The critical factor is peer influence," Blakemore said.

This fits our real-world picture of when teenagers start to take risks, such as smoking: it's when they're with others. And data from British car insurance companies show that adolescents have more accidents if they have a similar-aged passenger in the car, whereas in adults the pattern is reversed. What could it be about peer influence that has an effect on risk taking?

Blakemore suggested that adolescents have a vested interest in being accepted by their peer group, "probably for evolutionary reasons"—they need to become independent from their families.

In research with Catherine Sebastian, Blakemore showed the emotional side of this peer influence. Using a simple game-based paradigm of social exclusion, they found that adolescents reacted to apparent social exclusion with a significantly greater drop in mood than adults did. "This perhaps explains how perfectly intelligent, rational adolescents make risky decisions . . . the social factor weighs in particularly heavily on the see-saw of decision making." Imagine a 13-year-old girl whose friends all smoke, and they offer her a cigarette. Is it more risky to say yes to a cigarette, knowing the health risks of smoking, or to say no and risk being socially ostracized? "These decisions are not so crazy if we think about them in the context of the importance of their peer group," Blakemore concluded.

Referring to research she conducted at the Science Museum, Blakemore explained that adolescents don't judge situations or decisions as objectively less risky—they do not feel invincible—they are just particularly influenced by the risk perceptions of other teenagers and less so by adults. "It always surprises me that health doesn't just focus on social norms and peer effects," Blakemore mused. Find the most popular kid in a class and educate them about various risky behaviors, she said: research suggests that the perceptions of the whole class can then change towards the views of that cool child.

But what about the neuroscience behind this behaviour? Blakemore pointed out that, until recently, it was unclear at what point the brain stopped developing. MRI and MRI data have taken us far closer to understanding, showing that brain development continues throughout adolescence and even into the 20s and 30s. The prefrontal cortex has a role in the assessment of risks and impulsivity and Jay Giedd's work has shown that the gray matter volume in this area peaks in late childhood and early adolescence, followed by a significant decline during adolescence. What does this correspond to? Blakemore discussed "synaptic pruning," a "molding of the brain during adolescence" that is heavily dependent on the environment, as one factor.

Turning to "theory of mind," the ability to infer the mental states of others, Blakemore outlined MRI data showing that each of the four areas within the so-called "social brain network" parallel the increase in gray matter volume in childhood and decrease during adolescence seen in the prefrontal cortex. Yet nine developmental fMRI studies show that medial prefrontal cortex activity in social cognition tasks is higher in adolescents than in adults. Blakemore feels this may reflect a different cognitive strategy for adolescents in this kind of perspective taking task. She also pointed to a potential mismatch between the maturity of the emotion-led limbic system and the under developed prefrontal cortex to explain the greater propensity for adolescents to take risks.

Blakemore closed her talk with a startling example of how looking solely at average data can give us a false picture of brain development in adolescence—showing the huge differences among individuals in their brain development during this period. She concluded that individual differences should be the subject of further investigation, particularly looking into how genetics, culture, a person's environment and social group affect brain development. "It's the individual differences that are going to be more meaningful and interesting than the averages."

Critical Thinking

1. Are we limiting cognitive growth during adolescence?
2. Given the types of decisions that adolescents make, how can we develop a safer environment for our adolescent population?

Internet References

Adolescent Development in East Asia and the Pacific: Realizing Their Potential a Summary of Trends, Programming, and Policy Experiences
   https://www.unicef.org/ADAP_series_2.pdf

Center for Disease Control and Prevention: Teens (Ages 12–19)—Risk Behaviors
   https://www.cdc.gov/parents/teens/risk_behaviors.html

Fast Facts: How Does the United States Compare?
   https://thenationalcampaign.org/resource/fast-facts-how-does-united-states-compare

How Cultural Differences Influence Adolescent Development
   http://www.livestrong.com/article/560306-how-cultural-differences-influence-adolescent-development/

Article   Prepared by: Claire N. Rubman, *Suffolk County Community College*

How America Outlawed Adolescence

At least 22 states make it a crime to disturb school in ways that teenagers are wired to do. Why did this happen?

AMANDA RIPLEY

Learning Outcomes

After reading this article, you will be able to:

- Describe the types of crimes committed by 275,000 Texas students.

- Give two reasons why typical adolescent behavior should be "corrected" instead of prosecuted.

- Explain the 6 percent drop in criminal charges in Texas schools in 2013.

One Monday morning last fall, at Spring Valley High School in Columbia, South Carolina, a 16-year-old girl refused to hand over her cellphone to her algebra teacher. After multiple requests, the teacher called an administrator, who eventually summoned a sheriff's deputy who was stationed at the school. The deputy walked over to the girl's desk. "Are you going to come with me," he said, "or am I going to make you?"

Niya Kenny, a student sitting nearby, did not know the name of the girl who was in trouble. That girl was new to class and rarely spoke. But Kenny had heard stories about the deputy, Ben Fields, who also coached football at the school, and she had a feeling he might do something extreme. "Take out your phones," she whispered to the boys sitting next to her, and she did the same. The girl still hadn't moved. While Kenny watched, recording with her iPhone, Fields wrenched the girl's right arm behind her and grabbed her left leg. The girl flailed a fist in his direction. As he tried to wrestle her out of her chair, the desk it was attached to flipped over, slamming the girl backward. Then, he reached for her again, extracting her this time, and hurled her across the classroom floor.

The other kids sat unmoving, hunched over their desks. The teacher and the administrator stood in silence. As Fields crouched over the girl to handcuff her, Kenny tried to hold her phone steady. Her legs were shaking and her heart was hammering in her chest. If this was really happening, she thought, someone needed to know about it—someone, apparently, outside that room. "Put your hands behind your back," Fields ordered the girl, sounding excited, out of breath. "Gimme your hands! Gimme your hands!"

Finally, in an unnaturally high voice, Kenny blurted: "Ain't nobody gonna put this shit on Snapchat?" The administrator tried to quiet her down, saying her name over and over, but she would not be silenced. "What the fuck?" she said, her voice rising further. "What the fuck?" Then, she hit the Post button on her phone's Snapchat app.

Videos taken by Kenny and other students ended up online, and the story went viral that night. The girl who was thrown was black, like Kenny, and the footage of her being flung across the classroom by a white police officer inflamed debates about race and law enforcement. Hillary Clinton tweeted that there was "no excuse" for such violence, while the singer Ted Nugent praised Fields for teaching a lesson to "a spoiled, undisciplined brat."

After Fields handcuffed the girl, another deputy arrived to escort her out of the classroom. She would be released to her guardian later that day. Then, according to Kenny, Fields turned to her. "You got so much to say?," Fields asked. "Come on."

Kenny did not speak. She got up and put her hands behind her back.

THE NEXT DAY, the principal called the incident "horrific," and the school-board chair said it represented an "outrageous exception to the culture, conduct, and standards in which we so strongly believe." Richland County Sheriff Leon Lott, who oversees the officers at Spring Valley, said he was sickened by the videos and was investigating his deputy's actions. He added in passing that Niya Kenny had been arrested for "contributing to the chaos." None of the other officials mentioned her name.

Kenny's case did not receive much attention from officials because it was not unusual. Her arrest was based on a law against "disturbing school," a mysterious offense that is routinely levied against South Carolina students. Each year, about 1,200 kids are charged with disturbing school in the state—some for yelling and shoving, others for cursing. (In fact, the girl who was thrown from her desk was charged with disturbing school too, though the public uproar focused on the use of force.) State law makes it a crime to "disturb in any way or in any place the students or teachers of any school" or "to act in an obnoxious manner." The charge, which has been filed against kids as young as 7, according to the American Civil Liberties Union, is punishable by up to 90 days in jail or a $1,000 fine.

At least 22 states and dozens of cities and towns currently outlaw school disturbances in one way or another. South Dakota prohibits "boisterous" behavior at school, while Arkansas bans "annoying conduct." Florida makes it a crime to "interfere with the lawful administration or functions of any educational institution"—or to "advise" another student to do so. In Maine, merely interrupting a teacher by speaking loudly is a civil offense, punishable by up to a $500 fine.

In some states, like Washington and Delaware, disturbing-school laws are on the books but used relatively rarely or not at all. In others, they have become a standard classroom-management tool. Last year, disturbing school was the second-most-common accusation leveled against juveniles in South Carolina, after misdemeanor assault. An average of seven kids were charged every day that schools were in session.

Each year in Maryland, Florida, and Kentucky, about 1,000 students face the charge. In North Carolina, the number is closer to 2,000. Nationwide, good data are hard to come by. Some states, like Nevada and Arizona, do not track how many times juveniles are charged with this offense. (In Arizona, a court official would tell me only that the number is somewhere between zero and 5,375 arrests a year.) But figures collected by *The Atlantic* suggest that authorities charge juveniles with some version of disturbing school more than 10,000 times a year. This number does not even include older teenagers who are charged as adults.

Over the years, judges around the country have landed on various definitions of *disturbance*. In Georgia, a court concluded, a fight qualifies as disturbing school if it attracts student spectators. But a Maryland court found that attracting an audience does not create a disturbance unless normal school activities are delayed or canceled. In Alabama, a court found that a student had disturbed school because his principal had had to meet with him to discuss his behavior; an appeals court

overturned the ruling on the grounds that talking with students was part of a principal's job.

Just this summer in New Mexico, a federal appeals court upheld a school police officer's decision to arrest and handcuff a 13-year-old who had repeatedly burped in gym class, ruling that "burping, laughing, and leaning into the classroom stopped the flow of student educational activities, thereby injecting disorder into the learning environment." The decision reads like an *Onion* article, albeit one that goes on for 94 pages.

When teenagers talk back, scream obscenities, or otherwise behave badly, adults must call them out and hold them accountable. That's how kids learn. In time, most kids outgrow their delinquent ways. Police and policy makers who defend these laws say they make classrooms safer. But the laws have also been used to punish behavior that few reasonable people would consider criminal. Defiance is a typical part of adolescence, so putting teenagers in jail for swearing or refusing to follow an order is akin to arresting a 2-year-old for having a meltdown at the grocery store. It essentially outlaws the human condition. And the vagueness of the laws means they are inevitably applied unevenly, depending on the moods and biases of the adults enforcing them. In South Carolina, black students like Kenny are nearly four times as likely as their white peers to be charged with disturbing school.

THE ORIGINAL SCHOOL "DISTURBANCE" in South Carolina, the one that started it all, was flirting.

During the Progressive era, with women beginning to vote and race riots breaking out across growing urban centers, lawmakers seized on flirting as a menace to social order. New York City police set up flirting dragnets, using "pretty blonde girls as bait," according to a syndicated newspaper column from June 1920. "The enormous recent growth of the crime of flirting . . . must be ascribed to a growing laxity of conduct in general, and also to the rise of the short skirt," the article continued. "It should be promptly and drastically suppressed."

In 1919, a South Carolina state lawmaker and attorney named John Ratchford Hart, distressed by incidents of men flirting with students at the all-white women's college in his district, proposed a law to prohibit any "obnoxious" behavior or "loiter[ing]" at any girls' school or college in the state. Violators would face up to a $100 fine or 30 days in jail.

From the beginning, the disturbing-school law was intended to keep young people in their place. But it would evolve with threats to the status quo. Forty-eight years later, after black students organized a series of nonviolent marches against segregation in the rural enclave of Orangeburg, South Carolina, the county's representative in the statehouse—a former teacher named F. Hall Yarborough—proposed a bill to broaden the law to criminalize obnoxious behavior at all schools, single-sex and coed. Yarborough was alarmed not only by the uprisings in his own district but by civil-rights and antiwar protests on campuses across the country. He spoke obliquely of the activists he hoped to fend off with the expanded law. "I'm interested in keeping outside agitators off campus," he told the Associated Press. The bill sailed through the statehouse. No hearings were held.

Not long after that, black students from South Carolina State College led a multiday protest against a segregated bowling alley in Orangeburg. One night, after the protesters had returned to campus, someone threw a banister that hit a state trooper in the head. Police opened fire, shooting 30 unarmed students and killing three black teenagers, in what would become known as the Orangeburg Massacre. The governor signed South Carolina's newly expanded disturbing-school bill into law three weeks later.

It's hard to overstate the tension that crackled through the country back then. Peaceful protests far outnumbered violent ones, but it did not necessarily feel that way. From January 1969 to April 1970, more than 8,200 bomb threats, attempted bombings, and actual bombings were attributed to student protests. "These are not just college students out on a panty raid," a Texas legislator warned his colleagues. "These are revolutionaries dedicated to destroying our system."

In the midst of the turmoil, the U.S. Supreme Court ruled in 1969 against a Des Moines, Iowa, school district, finding that students had a right to protest peacefully on school grounds. In this case, the Court said, the teenage plaintiffs could wear black armbands in protest of the Vietnam War, as long as they did so without "materially and substantially" disturbing class. Justice Hugo Black issued an ominous dissent. "It is the beginning of a new revolutionary era of permissiveness in this country," he wrote. "Groups of students all over the land are already running loose, conducting break-ins, sit-ins, lie-ins, and smash-ins."

Following the federal ruling, state and local officials passed a flurry of laws that would punish students who *were* disturbing class, anywhere from universities to elementary schools. At the time, it's worth remembering, black students weren't just protesting; they were also integrating white classrooms, backed by the federal government. "As soon as we started introducing black bodies into white schools, we got these laws," says Jenny Egan, a public defender for juveniles in Maryland who regularly represents clients charged with disturbing school. "That's not a coincidence."

The maneuvering was part of a broader legislative cold war: As Michelle Alexander documents in her book, *The New Jim Crow*, after the Civil Rights Act dismantled formal segregation, politicians stopped demanding "segregation forever" and began calling for "law and order."

In September 1970, President Richard Nixon's Commission on Campus Unrest reported that more than 30 states had passed nearly 80 laws to counter student unrest. It warned that "legislators in a majority of states have passed antistudent and antiuniversity laws that range from the unnecessary and ill-directed to the purely vindictive." Amid the hysteria, some legislators proposed laws that were already on the books: In Kansas City, Missouri, police came out against a new disturbing-school statute because it would have duplicated not one but five existing city laws. Maryland lawmakers worried that the state's disturbing-school law "could be applied to a kindergarten pupil throwing a temper tantrum."

Still, the laws did not become integral to school discipline until the 1990s, when fears of rising gang- and drug-related violence—followed by a series of high-profile school shootings—led to the widespread installation of police officers in school hallways. By 1998, more than 100 South Carolina school districts, including Niya Kenny's, had brought in police, formally known as "school resource officers." After the Columbine High School shootings in Colorado the next year, South Carolina's Safe Schools Task Force recommended increasing the number of officers, and the state's Department of Education requested $14 million to pay for them—double the previous year's budget. (The fact that a full-time officer was employed at Columbine but was unable to stop the shooters did not seem to discourage hiring in other districts.)

By the early '90s, America's juvenile crime rate had begun to drop, a trend that would continue for the next two decades. It would be logical to assume that school police officers contributed to this decline. But there is little reliable evidence to support or refute that theory. What we do know is that the drop in crime began before police arrived in most schools. And once police were in place, they tended to keep busy. According to an analysis of 2,650 schools published in the *Washington University Law Review* earlier this year, students at schools with police officers were significantly more likely to be reported to law enforcement for low-level offenses than students at schools without police, even after controlling for the neighborhood crime rate, the demographics of the schools, and a host of other variables.

Previously, principals had needed to call the police to make an arrest; by the late '90s, in many schools, the police were already there. And while they were not technically supposed to get involved in workaday school-discipline issues, the disturbing-school laws rendered all manner of common misbehavior illegal. Some officers worked hard to build relationships with students and resolve problems before they escalated. But most did not have adequate training to manage adolescents, who are wired to proclaim their independence. "Most law-enforcement officers are trained to assert authority, to take control of the situation," says Mark Soler, the executive director of the Center for Children's Law and Policy, who has trained school police officers. "In a school context, that's bad advice." From 2000 to 2016, according to South Carolina's data, the disturbing-school charge was filed against students in the state 33,304 times.

THE HANDCUFFS DEPUTY FIELDS used on Kenny were tight, pressing against her skin. "I just had this one tiny hope," she told me later, "that he might just try to scare me and let me go."

This was Kenny's second time taking Algebra I. She'd failed it as a freshman, too busy socializing to do math. But as a senior, she was more focused: She had to pass the class in order to graduate. Until that morning, everything had been going according to plan. She had an A, and the teacher seemed to like her. If, for example, she took out her phone in class, he would give her a look, and she'd put it away.

Fields took her to another room, where Kenny says he and the administrator started yelling at her. "What did you think you were doing in there?," Fields asked. Kenny started to wonder whether she had misjudged the situation. If the deputy's actions were so wrong, why was she the only one saying so? "I started thinking I was the bad guy," Kenny told me. "Like maybe I'd done the wrong thing." Suddenly, she thought of what her mother would say about her arrest. She started crying, and Fields asked for her phone. She handed it over but admitted that she'd already posted the video.

Around 12:30 in the afternoon, another deputy led Kenny outside—still in handcuffs—to meet a police van. (Officers at Spring Valley can decide to release a student to a guardian after an arrest, as they had done with the girl who was thrown, but not with Kenny.) Standing there, in front of her school on Sparkleberry Lane, where she'd run cross-country and sung in the gospel choir, she started sobbing. The handcuffs were not a prop. She was going to jail. That's when she decided she would never come back to Spring Valley High School. As with many kids who get arrested at school, something shifted in her head, and she concluded that she did not belong there anymore.

Kenny climbed into the police van, which took her to the Alvin S. Glenn Detention Center, in Columbia. She had recently celebrated her 18th birthday, and would be processed as an adult. Inside the facility, an officer ordered her to take off her boots so they could be searched. Then, she was fingerprinted, photographed, and led into a holding room with about 20 other detainees. The room was frigid, and she crossed her arms to keep warm. Someone asked her why she was there, and she said that she'd yelled at a police officer in school. "Yelling?" a correctional officer said. "And they booked you in here for that?"

After a bond hearing, where she was told she would be let go until her court date, Kenny was sent back to the holding room to wait for release. With nothing else to do, she watched a TV mounted in the corner, which was playing the evening news on mute. That's when Kenny saw a video of her Algebra I classroom flash across the screen. "Did you see that?," Kenny shouted. "That's my classroom! That is why I am in here!" The other detainees looked over to watch. "Everybody was like,

'Are you serious? You don't need to be in here,'" she told me. "I was like, 'All right, I'm not going to get in trouble with my mom.'"

Shortly after 8 o'clock in the evening, about nine hours after her arrest, Kenny was released. Her mother, Doris Ballard-Kenny, hugged her in the parking lot. "I saw the video," Ballard-Kenny said. "I am proud of you." Standing outside the jail's barbed-wire fence, Kenny looked tired but resolute as she spoke to a TV reporter. "I had never seen nothing like that in my life, a man use that much force on a little girl," she said, shaking her head back and forth. "A big man, like 300 pounds of full muscle. It was like, no way, no way. You can't do nothing like that to a little girl."

That night, Kenny couldn't sleep. She had a crushing headache, the kind that comes from crying for too long. In the morning, she asked her mother to take the day off work to be with her. For the first time since elementary school, she was scared to be home by herself.

"Before this, I had a sense of pride for Spring Valley High School," Kenny's mother told me later. "It's one of the better schools in Columbia. A lot of the affluent kids go there." Spring Valley regularly makes *The Washington Post*'s list of America's "most challenging" high schools, based on the number of advanced tests taken by students. It is not a violent school or a destitute one. But in the course of a single day, it had unraveled some of the most important lessons she had instilled in her daughter. "She has always been taught to speak up for people. If you see an injustice being done, help the person," Ballard-Kenny said. "That's what she was doing. And it's almost like it's making what I taught her obsolete."

Kenny's arrest was not the first disciplinary controversy in her school district; in fact, a group of black parents had already created an association to help students who felt they'd been unfairly disciplined under the disturbing-school law and district policies. In the year leading up to the incident, the district had set up task forces on diversity and discipline, and hired a chief diversity officer to help address these concerns.

But the law-and-order culture remained powerful at Spring Valley—as it does across the state. Although Ben Fields was fired two days after the incident, he was not accused of committing any crime. Nor was the teacher or the administrator, both of whom kept their jobs (the administrator has since transferred to a school about an hour north of Spring Valley). None responded to requests for comment. In a survey of South Carolinians conducted by Public Policy Polling shortly after the videos went viral, almost half of the respondents said they opposed the decision to fire Fields. Only a third supported the decision. About 100 Spring Valley students—some of them football players who had been coached by Fields—walked out of class in protest of his dismissal. No one was arrested. An e-mail from the school-board chair, released to *The Atlantic* in response to a Freedom of Information Act request, shows that administrators knew about the protest in advance but felt that stopping it would have caused "more disruption of school" than allowing it.

"We were just upset," says Caleb, a black student who helped organize the walkout. (He requested that I use only his first name.) He acknowledged that Fields had used "definitely, probably, too much force—a little bit," but, he said, "we didn't think he deserved to be fired." Caleb did not know Kenny, but he had seen the video from the classroom, featuring her yelling "What the fuck?," and he had little sympathy for her. "I wouldn't have been surprised if someone had said, like, 'Man, this isn't right,'" he says. "But cursing, yelling, screaming like that definitely was not necessary." Like other students I met, Caleb seemed to expect more self-control from a teenage girl than from a sheriff's deputy.

As a society, our understanding of teenagers has not caught up to the science. In the past 15 years, neuroscientists have discovered that a teenager's brain is different in important ways from an adult's brain. It is more receptive to rewards than to punishment, and the parts that control impulses and judgment are still under construction. Which means that back talk and fake burps are predictable teenage acts—to be corrected, not prosecuted.

In September, almost a year after the arrests, the local solicitor, Dan Johnson, dropped the disturbing-school charge against the girl who had been thrown. The girl had indeed disturbed school, Johnson wrote in a 12-page explanation of his decision, but the case had been "compromised" by the firing of Fields—a punishment that might prejudice "prospective jurors" against the deputy's side of the story. (The fact that this girl was underage and therefore would have faced a judge, not a jury, went unmentioned.) He also noted that hospital X-rays taken after the arrest suggested that the girl's wrist had been fractured, but he declined to charge Fields, citing insufficient proof of a crime. (His report included a statement from Fields claiming that the girl had resisted arrest and punched him twice during the encounter, and that her desk had fallen over "because of the momentum that [her] movements had created.")

Johnson also dismissed the disturbing-school charge against Kenny. "There is simply not enough evidence to prove each and every element" of the alleged offense, he wrote. Kenny's attorney had expected such a dismissal, which happens in about ⅕ of juvenile arrests in South Carolina. But damage had already been done. Regardless of GPA, race, or prior offenses, students who have been arrested are nearly twice as likely as their peers to drop out of high school, even if they never go to court, according to a 2006 study by the criminologist Gary Sweeten. "Just being arrested can have long-term consequences," says Josh Gupta-Kagan, an assistant professor specializing in

juvenile justice at the University of South Carolina School of Law. "Teenagers start to see the school as out to get them."

"America generally loves crime and punishment—this idea that punishment somehow corrects behavior, that it teaches kids a lesson," says Jenny Egan, the Maryland public defender. In reality, the more involvement kids have with the legal system, the worse their behavior gets. Kids who get arrested *and* appear in court are nearly four times as likely to drop out of high school, Gary Sweeten found. But most people in the chain of decision making—from the state lawmaker to the teacher to the principal to the school police officer to the prosecutor—do not realize how much damage their actions can do, Egan says: "I don't think a majority of people in the system understand what it does to a child to put him in handcuffs and take him to court—at the very moment when he is trying to figure out who he is in the world."

Kids facing disturbing-school charges in South Carolina are typically offered punishment outside the court system, such as community service. If they've already taken this option in the past—or if they've been convicted of other charges on top of disturbing school—they can be incarcerated or placed on probation, a layer of surveillance that boosts their chances of getting rearrested for things as trivial as missing a day of school. In many juvenile cases, judges will make parents a party to the case, meaning that they are legally bound to report a child who comes home after a court-ordered curfew or violates any other probation condition.

"It's so easy to get into the system and so hard to get out," says Aleksandra Chauhan, a public defender for juveniles in Columbia. The system clings to kids. Which is why advocates like Chauhan argue that arrests should be a last resort, the nuclear option reserved for truly dangerous cases, not ejection buttons pressed whenever adults run out of patience. "We criminalize juvenile behavior that is considered normal by psychologists," she says. "We are creating criminals. I really believe that."

THE UNEXPECTED STANDOUT in reforming disturbing-school laws is the state of Texas. Until recently, Texas had one of the worst records in the country on juvenile justice. Police were charging 275,000 kids a year with "disrupting class" and other low-level offenses. Nearly, three in five students were suspended or expelled at least once between seventh and 12th grade, according to an in-depth analysis of nearly 1 million Texas students that came out in 2011. Over time, the Texas school system had become a quasi-authoritarian state, one that punished some kids far more than others.

When it came to clear-cut offenses, like using a weapon, African American students were no more likely than other students to get in trouble in Texas. But they were far more likely to be disciplined for *subjective* violations like disrupting class.

Even after controlling for more than 80 variables, including family income, students' academic performance, and past disciplinary incidents, the report found that race was a reliable predictor of which kids got disciplined.

Then, five years ago, a juvenile-court judge invited Wallace B. Jefferson, the chief justice of the Texas Supreme Court, to spend a day observing her courtroom. Jefferson watched in silence as parents and children, most without lawyers, stutter-stumbled through formal legal rituals many of them did not seem to understand. He was startled not just by the power imbalance but by the fact that he hadn't known about it before.

The first African American on the state's Supreme Court, Jefferson had spent most of his career defending organizations and corporations, not children. He'd never realized how the legal system was funneling kids from schools to detention centers. "These are families in distress—very often uneducated parents trying to deal with troubled youth, many of whom have mental-health issues," he told me. "If it were my kid, I would be in that courtroom filing pleadings to dismiss. But many of the kids were from broken homes and very modest financial means." After his day in juvenile court, Jefferson met with Texas legislators to see what could be done. It turned out that many were as disgusted by the status quo as he was. They were tired of reading news stories about kids getting charged with disrupting class for spraying perfume or throwing paper airplanes. It was a waste of taxpayer dollars, not to mention embarrassing.

"I guess it made some people feel good, like they were tough," John Whitmire, a state senator who joined forces with Jefferson, told me. He had chaired the Texas legislature's criminal-justice committee for almost two decades, and no one would have called him soft on crime. "I'm as tough as anybody there is on adults and on juveniles who will cut your throat and hurt you violently," he said. "But the screwups, whether adult or juvenile, I believe we have better results if we work with 'em." Like other lawmakers I interviewed, Whitmire made a point of mentioning that he himself may have been charged with disrupting school if the law had been enforced during his own childhood.

It took a lot of "talk, talk, talk," as Whitmire put it, but lawmakers on the left and the right answered Jefferson's call. Among other changes, they reined in the state's law against disrupting class. Texas students could no longer be charged with this offense at their own schools. Nor could students younger than 12 be charged with any low-level misdemeanor at school. Before charging older kids, officers had to write up formal complaints with sworn statements from witnesses—and some schools were required to try common-sense interventions (like writing a letter to parents or referring the student to counseling) before resorting to a legal charge.

The reforms took effect on September 1, 2013, the beginning of a new school year. Two months later, David Slayton, the head of the Texas Office of Court Administration, checked the charging data for juveniles. "I was floored," he told me. "It had dropped like a rock." He asked his staff to send him the data each subsequent month to make sure the numbers weren't a fluke. They weren't. That year, the number of charges filed for minor offenses like disrupting class dropped 61 percent. Thanks to the reforms, some 40,000 charges were *not* filed against kids. And there was no evidence that school safety suffered as a result. The number of juvenile arrests for violent crimes, which had been declining before the reforms, continued to fall, as did the number of expulsions and other serious disciplinary actions in schools. "It's been a remarkable achievement for our state," Slayton said. "The pendulum has swung back a little bit."

Over the years, South Carolina lawmakers have tried to do what Texas has done. After Kenny's arrest, several told me they were hopeful that reforms would finally happen, given all the bad press that the viral videos had brought to the state. Even Sheriff Lott, the official in charge of the officers in Kenny's district, has called for changes. "You could chew gum and be arrested, technically, for disturbing school," he told me. "There's too much discretion."

In April, a bill that would have eliminated the charge for students at their own school, like the one Texas had passed, came up for a subcommittee hearing in the South Carolina legislature. A solicitor and former teacher named Barry Barnette testified against the proposal. "There's kids that will not obey the rules. And you've got to have discretion for that officer," he said. "I wish it was a perfect world where the students were always well behaved and everything. It's not that way." A representative of the South Carolina Sheriffs' Association issued a statement arguing that the disturbing-school law should stay in place because without it, officers might be forced to charge students with more-serious offenses—like disorderly conduct or assault and battery.

This argument sounds sensible, but in fact both of those charges can carry less serious penalties under South Carolina code than the disturbing-school charge—a point that was not made at the hearing. Chauhan, the public defender in Columbia, testified in favor of the bill, as did an ACLU lawyer. In the end, it never made it past the subcommittee.

This year, lawmakers in Massachusetts and Virginia also tried to reform their disturbing-school laws. In each case, critics repeated the same essential objection: Police need to have this tool in their toolkit. It didn't seem to matter that police have access to hundreds of other tools, from disorderly conduct to disturbing the peace to a variety of other catchall charges.

In August, frustrated by a lack of action, ACLU lawyers filed a federal lawsuit against the state of South Carolina, alleging that the disturbing-school law is overly vague and violates due-process rights guaranteed under the Fourteenth Amendment. "The Disturbing Schools statute creates an impossible standard for school children to follow and for police to enforce with consistency and fairness," the complaint said. The lead plaintiff is Niya Kenny.

WHEN I LAST SAW KENNY, in March, over dinner at a Red Lobster near Spring Valley High School, she was wearing oversize glasses, a knit cardigan, and purple Puma sneakers. Her mother sat next to her, wearing an #EveryBlackGirl T-shirt. Kenny ordered raspberry lemonade and seafood pasta, apologizing for how tired she was. She hadn't slept the night before. A childhood friend had been robbed and shot to death a few days earlier, and she'd come directly from the funeral.

After dropping out of high school, Kenny had started taking classes four days a week at a continuing-education center for adults. Getting a GED had seemed like the fastest way to move on with her life. Still, she was aware that she was missing out. "I should be prom-dress shopping," she told me. "Paying my senior fees to get my cap and gown." Instead, she was spending most of her time outside of her GED classes working at a fast-food restaurant a mile from the high school. Every week or two, a stranger would recognize her: "Are you the girl from the news?" Sometimes, depending on her mood, she'd say, "No, that's not me."

Kenny said she was thinking about joining the military. Her arrest record should be expunged under South Carolina law, now that the charges have been dropped, but she will still have to disclose the arrest before she can enlist.

This is not the first time someone in her family has been accused of disturbing school, as it turns out. In 1968, the year South Carolina enacted the expanded disturbing-school law, Kenny's great-great-granduncle, the Reverend H. H. Singleton II, sent his children to a white school for the first time. Someone burned a cross on his lawn and another outside the church where he preached. Twenty years later, Singleton was fired from his job as a middle-school teacher, accused of causing a "disruption"—through his involvement in the local NAACP chapter, he had supported a group of black high-school football players who were protesting a coach's decision to bench a black quarterback. It took two years, but a court eventually ruled that he'd been wrongfully terminated, and he returned to school. Now Kenny and her mother are hoping the ACLU lawsuit will interrupt this pattern. "I'm looking at it long-term," Kenny's mother said. "Ten years from now, when kids are reading their South Carolina history, they will read the name Niya Kenny."

When I asked Kenny what else lawmakers should do to fix the system, besides changing the law, she answered without hesitation. Take police officers out of schools, she said, and replace them with counselors. It sounds sensible, particularly in schools, like Spring Valley, that have relatively few violent incidents. Starting this school year, the U.S. Department of Justice, which helps fund the officers in Richland County schools, is requiring more outside oversight and training to ensure that they are not involved in enforcing classroom discipline in the future—the result of an audit that began before Kenny's arrest. (The department is also conducting a civil-rights review of what happened at Spring Valley.) But the idea of removing officers altogether is not being considered in her district or across most of the country.

Once police are invited into the schoolhouse, they're rarely asked to leave. Debbie Hamm, the superintendent of Kenny's district, is quick to note that Spring Valley is a "very orderly school." But she would not recommend removing the officers: "The safety and security—and the feeling of safety and security—in our schools is really, really important."

Sheriff Lott says he has never considered removing the officers from any Richland County schools. "That one incident doesn't define our program," he told me. "Every day, we have 87 school resource officers who are doing a great job. Our focus is not on how many kids we arrest but on how many problems we prevent." Last school year, according to the sheriff's department, deputies "successfully resolved" 6,251 conflicts. Lieutenant Curtis Wilson, a spokesperson for the department, told me that a successful resolution includes a range of outcomes, from counseling students to arresting them. "Let's say you have a victim," says Wilson, "and we are able to successfully identify the [perpetrator] and remove him from the school. Now school can continue. So that is a successful resolution."

In September, Kenny moved to New York City for an internship at the African American Policy Forum, a think tank. After moving her into a Brooklyn apartment, she and her mother went to a nearby Chipotle. Kenny, social as always, chatted easily with one of the employees. The woman suggested that Kenny come work there for extra spending money, and they set up an interview for the next day. "They didn't even know who she was," Kenny's mother told me happily.

Critical Thinking

1. How can school districts promote a better attitude among their adolescent students?

2. How could we better differentiate between typical adolescent behavior and criminal acts?

3. Do all school districts and all countries experience the same issues with adolescent behavior—is it a systemic problem?

Internet References

Are Zero Tolerance Policies Effective in the Schools?
https://www.apa.org/pubs/info/reports/zero-tolerance.pdf

Center for Disease Control and Prevention: Teens (Ages 12–19)—Risk Behaviors
https://www.cdc.gov/parents/teens/risk_behaviors.html

How Cultural Differences Influence Adolescent Development
http://www.livestrong.com/article/560306-how-cultural-differences-influence-adolescent-development/

"Teen Brain" Non-Science Debunked
http://www.cjcj.org/news/11227

Why Teenage Boys Do Stupid Things
http://www.cbsnews.com/news/whats-wrong-with-the-teen-brain/

Article   Prepared by: Claire N. Rubman, *Suffolk County Community College*

Making the Bad Times Good

FRANCES MORRISON

Learning Outcomes

After reading this article, you will be able to:

- Explain why this teenager believes that she can help others.

- Give three constructive ways that counselors can help adolescents.

I want to be a youth counselor because I have been where most teenagers have been.

At six years old, I decided to be a teacher. At 13, I wanted to be a criminal lawyer and now, at 17, I have decided to be a youth counselor.

I've passed NCEA Level 2, I've decided to do my National Certificate in Youth Work (Level 4) with Workforce Development Limited, and I'm also volunteering for Youth Line.

I believe things do get better after you talk to someone about everything that's going on. I like to help people out, including my friends. I would still be a youth counselor even if I didn't get paid.

I feel everyone deserves a good life. I want to help ease all this hatred in this world because it makes me sad, to see people going suicidal because people are hurting each other.

If I had one wish, I would wish for no more hate in this world. It makes me happy when I think about being a youth counselor. I could actually save someone's life, I could make them feel better and I could help them find strategies for how to handle hurt.

Self-harming or suicide or fighting or drugs or bad behaviour will not provide solutions, just more problems.

Challenges

Young people are getting into the wrong crowds. They get peer pressured into fighting, smoking weed, other drugs and drinking. In their heart, they don't want to do these things, but they don't want to be unpopular with the crew they have befriended so it just becomes a normal day-to-day thing.

Weed makes you high and makes you happy but it damages your brain and can dominate your life. It stuffs up relationships with everyone except other dopers, and those relationships are already stuffed.

Helping Yourself

You can say "no" to fighting, smoking weed, drugs, and other bad stuff others do, because if they are your true friend, they would support what you chose, if they don't then make new friends, and if you can't then ask to move schools and explain to your parents why you want to move.

Parental Splits

Parents splitting up cause a lot of heartache, as I have experienced.

It can help to think about what life was like when they were together—was it mostly good or mostly bad? If it was bad then think about no more fighting in the house; and if it was mostly good and they split anyway then they probably have had their own problems and they just don't want to tell the children. Maybe they hid it and they are happier apart.

It's good to get your grief out now rather than later. Don't turn against one parent because usually it is a mutual decision.

It's hard to have your parents break up but I know my parents are happier apart, and it makes our household easier to live in because there is no more fighting.

All us children have had counseling and it has helped a lot. Counseling sometimes seems like it has done nothing to help, but it has.

Bullies Everywhere

Cyber bullying, physical bullying, and verbal bullying—sometimes young people can't get away from bullying. No matter where they turn they will get beaten up or get called names, and when they get home, they are bullied on the internet. Some young people have been driven to suicide as a result.

Bullying seems to never go away, but you can help yourself by ignoring bullies at school, blocking them on social media, or asking your parents if you can move schools. If it carries on, ask about home schooling and give your parents reasons home schooling would be good for you.

But remember to remain social. If you can't move schools or get home schooled then ignore the bullies, don't answer back because they just w ant a response from you. Give them no air, no energy.

Most bullies have something bad going on in their life or they have had a bad upbringing and they are taking it out on you. Hang with your friends and avoid the bullies.

Bullies need to think about being in the victim's shoes. How would you feel? You would feel like you didn't want to wake up and face another day. Step into their parents' shoes. How would they feel if their children finally give up because of you? Would you like your kids to go through that when you have kids? No you wouldn't, so you need to stop.

Self-harm

Self-harming can become an addiction. And it's hard to stop.

I have been there. I had counseling which made me stop for a while because my counselor gave me strategies, but when my life got hard again I self-harmed again. I finally stopped when I moved away.

I'm not qualified to advise anyone—yet, but here are a few things that worked for me.

I got my mum to lock up all the sharp items; I drew lines on my body with colored pens instead; I cried, just cried, and punched my pillow.

After self-harming, you have scars, burns on your body, and you might not be able to wear shorts tops or swimming gear or summer clothes because you are ashamed of your scars.

And it's okay—it's important—to talk to someone if you can't stop cutting. You can get a number of strategies to help you.

Suicide

This is definitely not the answer to anything.

It may seem like the answer at the time but it's not. I have tried suicide twice and each time the look on my parents' faces made me feel so stink. Their own child is not happy and they can't help.

Before you think it's a good path to go down think about how your parents will feel, your sisters and brothers, people around you. How will they feel? What about your other relatives, or even your friends? They will become depressed. You need to go counseling.

I believe suicide has a negative spiritual result, like a self-murder, and because I believe in an afterlife I think it may be spent in a negative experience as a result.

I also believe God can help you because He helped me. He helped me move away from Auckland and now my life is back to how I want it to be. I haven't self-harmed in a year and a half and I don't think about suicide. If you want God's help just call out for Him.

Peer Pressure

Peer pressure is a hard thing to say no to because you want to be like your friends.

But why copy them? You want a positive future and if you do what delinquent friends want you to do it's just going to crash down, and you have to try to stand up again.

Respect and decency from your friends measures the depth of the friendship. You can ask a counselor (if you have one) how to say no.

I would just say "No." I'm a very open person and when my friends try to pressure me I just say "No thanks."

But I know it's hard. I have done stuff because I felt pressured.

Coming Out

When you decide to go to counseling, you can tell your counselor anything because it's private. For example, if you need help to tell your parents that you think you're gay or bisexual you can get them to come into the room with your counselor and tell them.

Seeing the Traps

Self-harming, thinking about suicide, getting into the wrong crowd, being a bully and choosing between parents if you are stuck in any of these categories and others I haven't listed, there is help out there. Get in contact with a counselor. Make the move. Do it now.

Seeing the Future

What do you want your future to be? I hope everyone wants a good future. You need to get out of the wrong crowd. It is never too late. To help deal with suicidal feelings, think about everyone in your life. They all love you and care about you. At the moment, it may seem like they don't but they do, go ask them. Think about what job you want, what future you want. You need to make good choices.

If you find that hard ring Youthline free call: 0800 376 633, Text 234 and email: talk@youth-line.co.nz. Or find www.youthline.co.nz and go on live chat.

Think about the choice you are about to make and think what will happen if you do this. Is it really necessary?

Who to Confide in

If you tell a counselor something, they will keep it a secret. A counselor will ask you if they can tell your parents and they will respect your wishes. If you tell them you're thinking about killing yourself then they will need to tell your parents to keep you safe. You can trust a counselor.

Make Some One's Day

Stick post-it notes on people. Write what you like about them, for example "nice shirt" or "nice hair" then run off (so you're not waiting for a thank you). You could make their day.

Be who you are. Don't be different because one person or even 100 people don't like you or how you're dressing. Everyone is beautiful in their own way. Listen to Who You Are by Jessie J. Nobody's life is perfect, but you can get help to make your life a bit better. And remember, counselors are your friends. They are there to help. I hope to be one soon.

Critical Thinking

1. What are some of the potential problems when adolescents with no academic credentials give advice to others?

2. How can adolescents develop a more positive attitude toward life.

Internet References

Adolescent Non-Suicidal Self-Injury: Analysis of the Youth Risk Behavior Survey Trends
http://tpcjournal.nbcc.org/adolescent-non-suicidal-self-injury-analysis-of-the-youth-risk-behavior-survey-trends/

Consider the Source: Adolescents and Adults Similarly Follow Older Adult Advice More than Peer Advice
http://journals.plos.org/plosone/article?id=10.1371/journal.pone.0128047

Coping Skills and Adolescents
http://www.bbbswnc.org/wp-content/uploads/2014/09/adolescent_coping.pdf

Counseling Techniques for Adolescents
http://www.livestrong.com/article/212757-counseling-techniques-for-adolescents/

Educating Adolescents about Coping With Change
https://www.psychologytoday.com/blog/surviving-your-childs-adolescence/201204/educating-adolescents-about-coping-change

Article   Prepared by: Claire N. Rubman, *Suffolk County Community College*

"You've Got a Friend in Me"

PEG GRAFWALLNER

Learning Outcomes

After reading this article, you will be able to:

- Develop a deeper understanding of the impact of social isolation
- Discuss how "Ani's people" contributed to her development
- Give an example of Ani's childhood deprivation

Friendships have always been difficult for Ani. She would much rather be with adults than people her own age. I think it's because adults have always shown more patience when speaking with her. At times, Ani can be difficult to understand. When she doesn't speak slowly and clearly (concepts we work on every day), her language is garbled; as a result, most children grow impatient and walk away, and some adults just smile and nod, having no idea what she actually said. Also, adults are quick to praise her which she loves; whereas, those close in age to her don't offer compliments as part of typical conversation.

When we brought Ani home from the Bulgarian orphanage in 2001, she was 5 years, 11 months. As a result of Ani's years in the orphanage, she learned to soothe herself and developed coping mechanisms for trauma; such as patting her chest, rocking, and rapid finger movements. Since Ani's challenges were extensive and exhausting, we began to see a psychologist to help her and support us. During one our sessions many months later, I explained that Ani seemed to have a difficult time relating to children her own age and gravitated toward much younger children or young adults. The psychologist thought that perhaps, around younger children, Ani found herself to be a capable equal and maybe around older kids, she appreciated the direction and guidance they provided.

In addition, Ani had never learned to play with toys. There was a "toy room" in the orphanage where the children were allowed to go when meeting a potential adoptive parent. When I first met Ani, I met her in the toy room. She was so overwhelmed by the toys that she hardly noticed me. She wanted to push the baby stroller, listen to the animal noises on the Speak n' Say and watch the balls bounce in the Corn Popper. In one session with our psychologist, I lamented about her inability to play with toys. He set up a dollhouse (*I* wanted to play with the dollhouse!) and gave Ani a female figure and gave me the male figure. She picked it up, looked at it in wonder, and looked at him in confusion. I tried engaging her by asking her doll to sit with mine on the couch. You could see her eyes moving from him to me; searching for some kind of sign of what to do and questioning what we wanted. She was lost. She carefully placed the figure on the floor, grabbed one of the little plastic chairs from the house, and laid on the psychologist's couch. She began to gently stroke the chair. I was shocked. What little girl wouldn't want to play with a wonderful dollhouse, complete with furniture, dolls, and their accessories? I began shaking my head and bemoaned, "What's wrong with her? Why won't she play with it? This is so weird!" He responded, "Peg, this isn't weird. This is deprivation." It was at that point that I knew Ani's challenges were severe. Children use toys to make friends and build friendships. Ani didn't even know what to do *with* a toy.

Our son, Max, tried to play with Ani and offer his expertise on being the big brother. He was 10 when Ani came home to us, and even though he wanted a little brother, he tried to be the role model. Unfortunately, I was suffering from my own torment and guilt of "destroying" my family because I had brought home a damaged little girl. I didn't give Max the space to teach Ani how to play nor did I give him the opportunity to learn how to be a part of her life.

We began in-home intensive therapy when Ani was eight-years old. All of her therapists were college age students or slightly older. One of our therapists, Corrine, actually went to recesses with Ani throughout the school day. Most days, Ani just ran around the perimeter of the playground by herself. However, a plan was created where Corrine offered children stickers to include Ani in their games or interact with her. The children loved the stickers and Ani began to emulate play.

In addition, I scoured rummage sales for age-appropriate toys. Ani wanted to play with baby toys–anything that made noise and had bright, cheerful colors. But, I bought toys meant for a typical eight-year-old girl: dolls, a dollhouse, crib, high chair, stroller, and make-up vanity. I bought all the things I loved as a little girl and hoped that eventually Ani would love them, too. One day as I walked past Ani's bedroom, she was feeding her doll, Emily, in the high chair. Then, I suggested we take Emily for a walk in her stroller. Play was beginning to sink in.

When I would host birthday parties for Ani, her therapists always attended because they cued and prompted Ani on how to make conversation. Her therapists wrote social stories for her and all play was directed so Ani could learn how to play and what language to use when playing.

We immersed Ani in our community and signed her up for Special Olympics. As she grew, her athletic gifts became apparent. She was a determined runner and a good swimmer. As a member of Special Olympics, Ani took part in track, bowling, gymnastics, volleyball, basketball, and tennis. We refer to the Special Olympics athletes as "Ani's people." Among this group, we don't have to worry about her behavior or what she might say. Her peers "understand" her as best as they can and, as parents, we are all flexible, patient, and sympathetic.

In high school, Ani became a member of the track team and a member of the girls swim team. She was the only girl on the team who ran cross-country and her teammates were helpful and supportive. However, Ani "retired" from track in her junior year of high school, deciding that she had enough. Ani became a member of the girls swim team in her freshmen year and stayed with it all four years. The swim manager became her swim mentor. Alana explained appropriate behavior on the swim deck, demonstrated proper etiquette at swim meets, and rewrote Ani's swim notes and sent them home with her. She went with Ani to the pasta parties and introduced Ani to her friends so Ani had a lunch group. However, Alana was a senior and the following year things changed. Ani didn't have a mentor and the swim captain was expected to help her out. While Ani muddled through, it was clear she was lost without Alana and the other girls weren't interested in picking up the slack. By junior year, Ani was no longer a team member. Yes, she was on the roster, and yes, she swam with a group of girls. But, as we watched from the gallery, it was obvious she was alone. In Ani's senior year, an e-mail from the parent of the captain was sent to the swim girls. The parent asked that the girls pick up all of the "stuff" they had left the night before. Apparently, there

had been a swim team sleepover and all members of the swim team were invited–except Ani. She was the only one from the team who wasn't invited. When I emailed the parent and asked for clarification, she apologized and said Ani's invitation must have been "lost" in the mail. Thankfully, Ani didn't understand their behavior toward her and I made sure the lost invitation was never mentioned.

Finally, "friendships" in the sense that we understand them, continue to elude Ani. She does not have a "best" friend or someone to share girl secrets. She has friends through Special Olympics; but, we always have to remind her to make conversation and be part of the group, since she is content to watch the activities around her. In addition, we hope that someday Max and Ani will be able to form a friendship—whatever that may look like—and take the role of brother and sister. Lastly, we are appreciative for those continued opportunities to support Ani in learning what friendship is and how to make friends, and we are indebted to those who help us along the way.

Critical Thinking

1. Can adolescents recover from an impoverished early childhood experience?

2. How can adolescents be more inclusive of children like Ani as they struggle with their own adolescent issues?

Internet References

Disabilities Complicate Adolescence
http://www.post-gazette.com/news/health/2005/09/28/Disabilities-complicate-adolescence/stories/200509280235

From Neurons to Neighborhoods: The Science of Early Childhood Development: Making Friends and Getting Along with Peers
https://www.ncbi.nlm.nih.gov/books/NBK225544/

Helping the Socially Isolated Child Make Friends
http://www.ldonline.org/article/19272/

Making (and Keeping) Friends: A Model for Social Skills Instruction
https://www.iidc.indiana.edu/pages/Making-and-Keeping-Friends-A-Model-for-Social-Skills-Instruction

Special at School But Lonely at Home: An Alternative Friendship Group for Adolescents with Down Syndrome
https://www.down-syndrome.org/practice/2012/

PEG GRAFWALLNER adopted Ani from a Bulgarian orphanage when she was five years, 11 months. Not knowing what to do or where to go for assistance, her family began a journey to learn, ask, and eventually educate. There were extremely dark times when they felt completely alone. But, Ani's inspiring smile and beautiful spirit has kept the family grounded.

Article   Prepared by: Claire N. Rubman, *Suffolk County Community College*

Childhood Lost

Girls are entering puberty sooner than ever and jeopardizing their health and happiness.

SUSAN SCUTTI

Learning Outcomes

After reading this article, you will be able to:

- Define "precocious puberty."
- Give three possible reasons for early maturation.
- Describe the social, emotional, and psychological impact of early onset puberty.
- Explain hormone therapy in more detail.

At age 6, Rebecca's body began to develop in ways that seemed unusual. Her mother, Ellen, had noticed a change in Rebecca's breast area, but some of the other little girls, the chubbier ones at least, also seemed to be carrying extra weight there. But there was also the hair that had begun to appear under her daughter's arms.

"People assumed she was so much older than she was, but still she would cry sometimes, and people would look at you like, *How old is that kid?*" says Ellen, who spoke to *Newsweek* under condition of anonymity.

When a test showed Rebecca's bone age to be 10½, a pediatric endocrinologist diagnosed "precocious puberty." While the exact cause is unknown, this endocrine disorder is triggered by the early release of hormones in the brain, a circumstance that hurls a child into sexual maturation years before the usual age.

This sudden sexual development in a child so young can be unnerving to parents. "My daughter is 7 years and 10 months old. She started having body odor at 5 and breast buds at 6," one mother wrote recently in a group chat about the condition. She wrote, too, of her daughter's "roller-coaster emotions," a common complaint from parents observing massive mood swings, PMS-like symptoms and other "teen emotions" in daughters just beginning the first grade—and in some cases even younger.

The condition affects individuals in different ways. According to Ellen, the most troubling sign in Rebecca was growing six inches in one year. "There was a lot of stress mainly due to her height," says Ellen. "People would say, '*Oh, she's so tall!*,' not thinking or anything, and you could see her little face get sad."

"People thought I was older," says Rebecca, who is now 14. "[Like] I had failed kindergarten or something." Her mother says, "She had to be very mature a lot of the time, but on the flip side, she was all into Disney and still a little girl."

Unlike Rebecca, many precocious kids lose their interest in Disney and little-girl things and begin to act, well, the age of their bodies. The mother of one 8-year-old wrote that her daughter "is a very sexual being. Although she does not by definition understand what 'sexiness' means, she exhibits a very particular awareness of her body and wants other people to notice her." Another mother observed, "It is really as if my 6-year-old has a 12-year-old trapped in her body."

Living in a Sea of Chemicals

In girls, puberty is commonly defined as breast development, growth of pubic hair, and menarche, the beginning of the menstrual cycle. At the turn of the 20th century, the average age for an American girl to get her period was 16 to 17. Today, that number has plummeted to under 13, according to data from the National Health and Nutrition Examination Survey. The trend has been attributed to the epidemic of overweight children and a greater exposure to pollution, which does bad things to developing bodies and accelerates the timing of a girl's first menstruation.

Environmental toxins also cause many girls to develop breasts at an earlier age than in the past. Compared with 20 years ago, American girls today begin developing breasts anywhere from one month to four months earlier, a significant difference. At the same time, the number of girls who begin to develop early is increasing. "Just a generation ago, less than five percent of girls started puberty before the age of 8; today that percentage has more than doubled," note Dr. Louise Greenspan and Julianna Deardorff in *The New Puberty: How to Navigate Early Development in Today's Girls*.

Among the toxins causing this trend, the biggest offenders are plastic compounds, in particular phthalates, man-made chemicals found all over the place: in plastic food and beverage containers, carpeting, shampoos, insect repellents, vinyl flooring, shower curtains, plastic toys, and in the steering wheels and dashboards of most cars. Our bodies cannot metabolize phthalates, which interfere with the endocrine system—the body's system of glands and hormones—and harm fat cells. Indirectly, phthalates may cause weight gain and so influence the timing of puberty. "The No. 1 factor that was pushing girls into puberty early was their body mass index," says Dr. Frank Biro, director of education and a professor in the Division of Adolescent Medicine at Cincinnati Children's Hospital Medical Center.

Our children are living in a "sea of chemicals," says Dr. Marcia E. Herman-Giddens, a professor of public health at the University of North Carolina. She argues that children are speeding into puberty before they're ready, and that this early maturation is both the symptom of bodily damage that has already occurred and the probable cause of health consequences they may expect in the future.

Getting Hit On

"It's one of the most robust findings in studies of psychological development," says Laurence Steinberg, a professor of psychology at Temple University, and author of *Age of Opportunity: Lessons from the New Science of Adolescence*. He is referring to recent research demonstrating how earlier-maturing girls are more likely to become depressed. One 2014 study, for instance, finds "girls with earlier [puberty] timing had higher levels of depression symptoms at age 10 years." Another study echoes these findings, while also suggesting such effects may be long-lasting. Along with higher rates of depression, younger girls who enter puberty earlier than their peers are more prone to obesity and drug abuse.

When children enter puberty, their brains undergo changes—brought on by the flood of pubertal hormones—that "makes them especially attentive to what other people think of them and especially responsive to social reward," says Steinberg.

Dopamine, a neurotransmitter crucial to the experience of pleasure, floods and effectively remodels the pathway between the behavior-regulating prefrontal cortex and the brain's reward center. "The adolescent brain is one where the accelerator is pressed to the floor before there's a good braking system in place," says Steinberg. "This gap between when the brain is easily aroused and when the braking is in place creates a period of vulnerability." With puberty occurring at a younger age, this period begins earlier, when a girl may be inadequately prepared.

After all, early maturing girls naturally attract unwanted attention. "You encounter a young lady in the mall and she looks like she's 15 years old," says Biro. "You will interact with her like she's 15, but suppose she's 11?" And because of the way her brain is being flooded with hormones, a young girl hanging out with older kids most likely wants to please and may be more inclined to go along with the crowd.

Meanwhile, no matter how physically developed a girl is, her psychosocial maturation remains anchored to her chronological age. "These young girls get, let's use the term *hit on*, by older boys and men and how can they be prepared to deal with it? Obviously, grown women have a hard [enough] time dealing with unwanted sexual attention," observes Herman-Giddens.

The brain is highly plastic, and stressful experiences like these take their toll. Early-maturing girls are more likely to smoke cigarettes, they are at high risk for substance use, and they have higher rates of eating disorders. Though most of this fallout is experienced while they are young, some of the consequences extend into adult life. Substance problems and depression experienced at a young age can easily return, for instance. Then there are health problems that those who undergo early puberty are more likely than the general population to experience later on in their lives, like higher blood pressure and cardiovascular problems.

"Puberty is considered one of those windows of susceptibility," says Biro, when the body is especially sensitive to the negative health impact of social and environmental stressors. In particular, the actively maturing breast tissue of a girl, unlike the breast tissue of a full-grown woman, is more vulnerable to damaging environmental pollutants.

Today's girl is both starting puberty earlier and going through it more slowly, according to Biro, which means a girl remains in this high-risk state for a longer. In an article, he coauthored with Deardorff and others, Biro found up to a 30 percent increased risk for breast cancer when a woman experiences her first period at a younger age. And "for each year that age of menarche was delayed, the risk of premenopausal breast cancer was reduced by 9 percent, and risk of postmenopausal breast cancer was reduced by 4 percent."

Early breast development also opens the door to reproductive tract cancers, says Herman-Giddens, since "if you're starting to develop breasts, your body is making estrogen." Estrogen, especially when combined with stress hormones, is a known cancer-causing agent. Having had an earlier start to puberty, an early-maturing girl produces more estrogen over the years and so elevates her lifetime risk of reproductive cancers.

Able to Conceive in Kindergarten

There is a medical solution for patients who, like 6-year-old Rebecca, are diagnosed with precocious puberty. Hormone treatments can essentially halt the process of sexual maturation. Then, at an appropriate age, the drugs are withdrawn and puberty plays out. Some girls diagnosed with precocious puberty have no choice but to medicate in order to prevent serious bone and growth problems. Rebecca fell into this category. While precocious children may stand half a foot taller than their peers in kindergarten, these same children also tend to stop growing at a young age and so never reach their predicted adult heights. Often, they fail to reach five feet tall.

As the average age of the onset of puberty continues to rapidly decrease, the line between endocrine disorder and so-called normal development has begun to blur. "A lot of girls who we are labeling as premature puberty now are probably normal, healthy girls who are at the lower end of the new normal," says Dr. Paul Kaplowitz of Children's National Medical Center. Which makes it pretty difficult for parents to know whether they should be medicating their young daughters.

In these edge cases, the decision to undergo hormone therapy is a matter of balancing potential benefits and harms. According to Dr. Alan Christianson, author of *The Adrenal Reset Diet*, the medications themselves may have both short-term side effects, such as headaches, hot flashes and vaginal bleeding, and possible lasting complications, such as thyroid gland disorders.

Another barrier to treatment is the expense: The drugs cost a minimum of $15,000 a year, excluding lab costs. In Ellen's case, most of this was covered by insurance, but she still ended up having to pay a few thousand dollars a year.

Which is why many parents decide there's nothing more to do for an early-maturing daughter other than guiding her, the best they can, through the vulnerable years. That, though, is often a difficult and solitary road to walk. As Ellen says, "Precocious puberty is not like allergies or something where you can just find other mothers on the playground or at the school going through the same thing with their kids."

But many other parents do choose medication. Having seen very young girls struggle with their periods, Kaplowitz says he's "OK" with treating those early-maturing girls who "are likely to start their period well before age 10." More than a few girls today begin breast development shortly after turning 8 and then continue growing at a rapid pace.

Outward manifestations of maturation are one thing. Usually, though, it's not height problems or breast development that propel parents to opt for medical treatment. "In my experience, it is largely because parents are worried about whether their girls can handle periods at an early age," says Kaplowitz.

In the words of one mother in a chat room, the possibility that her daughter "could menstruate at any time (she was already having discharge by about 3 or 4) trumped the height factor . . . The mere possibility of her being able to conceive in kindergarten was enough for me to decide to treat her."

Critical Thinking

1. If you were the parent of a child who was experiencing precocious puberty, what would you do to help your child?

2. What can we, as a society, do to reduce some of the unintended contributors to precocious puberty in a child's environment?

Internet References

Early Puberty in Girls Is Becoming Epidemic and Getting Worse
   http://www.alternet.org/personal-health/early-puberty-girls-epidemic

Precocious Puberty: Genetic and Rare Diseases Information Center
   https://rarediseases.info.nih.gov/diseases/7446/precocious-puberty

Precious Puberty Symptoms and Causes
   http://www.mayoclinic.org/diseases-conditions/precocious-puberty/symptoms-causes/dxc-20266003

Puberty Comes Earlier and Earlier for Girls
   http://www.newsweek.com/2015/02/06/puberty-comes-earlier-and-earlier-girls-301920.html

Unit 2

UNIT

Prepared by: Claire N. Rubman, *Suffolk County Community College*

Developmental Changes in Adolescence: Cognitive, Physical, Social, and Emotional

In this section, we will focus on what happens within the developing adolescent brain and how those changes manifest themselves from a physical, social, and emotional perspective.

We have learned a great deal about the brain through MRI's and PET scans. We know that we have an abundance of neurons that fire and become "wired together." This is referred to as brain connectivity. As the frontal lobe increases in connectivity, so we gain "white matter." The myelination process helps to speed up those communications in our brain. The price that we pay for this speed is a loss of flexibility as we enter adulthood. This makes the adolescent years a critical time for exploration and discovery. During this critical period of growth, our brains increase in power but also become more vulnerable (Perkins-Gough, 2015).

One byproduct of all of this increased growth is that our brain stokes our desire to seek out new sensations and take risks. The down side of this discovery and exploration is that adolescents face an increased 200 percent chance that they will die (Miller, 2015). Car accidents, homicides, and suicide are the main causes of adolescent accidents and deaths. Despite this, humans are more successful at adapting to new environments than Neanderthals, polar bears and gorillas—mainly because we take longer to mature and there we can adapt to changing environments. This is how we survive!

The frontal lobe is the "seat" of our executive functioning. This is where we make judgments and control our impulses. Adolescents develop control over this region in time, but it is a slow process.

One ideal way to nurture this slow moving development is to create the ideal set of circumstances for experience and growth. Goeller (2016) touts the benefit of summer camps that are designed exclusively for adolescents to learn about the changes that they are experiencing in their thinking and reasoning. This is the ideal risk-free environment for teens to learn about the physical and biological changes that affect their decision-making and their behavior choices. Here, they can learn about their own emotional triggers. The frontal lobe does not fully mature until around 25 years of age, this gives adolescents plenty of time to role play and learn brain facts at summer camp!

Teens need to learn about their changing brains and how they can optimize their own development. This is especially true with regard to sleep. What do teens actually know about the importance of sleep during these critical years of brain growth? Do they know, for example, that adolescents need around nine hours of sleep each night but many only get as few as six hours? According to the National Sleep Foundation, this sleep deprivation or "sleep debt" contributes to poor decision-making, inattention, depression, driving errors, and the use of stimulants to stay awake (Amos & D'Andrea, 2012). The sleep debt is due to many factors including caffeine consumption, electronics in teen bedrooms, an excess of homework, too much socializing, and a lack of understanding about the importance of sleep.

Article   Prepared by: Claire N. Rubman, *Suffolk County Community College*

Grab the Teenage Window of Opportunity

KAREN GOELLER

Learning Outcomes

After reading this article, you will be able to:

- Describe the role of the "amygdala" in adolescence.
- Explain the value of the right brain, the left brain, and the relationship between both in adolescent development.

The camp experience provides an outstanding opportunity for personal growth. The adolescent brain, which is undergoing tremendous physical and neurological development, can benefit greatly from the unique attention of the camp environment. When approached with awareness, we can help adolescent children develop positive tools that they will be able to count on for the rest of their lives. It's often too easy to simply close our eyes and hope our kids will just grow out of some of the stereotypical negative adolescent behaviors including the predictably unpredictable mood swing, as well as the automatic barrage of hostility and anger. When we understand the neurological changes underlying these antisocial behaviors, we become more resilient in our ability to help our adolescent campers not only manage a more positive emotional response but generate healthier behavior.

Dr. Jill Bolte Taylor, respected scientist and *New York Times* bestselling author of *My Stroke of Insight: A Brain Scientist's Personal Journey* (2006), helps us imagine new possibilities for teenage campers. In her TEDxYouth talk the Neurological Transformation of the Teenage Brain (2013), Taylor shares that the teenage years represent one of the brain's most vulnerable stages. When she draws parallels between recovery from her own experience with a stroke, and the last 20 years of research about the teenage brain, she helps us understand that as adults we have the ability (and the responsibility) to help our teenagers

better understand the biology underlying what they are thinking and feeling. Taylor's inspirational message emphasizes that we have this one-time window of opportunity as hands-on camp leaders to deeply and profoundly impact how our campers live their lives.

Taylor grew up as a camper herself. Camp provided a powerful social setting for character and relationship building that helped Taylor and her friends go on to lead meaningful lives. And now, even as she has achieved much fame, Taylor comes back to her background as a camper to illustrate firsthand the possibilities for teenagers to make extraordinary neurological connections. Her lessons provide a starting point for us to reassess our own beliefs, daily routines, and interactions with adolescents and uncover new ways to strengthen the camp experience.

Lesson 1: Learn More about the Developing Teenage Brain

"Keep them alive 'til 25!" is Taylor's rallying cry and her best advice for camp directors and staff who provide programming for adolescents. The adolescent brain functions very differently from that of an adult brain, and we cannot afford to forget this. The frontal lobe of the brain, responsible for personality make-up, impulse control, and judgment about what is right and wrong, is not completely developed until about age 25. So, Taylor's eye-opening message is directed first at the adults who work with adolescents. We are the ones who must become more observant about the mental health of adolescents. Teenage campers experience neurological shifts as part of normal development, and we must be on constant alert that these teenagers are thinking, speaking, and acting with brains that are not yet fully mature. We need heightened awareness about everything

Teenage Brain-focused Activities for Camping Staff to Try Now

- Right from the start, open campfire talks with thought-provoking, brain-based learning. Share a basic brain fact about *neuroplasticity*, the ability of cells to reconnect, and explain that the brains we bring to camp will not be the ones with which we leave. Talk to campers about the importance of being open-minded and trying new skills. Mix campers in small groups and ask them to think about ways they will grow their own brains at camp. To stimulate conversation, give each group chart paper and colored markers. Ask them to draw a brain and brainstorm possibilities around it. All ideas are good ones!

- Tweens and teens like learning new and challenging words. Introduce campers to the *amygdala*, structures in each hemisphere of the brain that regulate emotions such as fear and anger. Share that teenage brains are different from those of adults because the teenage brain's frontal lobe is not yet fully developed, which can easily cause teens to engage in impulsive and immature behavior. Put them in pairs and let them act out risk-taking situations, inserting the voice of the amygdala by asking themselves questions, such as "Do I feel angry and fearful now, or do I feel safe and calm?" Have fun with the activity and teach campers the importance of slowing down and confronting a situation in a more mindful and peaceful manner. You could extend the activity to give the Amygdala Award daily to a camper who handles a difficult situation in a calm and positive way.

- Give campers a brief explanation of both right-brain (compassionate, artistic, creative, playful) and left-brain (methodical, focused on details, judgement of right and wrong) thinking. Give campers each a sketch pad and take them on a nature walk. Tell them to look for animals or plants in their natural settings and ask them to draw one of their choosing. Underneath the drawn object, have them write about it from a left-brain perspective. Then ask them to write about the same object as it might be perceived by someone with a right-brain perspective.

- Provide families with a brain-based, postcamping reflection activity to engage them in meaningful discussions with their teens after camp. Having conversations together will help families be a part of their

teenager's growth process. Suggest some open-ended questions:

- What new and different activities did you participate in at camp?
- What activities did you most enjoy and why?
- What relationships did you develop at camp?
- What were some of the qualities in these friends that you admired?
- How can you continue to build upon the connections you made with ideas, activities, and friends after camp?

adolescent to step up in our supervisory roles to help adolescents through this challenging stage of change.

We must seek out ways to teach adolescents about what is going on in their own brains. Creating simple learning activities about the brain can help teenagers better understand not only their own behaviors but also the actions of those teens around them. Excellent kid-friendly materials that explain adolescent neurological changes are available on sites such as the Society for Neuroscience (brainfacts.org).

Camp is a relaxing setting in which to learn about physical and hormonal brain development and its impact on behavior and then to practice behavior modification in a less threatening environment. For instance, when adolescents learn about their brain's frontal lobe not yet being fully developed and their predisposition to impulsive behavior, they can have fun role-playing various strategies with peers to learn how to react in more positive ways during stressful situations.

Families will be reassured to hear that adolescent brain development is recognized (and celebrated) at camp. As camp directors, you should communicate clearly with families about the benefits of camp for allowing teenagers to explore and attempt new skills during this growth stage. Having camp personnel who are knowledgeable about adolescent brain development will give families confidence that they have made a wise investment in their children's emotional health. Then, designing pre- and postcamp activities for the adolescent brain can engage families and extend learning to support campers at home.

Lesson 2: Understand and Question the Status of the Amygdala

Camp personnel quickly notice the height, weight, and skin changes occurring in the bodies of adolescent campers, but do we just as readily recognize the neurological shifts taking place? Taylor shares that because the frontal lobe is not fully developed in adolescence, teenagers' actions are controlled largely by the amygdala (one in each hemisphere of the brain) that regulate emotions such as fear and anger.

There is a biological reason why adolescents process information differently from adults. Information streams in through the sensory systems and heads directly for the amygdala within the brain's limbic system, determining adolescents' perceived levels of safety in the world. When enough of the information coming in feels familiar, the amygdalae are calm; adolescents feel safe, and they are capable of learning new information. On the contrary, when the amygdalae feel unsafe, Taylor explains that adolescents experience this as anxiety, and it is harder for adolescents to think clearly and concentrate. Having a basic knowledge about the amygdala will help us understand that adolescent campers will not always respond thoughtfully or make good decisions. In fact, we should anticipate and plan for their impulsivity and immaturity as part of their normal neurological development.

Taylor urges adults to help adolescents learn to recognize emotional triggers. She shares that to some degree adolescents have the cognitive ability to control the circuitry in their brains and consciously choose to remain in the present moment and not engage with negative behavior. As our adolescent campers begin to feel anxious, frustrated, or become angry easily, we can help them slow down and confront the situations in a calmer manner. Knowing the importance of remaining calm and learning how to stay even-tempered in threatening situations will enable adolescents to think before acting impulsively or irrationally.

Lesson 3: Nurture Multiple and Different Brain Connections

Taylor had a stroke in the left hemisphere of her brain, and her trauma gave her an unparalleled opportunity to experience the redeveloping brain. Her rehabilitation took place in the same order, with the same circuits and the same subjects, as a young child going through normal development. She spent eight years making new connections and recovering all of her mental and physical functions.

Taylor speaks of neuroplasticity, the ability of cells to reconnect. She explains that the neurons in our brains are the same, but as time passes, their connections are altered based upon our experiences. Taylor asserts that the teenage brain is in an ongoing state of development, which is very different from the mature adult brain. Because of the major neurological changes that happen during the teenage years, it is important that we pay

attention to which circuits we are enabling and which ones we are discouraging.

As an example, if a child is a good singer while in elementary school, Taylor urges that child to keep singing throughout the teenage years to keep this circuitry strong during adult life. She cautions that a pruning back of 50 percent of connections takes place during adolescence, but the good news is that adolescents can now nurture the other half that they are going to keep. Taylor optimistically claims the beauty of the teenage years is that adolescents are "tending the gardens of their minds." Adolescence brings a time of great promise as teenagers can explore and think expansively about who and how they want to be when they get older.

Camp directors and staff need to know that the brains our adolescents bring to camp will not be the ones with which they will leave. What a tremendous obligation we have in helping adolescents nourish those brain connections! The camp setting is a natural haven for teenagers to ask questions and problem solve independently and with peers. Camp offers so many possibilities for adolescent campers in trying out new skills, exploring new hobbies, or beginning new activities that they can then continue into adulthood. What is most important is that we encourage adolescents to take safe risks, play, and open themselves up to more possibilities and options. And, as adults, we need to keep asking ourselves how we are seeking out creative ways to encourage and reward our adolescents for pursuing and practicing unfamiliar skills and hobbies.

Camps are unique places where adolescents don't have to be the best and, instead of competing, they cheer each other on. Camps are safe, nurturing spaces where adolescents can try and fail without the pressures that might exist elsewhere. For instance, adolescents can become discouraged and alienated when they try out and are cut from competitive sports at school or in community clubs; instead, at camp, teens can join, join, and join again. Participation itself is our goal as we encourage and stimulate new and multiple brain connections.

Lesson 4: Explore Learning from Both the Right and Left Minds

Understanding what the brain can do and what each part of the brain is doing at different times during daily activities helps us make sense of our world. Taylor explains how, on the morning of her stroke, the language centers in her left hemisphere became silent. Instead of feeling anxious, she became comforted by a growing sense of peacefulness. We have two very unique ways of processing information and of perceiving the world. Our right brain looks at the collective whole; it looks for similarities, and it is compassionate, loving, artistic, creative, and supportive. Our left brain focuses on the individual; it seeks differences, and it thinks linearly, creates and understands language, and is the source of judgment of what is right or wrong.

Taylor advocates that we need to teach adolescents about the most important relationship they have, which exists between the characters of their right and left brains. She adds that much of the new research in the last 15 years has focused on mindfulness, the ability to alter our thoughts and change the circuitry underneath, enabling us to think in different ways. Adolescents need to be more aware of their own mental health, recognizing that they are products of what is going on within their brain cells. Perhaps adolescents cannot always choose, but they can become cognizant of "right brain" and "left brain" characteristics. Often, we recognize the need for left brain sequential, analytical, and logical intentional leaders, organizers, and doers. Yet, as Taylor shares, the right mind provides us with holistic, innovative, and intuitive perspectives that enable us to develop deeper capacities for empathy, inventiveness, and passion.

As camp directors and staff, we should strive to enrich both right brain and left brain thinking in the activities we design for our campers. To illustrate, right brain activities will lead adolescents to become more compassionate, expansive, open, and supportive of others. Left brain activities will give adolescents opportunities to create and understand language, define the boundaries of where we begin and end, judge right from wrong, and focus on details and more details. As adults, we need to help adolescents draw from strengths in both hemispheres of their brains to assist them in leading more balanced, healthy, and meaningful lives.

Final Camp Reflections

Taylor illuminates our thinking about the adolescent brain and its vast potential, power, and possibilities. Her neuroscience research and firsthand experience suggest we should re-evaluate and readjust how we work with adolescent campers. Yes, the brain is a complex organ, but it doesn't have to be intimidating.

Adolescents who are fortunate enough to participate in the camp experience are truly taking care of their brain cells. What power we have to observe and shape the biological circuitry of our adolescents. However, as adults we must remember that these changes are taking place and think about our power

in guiding their behavior accordingly. Those of us who work with adolescent campers must challenge our own thinking and capitalize on this one-time, exciting maturation period. When armed with impactful, brain-based lessons, we can open up unlimited possibilities and unparalleled growth for our adolescent campers.

References

Taylor, J. B. (2006). *My stroke of insight: A brain scientist's personal journey*. New York, NY: Penguin Group.

Taylor, J. B. (2013, February). *The neurological transformation of the teenage brain*. TEDxYouth. Retrieved from youtube.com/watch?v=PzT_SBl31-s

Critical Thinking

1. How can we encourage adolescents to readjust and reevaluate their thinking in their daily lives?

2. How could we modify our immediate environment to better accommodate the needs of adolescents?

Internet References

Developmental Characteristics of Young Adolescents
https://www.amle.org/BrowsebyTopic/WhatsNew/WNDet/TabId/270/ArtMID/888/ArticleID/455/Developmental-Characteristics-of-Young-Adolescents.aspx

My Stroke of Insight
https://www.ted.com/talks/jill_bolte_taylor_s_powerful_stroke_of_insight

Summer Camps Make Kids Resilient
https://www.psychologytoday.com/blog/nurturing-resilience/201202/summer-camps-make-kids-resilient

The Workings of the Adolescent Brain
http://www.brainfacts.org/across-the-lifespan/youth-and-aging/articles/2016/the-workings-of-the-adolescent-brain-091616/

KAREN GOELLER, PhD, lives in Terre Haute, Indiana, with her husband Michael. She has two grown children, Scott and Kate. She currently serves as a deputy superintendent of the Vigo County School Corporation. Karen and Jill Bolte Taylor spent summers camping together at Camp Na Wa Kwa in Poland, Indiana, with Barbara Webster's Girl Scout Troop.

Article   Prepared by: Claire N. Rubman, *Suffolk County Community College*

The Sleepy Teenager: Waking Up to the Unique Sleep Needs of Adolescents

Biologic changes in the sleep–wake cycle in conjunction with environmental and social influences contribute to inadequate sleep and hypersomnolence in adolescents. Pediatricians should counsel their teenaged patients about the many consequences of sleep debt to keep them functioning well in school as well as at home.

LOUELLA B. AMOS AND LYNN A. D'ANDREA

Learning Outcomes

After reading this article, you will be able to:

• List seven possible consequences of insufficient sleep in adolescence.

• Discuss how much sleep adolescents think that they need versus how much sleep they actually get.

• Explain two possible contributors to the "night owl" tendency among adolescents.

Teenagers generally require 8.5 to 9.5 hours of sleep per night.[1] The National Sleep Foundation (NSF) 2006 Sleep in America Poll revealed that adolescents report sleeping 7.6 hours on school nights, even though they feel that they need an average of 8.2 hours of sleep for optimal daytime function.[2]

More than 50 percent of teenagers feel sleepy during the day.[2] Only approximately 20 percent of all surveyed adolescents (6th- to 12th-graders) report an adequate amount of nightly sleep (≥9 hours per night); among high school students (9th- to 12th-graders), the percentage decreases to 9 percent, suggesting that sleep deprivation is more common in older adolescents. Interestingly, 90 percent of parents believe that their adolescent gets enough sleep on most school nights.

Adolescent Sleep Physiology

Circadian rhythms organize the timing of various biologic processes, including sleep regulation. Light is the main environmental stimulus that synchronizes the intrinsic human circadian period to the 24-hour day. Melatonin, a hormone secreted by the pineal gland, induces evening drowsiness and also maintains the inherent sleep–wake cycle. Light blocks the secretion of melatonin; therefore, light exposure at bedtime can delay sleep initiation. Advanced Tanner stage has been associated with a delay in melatonin secretion in adolescents aged 11 to 14 years.[3] In addition, adolescents seem to have a longer circadian period (24.3 hours), and difficulty entraining their sleep-wake cycle to the 24-hour solar day causes circadian phase delay or a "night owl" tendency to stay up late at night.[4] This circadian alteration during adolescence has been observed across various cultures throughout the world and even across several mammalian species.[5]

Sleep–wake homeostasis refers to the buildup of "sleep drive" throughout the day. A prolonged period of wakefulness increases the intrinsic need for sleep, or sleep pressure. Taking a nap in the afternoon affects sleep homeostasis by decreasing this drive to sleep, thereby delaying sleep onset at bedtime. Adolescents with more advanced Tanner stage have a slower accumulation in sleep pressure compared with younger, less mature adolescents.[6] This pubertal decrease in sleep drive may promote delayed sleep initiation in teenagers.

Together, the circadian timing and homeostatic sleep systems regulate the sleep–wake cycle.[7] Developmental changes in both systems contribute to the struggle to fall asleep at night during adolescence. The combination of difficulty initiating sleep and the adolescent sleep need (≥9 hours per night) yields chronic sleep debt and daytime sleepiness for many teenagers.

Sleep Behaviors

Based on the 2006 NSF poll, most adolescents (97 percent) have an electronic device in their bedrooms.[2] Seventy-six percent of adolescents report watching television within an hour of bedtime. One study found that among adolescents aged 12 to 18 years, 82 percent watched television and 55 percent used their computers after 9 p.m.[8] Other nighttime activities include watching DVDs, cell phone use, and playing video/computer games. It has been hypothesized that adolescents experience an exaggerated response to the circadian phase-delaying effects of nighttime light exposure; therefore, light stimulation associated with use of electronics close to bedtime may exacerbate their natural night owl tendency.[5]

Caffeine consumption is highly prevalent among adolescents. The 2006 NSF poll found that 31 percent of adolescents who reported drinking two or more caffeinated beverages per day were more likely not to sleep enough on school nights compared with those who drink 1 or fewer.[2] Of 191 middle school students, average caffeine consumption was 52.7 mg per day, and 19 percent of students consumed more than 100 mg per day. Students may be unaware of the caffeine content of many commonly consumed beverages and over-the-counter medications (Table 1).[9] Increased caffeine consumption in this cohort correlated with a later bedtime, more disrupted sleep, and daytime sleepiness.[10] In healthy adults, the elimination half-life of caffeine is 5 hours; therefore, caffeine lingers in the body well after consumption and can affect sleep.[11]

Other activities that keep teenagers up at night include evening homework, extracurricular activities (e.g., athletics), jobs, and socializing. Adolescents who work 20 or more hours per week attain less sleep, tend to oversleep more on school days, and report increased use of caffeine, alcohol, and tobacco compared with adolescents who work fewer than 20 hours per week.[12] Parental influence on setting bedtimes dramatically decreases as adolescents get older. Adolescents who have a curfew get to sleep earlier, wake up earlier in the morning, and have less daytime sleepiness.

Implications of Insufficient Sleep

Chronic sleep debt in adolescents negatively affects various aspects of their lives. Difficulty waking up in the morning results in tardiness or absence from school. Poor attendance and inattentiveness in class adversely affect grades. Adequate sleep is also essential for memory consolidation and learning enhancement.[13] Researchers found that high school students with self-reported earlier bedtimes and longer, more regular sleep had higher grades (A's and B's) compared with students with later bedtimes and shorter or more irregular sleep (C's, D's, and F's).[14] They also found more depressed mood in adolescents who slept fewer than 6 hours, 45 minutes, on school nights compared with those who slept 8 hours, 15 minutes, or more on school nights.

Sleep deprivation not only adversely affects grades but also decision-making skills, executive function, and behavioral inhibition.[15,16] In an emotionally labile age group such as adolescents, this presents a potentially dangerous public health problem, particularly with regard to substance abuse and drowsy driving.[17] Most college students do not sleep enough, use alcohol as sleep aids, and take stimulants to improve daytime alertness; 16 percent of these same students have fallen asleep while driving.[18]

According to the 2006 NSF poll, more than 50 percent of surveyed adolescents who drive reported driving sleepy in the past year.[2] The National Young Driver Survey by Children's Hospital of Philadelphia discovered that 75 percent of teenagers saw peers driving drowsy, but only 42 percent saw fatigue as a risk factor for unsafe driving.[19,20] In 2005, approximately 7,500 drivers aged between 15 and 20 years were involved in fatal motor vehicle crashes, and about 3,500 adolescent drivers were killed in these crashes.[21] In an analysis of all US motor vehicle accidents occurring between 1999 and 2008, 16.5 percent of fatal crashes involved a drowsy driver.[22]

Evaluation

The first step in evaluating sleepy teenagers is to determine whether they are getting enough sleep. It is important to elicit information about their sleep–wake cycle (Table 2). If they sleep fewer than 8 to 9 hours and have difficulty waking up spontaneously in the morning with or without an alarm, they may not be sleeping enough. Falling asleep at school, daytime naps, and "oversleeping" or "sleeping-in" on the weekends are other signs of insufficient sleep during school days.

Table 1   Caffeine Content Chart

Product	Serving size	Caffeine content, mg
Coca-Cola	12 oz	35
Diet Coke	12 oz	47
Pepsi	12 oz	38
Diet Pepsi	12 oz	36
Dr. Pepper	12 oz	42
Mountain Dew	12 oz	54
Coffee	8 oz	133
Cappuccino	6 oz	35
Starbucks coffee, grande	16 oz	320
Einstein Brothers coffee	16 oz	300
Dunkin Donuts coffee	16 oz	206
Tea, brewed	8 oz	53
Iced tea, Snapple	16 oz	42
Chocolate milk	8 oz	5
Dark chocolate	1 oz	20
Hershey's Kisses	9 pieces	9
Dexatrim	1 tablet	200
Excedrin, extra strength	2 tablets	130
No Doz, max strength	1 tablet	200
Red Bull	8.3 oz	80
Enviga	12 oz	100
Monster Energy	16 oz	160
Spike Shooter	8.4 oz	300
Five-Hour Energy Drink	1.93 oz	207

From Center for Science in the Public Interest.[9]

Why are many teenagers not sleeping enough? The most common reason is a late bedtime. Teenagers fall asleep later but need to wake up early in the morning for school or other morning activities. Although there are physiologic reasons for this night owl tendency, sleep hygiene and environment also play a role (Table 3). As mentioned earlier, after-school employment, homework, and sports activities also keep teenagers up late at night.

If sleep behaviors and environment have been optimized but teenagers still struggle with sleep, they may need a formal evaluation for sleep disorders. Psychophysiologic insomnia, delayed sleep-phase disorder, and restless legs syndrome (RLS) manifest as difficulty falling sleep. Sleep disorders that affect sleep quality and/or cause daytime sleepiness include obstructive sleep apnea, periodic limb movement disorder (PLMD), and intrinsic sleep disorders of hypersomnia (e.g., narcolepsy or idiopathic hypersomnia).[23]

Restless legs syndrome and PLMD are sleep-related movement disorders: RLS is a clinical diagnosis based on subjective nocturnal leg discomfort that affects the ability to initiate sleep, and PLMD is diagnosed by polysomnographic evidence of increased "periodic limb movements" coupled with the complaint of nonrestorative sleep.[23] Assessment and diagnostic testing for these sleep disorders may warrant referral to a pediatric sleep specialist.

Treatment

Informing teenagers about their sleep need, either in the pediatrician's office or in the classroom, empowers them in the treatment process (Figure 1). Teenagers and their parents need to work together to figure out how to get the teenager to bed early enough and maintain a consistent sleep schedule that ensures adequate sleep on weekdays and weekends. Staying up late on weekends sabotages the good sleep pattern established during the week, particularly with teenagers' physiologic predisposition for sleep phase delay. Adolescents should avoid exposure to any electronic devices within 1 hour of bedtime to prevent light stimulation and prolongation of sleep onset. If possible, they should refrain from caffeine consumption, particularly after lunchtime, because the stimulating effects can persist for hours after intake. Finally, attaining adequate sleep must be a concerted effort by all family members. Parental supervision and enforcement of bedtimes are often lacking in this age group but may be necessary to make sure adolescents obtain enough sleep.

In general, otherwise healthy adolescents produce sufficient melatonin; however, the timing of melatonin secretion is delayed. In 2007, the American Academy of Sleep Medicine published *Practice Parameters for the Clinical Evaluation and Treatment of Circadian Rhythm Sleep Disorders*, which discussed the use of melatonin in patients with delayed sleep phase disorder (DSPD).[24]

In DSPD, physiologic doses of exogenous melatonin (e.g., 0.5 mg) given late afternoon or early evening may be more effective in advancing the inherent sleep phase than higher doses of melatonin (3–5 mg) given late at night.[25]

Most people are unaware that adolescents may require more than 9 hours of nightly sleep. Educating the public about the signs and symptoms of insufficient sleep and the sleep needs of teenagers may facilitate efforts to improve their sleep. Teachers can identify at-risk students and notify their parents. Parents can try to modify sleep behaviors or seek guidance from their

Table 2 Sleep–wake Cycle

- What time do your teenagers go to bed?
- What time do they fall asleep?
- Do they sleep through the night?
- What time do they wake up the next morning?
- Do their weekend sleep schedules deviate significantly from weekday sleep schedules?

pediatrician. Setting limits on the amount and complexity of evening homework, after-school job hours, and extracurricular activities may get teenagers home earlier. Ideally, if the insufficient sleep cycle is broken, teenagers are less sleepy during the day, and they may efficiently use "study halls" for completing homework rather than for a daytime nap and ultimately get to sleep earlier at night, perpetuating good sleep habits.

School Start Times

A societal debate that underlies insufficient sleep in teenagers is early school start times. Traditionally in the United States, the school day in high school begins earlier than in middle schools or elementary schools, and often the start time is before 8 a.m. The conflict between adolescents' inherent circadian phase delay and rigid school start times results in chronic sleep deprivation.

In 1997, school districts in Minnesota delayed high school start times by at least 1 hour. Benefits of this change included increased nightly sleep (approximately 1 more hour of sleep per night), improved attendance, decreased tardiness, increased daytime alertness, improved student behavior, and trended toward improved academic performance.[26]

Researchers compared adolescents at two different middle schools with a 1 hour or more difference in start times (7:15 a.m. vs. 8:37 a.m.).[27] Students at the school with the later start time obtained 1 more hour of sleep, were less tardy at school, and received better grades.

Table 3 Sleep Hygiene and Environment

- Before bedtime, do your teenagers watch TV, play video games, use their cell phones, or surf the Internet? Do they consume caffeine?
- What time do they drink their last caffeinated beverage?
- Do they have any electronic devices in their bedrooms?
- Are their rooms dark and quiet?

Why Should I Sleep?

- Sleep is important for growth. Your body produces a chemical called growth hormone during deep sleep.
- Sleep helps you fight off sickness. The immune system weakens with sleep deprivation.
- Sleep can help you do well on tests. The sleep stage when you dream, called REM sleep, strengthens your memory.
- You have more energy for afterschool activities. It's natural to feel tired between 2 p.m. and 4 p.m., when school ends. Not getting enough sleep makes it even harder to stay awake for afterschool activities.
- Getting good sleep improves your mood. It is easier to get angry when you're sleepy.

How Much Sleep Do I Need?

On average, most teenagers need approximately 9 hours of sleep per night; however, not everyone has the same sleep need. If you wake up feeling refreshed and are able to stay awake throughout the day without difficulty and without caffeine, you are probably sleeping enough.

How Do I Get Good Sleep?

- Establish a bedtime routine. Try taking a warm shower, reading, relaxing, and/or listening to soft music before bedtime.
- Turn off all electronic devices at least 1 hour before bedtime.
- Exercising several hours before bedtime may help you fall asleep and stay asleep at night.
- Do not consume caffeine after lunch.
- Set a consistent sleep schedule. Keep the weekday and weekend sleep schedule similar.
- Don't take an afternoon nap. If you feel you have to take a nap, limit it to 30 minutes in the early afternoon.
- Avoid tobacco and alcohol, because these substances disrupt sleep.

Figure 1. Sample patient handout. Go to CantempararyPediatrics.comISleepHandout to download a printable version for your office.

And, a school district in Kentucky delayed middle school and high school start times by 1 hour. The most compelling finding in this study was that motor vehicle crashes involving drivers aged 17 to 18 years in the respective county decreased by 16.5 percent after the change in start times.[28]

Easier Said than Done

Changing these bell times is a challenge. School bus transportation, public transportation, and traffic congestion depend on the current and predictable timetable of school start times. Delaying the start of the school day affects after-school activities, including jobs and sports practices. Parents coordinate their employment hours and family activities around the early start times and may be resistant to change. Therefore, altering school start times would need to be a group effort requiring input from everyone in the community.

Helping Adolescents Get the Sleep They Need

Most teenagers are sleepy because of insufficient sleep. Based on the 2006 NSF poll, they know they do not sleep enough but may not know how much sleep they truly need. Informing adolescents and the community about the developmental changes in their sleep-wake cycle and their sleep requirements is the initial step to getting them the sleep they need. *cp*

References

1. Carskadon MA, Harvey K, Duke P, Anders TF, Litt IF, Dement WC. Pubertal changes in daytime sleepiness. *Sleep.* 1980; 2(4):453–460.
2. National Sleep Foundation. *2006 Sleep in America Poll: Summary of Findings.* Washington, DC: National Sleep Foundation; 2006.
3. Carskadon MA, Acebo C, Richardson GS, Tate BA, Seifer R. An approach to studying circadian rhythms of adolescent humans. *J Biol Rhythms.* 1997;12(3):278–289.
4. Carskadon MA, Labyak SE, Acebo C, Seifer R. Intrinsic circadian period of adolescent humans measured in conditions of forced desynchrony. *Neurosci Lett.* 1999;260(2):129–132.
5. Hagenauer MH, Perryman JI, Lee TM, Carskadon MA. Adolescent changes in the homeostatic and circadian regulation of sleep. *Dev Neurosci.* 2009;31(4):276–284.
6. Jenni OG, Achermann P, Carskadon MA. Homeostatic sleep regulation in adolescents. *Sleep.* 2005;28(11):1446–1454.
7. Borbély AA. A two process model of sleep regulation. *Hum Neurobiol.* 1982;1(3):195–204.
8. Calamaro CJ, Mason TB, Ratcliffe SJ. Adolescents living the 24/ 7 lifestyle: effects of caffeine and technology on sleep duration and daytime functioning. *Pediatrics.* 2009;123(6):e1005–e1010.
9. Center for Science in the Public Interest. Caffeine content of food and drugs. www.cspinet.org/new/cafchart.htm. September 2007. Accessed September 17, 2012.
10. Pollak CP, Bright D. Caffeine consumption and weekly sleep patterns in US seventh-, eighth-, and ninth-graders. *Pediatrics.* 2003;111(1):42–46.
11. Kaplan GB, Greenblatt DJ, Ehrenberg BL, et al. Dose-dependent pharmacokinetics and psychomotor effects of caffeine in humans. *J Clin Pharmacol.* 1997;37(8):693–703.
12. Carskadon MA. Patterns of sleep and sleepiness in adolescents. *Pediatrician.* 1990;17(1):5–12.
13. Stickgold R, Hobson JA, Fosse R, Fosse M. Sleep, learning, and dreams: off-line memory reprocessing. *Science.* 2001;294(5544):1052–1057.
14. Wolfson AR, Carskadon MA. Sleep schedules and daytime functioning in adolescents. *Child Dev.* 1998;69(4):875–887.
15. Harrison Y, Horne JA. The impact of sleep deprivation on decision making: a review. *J Exp Psychol Appl.* 2000;6(3):236–249.
16. Pace-Schott EF, Nave G, Morgan A, Spencer RM. Sleep-dependent modulation of affectively guided decision-making. *J Sleep Res.* 2012;21(1):30–39.
17. Carskadon MA. Adolescent sleepiness: increased risk in a high-risk population. *Alcohol Drugs Driving.* 1990;5/6(4/1):317–328.
18. Taylor DJ, Bramoweth AD. Patterns and consequences of inadequate sleep in college students: substance use and motor vehicle accidents. *J Adolesc Health.* 2010;46(6):610–612.
19. Winston FK, Durbin DR, Ginsburg KR, et al; Young Driver Research Initiative Research Team. *Driving: Through the Eyes of Teens. A Research Report of the Children'S Hospital of Philadelphia and State Farm.* Philadelphia, PA: Center for Injury Research and Prevention at the Children'S Hospital of Philadelphia; 2007.
20. Ginsburg KR, Winston FK, Senserrick TM, et al. National young-driver survey: teen perspective and experience with factors that affect driving safety. *Pediatrics.* 2008;121(5):e1391–e1403.
21. National Highway Transportation Safety Administration. *Traffic Safety Facts 2005 Data: Young Drivers.* Washington, DC: US Department of Transportation; 2006.
22. Tefft BC. Prevalence of motor vehicle crashes involving drowsy drivers, United States,1999–2008. *Accid Anal Prev.* 2012;45:180–186.
23. American Academy of Sleep Medicine. *The International Classification of Sleep Disorders: Diagnostic and Coding Manual.* 2nd ed. Westchester, IL: American Academy of Sleep Medicine; 2005.
24. Morgenthaler TI, Lee-Chiong T, Alessi C, et al; Standards of Practice Committee of the American Academy of Sleep Medicine. Practice parameters for the clinical evaluation and treatment of circadian rhythm sleep disorders. An American Academy of Sleep Medicine report. *Sleep.* 2007;30(11):1445–1459. Erratum in: *Sleep.* 2008;31(7):table of contents.
25. van Geijlswijk IM, Korzilius HP, Smits MG. The use of exogenous melatonin in delayed sleep phase disorder: a meta-analysis. *Sleep.* 2010;33(12):1605–1614.
26. Wahlstrom KL. Changing times: findings from the first longitudinal study of later high school start times. *NASSP Bull.* 2002;86(633):3–21.
27. Wolfson AR, Spaulding NL, Dandrow C, Baroni EM. Middle school start times: the importance of a good night's sleep for young adolescents. *Behav Sleep Med.* 2007;5(3):194–209.
28. Danner F, Phillips B. Adolescent sleep, school start times, and teen motor vehicle crashes. *J Clin Sleep Med.* 2008;4(6):533–535.

Critical Thinking

1. What can parents do to encourage their adolescents to maintain good sleep habits?

2. What do adolescents know about the deleterious effects of insufficient sleep on driving, education and learning?

3. How could adolescents be better informed about the benefits of sleep?

Internet References

Facts about Drowsy Driving Teens
   http://drowsydriving.org/wp-content/uploads/2009/10/DDPW-Teens-Drowsy-Driving-Facts.pdf

Sleep Deprivation May Be Undermining Teen Health
   http://www.apa.org/monitor/oct01/sleepteen.aspx

Sleep-deprived Teenagers May Be at Risk of Long-term Damage to Wiring of the Brain
   http://www.dailymail.co.uk/health/article-2047322/Sleep-deprived-teenagers-risk-long-term-damage-wiring-brain.html

Why Are Teenagers So Sleep-Deprived?
   https://childmind.org/article/teenagers-sleep-deprived/

LOUELLA B. AMOS is an assistant professor of pediatrics, Division of Pulmonary and Sleep Medicine, Medical College of Wisconsin, Milwaukee.

LYNN A. D'ANDREA is a professor of pediatrics, Division of Pulmonary and Sleep Medicine, Medical College of Wisconsin, Milwaukee.

Article Prepared by: Claire N. Rubman, *Suffolk County Community College*

Go to Bed

Social and school pressures prompt many stressed teens to forsake sleep.

RUTHANN RICHTER

Learning Outcomes

After reading this article, you will be able to:

- Describe the phenomenon known as the "sleep phase delay."

- Explain the term "social jet lag."

- Discuss the impact of sleep loss on suicidal thoughts and behaviors.

Carolyn Walworth, 17, often reaches a breaking point around 11 p.m., when she collapses in tears. For 10 minutes or so, she just sits at her desk and cries, overwhelmed by unrelenting school demands. She is desperately tired and longs for sleep. But she knows she must move through it, because more assignments in physics, calculus, or French await her. She finally crawls into bed around midnight or 12:30 a.m.

The next morning, she fights to stay awake in her first-period U.S. history class, which begins at 8:15. She is unable to focus on what's being taught, and her mind drifts. "You feel tired and exhausted, but you think you just need to get through the day so you can go home and sleep," says the Palo Alto, California, teen. But that night, she will have to try to catch up on what she missed in class. And the cycle begins again. "It's an insane system. . . . The whole essence of learning is lost," she says.

Walworth is among a generation of teens growing up chronically sleep-deprived. According to a 2006 National Sleep Foundation poll, the organization's most recent survey of teen sleep, more than 87 percent of high school students in the United States get far less than the recommended eight to 10 hours, and the amount of time they sleep is decreasing—a serious threat to their health, safety, and academic success. Sleep deprivation increases the likelihood teens will suffer myriad negative consequences, including an inability to concentrate, poor grades, drowsy driving incidents, anxiety, depression, thoughts of suicide, and even suicide attempts. It's a problem that knows no economic boundaries.

While studies show that both adults and teens in industrialized nations are becoming more sleep-deprived, the problem is most acute among teens, says Nanci Yuan, MD, director of the Stanford Children's Health Sleep Center. In a detailed 2014 report, the American Academy of Pediatrics calls the problem of tired teens a public health epidemic.

"I think high school is the real danger spot in terms of sleep deprivation," says William Dement, MD, PhD, founder of the Stanford Sleep Disorders Clinic, the first of its kind in the world. "It's a huge problem. What it means is that nobody performs at the level they could perform," whether it's in school, on the roadways, on the sports field or in terms of physical and emotional health.

Social and cultural factors as well as new forms of information technology all have collided with the biology of the adolescent to prevent teens from getting enough rest. Since the early '90s, it's been established that teens have a biologic tendency to go to sleep later—as much as two hours later—than their younger counterparts.

Yet when they enter their high school years, they find themselves at schools that typically start the day at a relatively early hour. So their time for sleep is compressed, and many are jolted out of bed before they are physically or mentally ready. In the process, they not only lose precious hours of rest, but their natural rhythm is disrupted, as they are being robbed of the dream-rich, rapid-eye-movement stage of sleep, some of the deepest, most productive sleep time, says pediatric sleep specialist Rafael Pelayo, MD, with the Stanford Sleep Disorders Clinic.

"When teens wake up earlier, it cuts off their dreams," says Pelayo, a clinical professor of psychiatry and behavioral sciences. "We're not giving them a chance to dream."

Understanding Teen Sleep

On a sunny June afternoon, Dement maneuvered his golf cart, nicknamed the Sleep and Dreams Shuttle, through the Stanford University campus to Jerry House, a sprawling, Mediterranean-style dormitory where he and his colleagues conducted some of the early, seminal work on sleep, including teen sleep.

Beginning in 1975, the researchers recruited a few dozen local youngsters between the ages of 10 and 12 who were willing to participate in a unique sleep camp. During the day, the young volunteers would play volleyball in the backyard, which faces a now-barren Lake Lagunita, all the while sporting a nest of electrodes on their heads.

At night, they dozed in a dorm while researchers in a nearby room monitored their brain waves on 6-foot electroencephalogram machines, old-fashioned polygraphs that spit out wave patterns of their sleep.

One of Dement's colleagues at the time was Mary Carskadon, PhD, then a graduate student at Stanford. They studied the youngsters over the course of several summers, observing their sleep habits as they entered puberty and beyond.

Dement and Carskadon had expected to find that as the participants grew older, they would need less sleep. But to their surprise, the youngsters' sleep needs remained the same throughout the teen years—roughly nine hours. "We thought, 'Oh, wow, this is interesting,'" says Carskadon, now a professor of psychiatry and human behavior at Brown University and a nationally recognized expert on teen sleep.

Moreover, the researchers made a number of other key observations that would plant the seed for what is now accepted dogma in the sleep field. For one, they noticed that when older adolescents were restricted to just five hours of sleep a night, they would become progressively sleepier during the course of the week. The loss was cumulative, accounting for what is now commonly known as sleep debt.

"The concept of sleep debt had yet to be developed," says Dement, the Lowell W. and Josephine Q. Berry Professor and a professor of psychiatry and behavioral sciences. It's since become the basis for his ongoing campaign against drowsy driving among adults and teens. "That's why you have these terrible accidents on the road. People carry a large sleep debt, which they don't understand and cannot evaluate."

The researchers also noticed that as the kids got older, they were naturally inclined to go to bed later. By the early 1990s, Carskadon established what has become a widely recognized phenomenon—that teens experience a so-called sleep-phase delay. Their circadian rhythm—their internal biological clock—shifts to a later time, making it more difficult for them to fall asleep before 11 p.m.

Teens are also biologically disposed to a later sleep time because of a shift in the system that governs the natural sleep–wake cycle. Among older teens, the push to fall asleep builds more slowly during the day, signaling them to be more alert in the evening.

"It's as if the brain is giving them permission, or making it easier, to stay awake longer," Carskadon says. "So you add that to the phase delay, and it's hard to fight against it."

Pressures Not to Sleep

After an evening with four or five hours of homework, Walworth turns to her cellphone for relief. She texts or talks to friends and surfs the Web. "It's nice to stay up and talk to your friends or watch a funny YouTube video," she says. "There are plenty of online distractions."

While teens are biologically programmed to stay up late, many social and cultural forces further limit their time for sleep. For one, the pressure on teens to succeed is intense, and they must compete with a growing number of peers for college slots that have largely remained constant. In high-achieving communities like Palo Alto, that translates into students who are overwhelmed by additional homework for Advanced Placement classes, outside activities such as sports or social service projects, and in some cases, part-time jobs, as well as peer, parental and community pressures to excel.

At the same time, today's teens are maturing in an era of ubiquitous electronic media, and they are fervent participants. Some 92 percent of U.S. teens have smartphones, and 24 percent report being online "constantly," according to a 2015 report by the Pew Research Center. Teens have access to multiple electronic devices they use simultaneously, often at night. Some 72 percent bring cellphones into their bedrooms and use them when they are trying to go to sleep, and 28 percent leave their phones on while sleeping, only to be being awakened at night by texts, calls, or e-mails, according to a 2011 National Sleep Foundation poll on electronic use. In addition, some 64 percent used electronic music devices, 60 percent used laptops and 23 percent played video games in the hour before they went to sleep. More than half reported texting in the hour before they went to sleep, and these media fans were less likely to report getting a good night's sleep and to feel refreshed in the morning. They were also more likely to drive when drowsy, the poll found.

They say they are tired, but they don't realize they are actually sleep-deprived. And if you ask kids to remove an activity, they would rather not. They would rather give up sleep than an activity.

The problem of sleep-phase delay is exacerbated when teens are exposed late at night to lit screens, which send a message via the retina to the portion of the brain that controls the body's circadian clock. The message: It's not nighttime yet.

Yuan, a clinical associate professor of pediatrics, says she routinely sees young patients in her clinic who fall asleep at night with cellphones in hand.

"With academic demands and extracurricular activities, the kids are going nonstop until they fall asleep exhausted at night. There is not an emphasis on the importance of sleep, as there is with nutrition and exercise," she says. "They say they are tired, but they don't realize they are actually sleep-deprived. And if you ask kids to remove an activity, they would rather not. They would rather give up sleep than an activity."

Adolescents are also entering a period in which they are striving for autonomy and want to make their own decisions, including when to go to sleep. But studies suggest adolescents do better in terms of mood and fatigue levels if parents set the bedtime—and choose a time that is realistic for the child's needs. According to a 2010 study published in the journal *Sleep*, children are more likely to be depressed and to entertain thoughts of suicide if a parent sets a late bedtime of midnight or beyond.

In families where parents set the time for sleep, the teens' happier, better-rested state "may be a sign of an organized family life, not simply a matter of bedtime," Carskadon says. "On the other hand, the growing child and growing teens still benefit from someone who will help set the structure for their lives. And they aren't good at making good decisions."

According to the national sleep poll, by the time U.S. students reach their senior year in high school, they are sleeping an average of 6.9 hours a night, down from an average of 8.4 hours in the sixth grade. The poll included teens from across the country from diverse ethnic backgrounds.

American teens aren't the worst off when it comes to sleep, however; South Korean adolescents have that distinction, sleeping on average 4.9 hours a night, according to a 2012 study in *Sleep* by South Korean researchers. These Asian teens routinely begin school between 7 and 8:30 a.m., and most sign up for additional evening classes that may keep them up as late as midnight. South Korean adolescents also have relatively high suicide rates (10.7 per 100,000 a year), and the researchers speculate that chronic sleep deprivation is a contributor to this disturbing trend.

By contrast, Australian teens are among those who do particularly well when it comes to sleep time, averaging about nine hours a night, possibly because schools there usually start later.

Regardless of where they live, most teens follow a pattern of sleeping less during the week and sleeping in on the weekends to compensate. But many accumulate such a backlog of sleep debt they don't sufficiently recover on the weekend and still wake up fatigued when Monday comes around.

Moreover, the shifting sleep patterns on the weekend—late nights with friends, followed by late mornings in bed—are out of sync with their weekday rhythm. Carskadon refers to this as "social jet lag."

"Every day we teach our internal circadian timing system what time it is, is it day or night, and if that message is substantially different every day, then the clock isn't able to set things appropriately in motion. In the last few years, we have learned there is a master clock in the brain, but there are other clocks in other organs, like liver or kidneys or lungs, so the master clock is the coxswain, trying to get everybody to work together to improve efficiency and health. So if the coxswain is changing the pace, all the crew become disorganized and don't function well. . . . So nothing goes as it's supposed to."

This disrupted rhythm, as well as the shortage of sleep, can have far-reaching effects on adolescent health and well-being, she says.

"It certainly plays into learning and memory. It plays into appetite and metabolism and weight gain. It plays into mood and emotion, which are already heightened at that age. It also plays into risk behaviors—taking risks while driving, taking risks with substances, taking risks maybe with sexual activity. So the more we look outside, the more we're learning about the core role that sleep plays," Carskadon says.

We hypothesize that when teens sleep, the brain is going through processes of consolidation—learning of experiences or making memories. It's like your brain is filtering itself.

Many studies show students who sleep less suffer academically, as chronic sleep loss impairs the ability to remember, concentrate, think abstractly, and solve problems. In one of many studies on sleep and academic performance, Carskadon and her colleagues surveyed 3,000 high school students and found that those with higher grades reported sleeping more, going to bed earlier on school nights, and sleeping in less on weekends than students who had lower grades.

Sleep is believed to reinforce learning and memory, with studies showing that people perform better on mental tasks when they are well-rested.

"We hypothesize that when teens sleep, the brain is going through processes of consolidation—learning of experiences or making memories," Yuan says. "It's like your brain is filtering itself—consolidating the important things and filtering out those unimportant things." When the brain is deprived of that opportunity, cognitive function suffers, along with the capacity to learn.

"It impacts academic performance. It's harder to take tests and answer questions if you are sleep-deprived," she says.

That's why cramming, at the expense of sleep, is counterproductive, says Pelayo, who advises students: "Don't lose sleep to study" or you'll lose out in the end.

The Panic Attack

Chloe Mauvais, 16, hit her breaking point at the end of a very challenging sophomore year when she reached "the depths of frustration and anxiety." After months of late nights spent studying to keep up with academic demands, she suffered a panic attack one evening at home.

"I sat in the living room in our house on the ground, crying and having horrible breathing problems. It was so scary. I think it was from the accumulated stress, the fear over my grades, the lack of sleep and the crushing sense of responsibility. High school is a very hard place to be," says the senior at Menlo-Atherton High School.

Where she once had good sleep habits, she had drifted into an unhealthy pattern of staying up late, sometimes until 3 a.m., researching and writing papers for her AP European History class and prepping for tests.

"I have difficulty remembering events of that year, and I think it's because I didn't get enough sleep. The lack of sleep rendered me emotionally useless. I couldn't address the stress because I had no coherent thoughts. I couldn't step back and have perspective. . . . You could probably talk to any teen and find they reach their breaking point. You've pushed yourself so much and not slept enough and you just lose it."

The experience was a kind of wake-up call, as she recognized the need to return to a more balanced life and a better sleep pattern, she says.

But for some teens, this toxic mix of sleep deprivation, stress and anxiety, together with other external pressures, can tip their thinking toward dire solutions.

Research has shown that sleep problems among adolescents are a major risk factor for suicidal thoughts and death by suicide, which ranks as the third-leading cause of fatalities among 15- to 24-year-olds. And this link between sleep and suicidal thoughts remains strong, independent of whether the teen is depressed or has drug and alcohol issues, according to some studies.

"Sleep, especially deep sleep, is like a balm for the brain," says Shashank Joshi, MD, associate professor of psychiatry and behavioral sciences at Stanford. "The better your sleep, the more clearly you can think while awake, and it may enable you to seek help when a problem arises. You have your faculties with you. You may think, 'I have 16 things to do, but I know

where to start.' Sleep deprivation can make it hard to remember what you need to do for your busy teen life. It takes away the support, the infrastructure."

Sleep is believed to help regulate emotions and its deprivation is an underlying component of many mood disorders, such as anxiety, depression and bipolar disorder. For students who are prone to these disorders, better sleep can help serve as a buffer and help prevent a downhill slide, Joshi says.

Rebecca Bernert, PhD, who directs the Suicide Prevention Research Lab at Stanford, says sleep may affect the way in which teens process emotions. Her work with civilians and military veterans indicates that lack of sleep can make people more receptive to negative emotional information—which they might shrug off if they were fully rested, she says.

"Based on prior research, we have theorized that sleep disturbances may result in difficulty regulating emotional information, and this may lower the threshold for suicidal behaviors among at-risk individuals," says Bernert, an instructor in psychiatry and behavioral sciences. Now she's studying whether a brief nondrug treatment for insomnia reduces depression and risk for suicide.

Sleep deprivation also has been shown to lower inhibitions among both adults and teens. In the teen brain, the frontal lobe, which helps restrain impulsivity, isn't fully developed, so teens are naturally prone to impulsive behavior.

"When you throw into the mix sleep deprivation, which can also be disinhibiting, mood problems and the normal impulsivity of adolescence, then you have a potentially dangerous situation," Joshi says.

Some Schools Shift

Given the health risks associated with sleep problems, school districts around the country have been looking at one issue over which they have some control: school start times. The trend was set by the town of Edina, Minnesota, a well-to-do suburb of Minneapolis, which conducted a landmark experiment in student sleep in the late 1990s. It shifted the high school's start time from 7:20 a.m. to 8:30 a.m. and then asked University of Minnesota researchers to look at the impact of the change. The researchers found some surprising results: Students reported feeling less depressed and less sleepy during the day and more empowered to succeed. There was no comparable improvement in student well-being in surrounding school districts where start times remained the same.

With these findings in hand, the entire Minneapolis Public School District shifted start times for 57,000 students at all of its schools in 1997 and found similarly positive results. Attendance rates rose, and students reported getting an hour's more sleep each school night—or a total of five more hours of sleep a week—countering skeptics who argued that the students would respond by just going to bed later.

Parents and teachers need to trim back their expectations and minimize pressures that interfere with teen sleep.

Other studies have reinforced the link between later start times and positive health benefits. One 2010 study at an independent high school in Rhode Island found that after delaying the start time by just 30 minutes, students slept more and showed significant improvements in alertness and mood. And a 2014 study in two counties in Virginia found that teens were much less likely to be involved in car crashes in a county where start times were later, compared with a county with an earlier starting bell.

Bolstered by the evidence, the American Academy of Pediatrics in 2014 issued a strong policy statement encouraging middle and high school districts across the country to start school no earlier than 8:30 a.m. to help preserve the health of the nation's youth. Some districts have heeded the call, though the decisions have been hugely contentious, as many consider school schedules sacrosanct and cite practical issues, such as bus schedules, as obstacles.

In Fairfax County, Virginia, it took a decade of debate before the school board voted in 2014 to push back the opening school bell for its 57,000 students. And in Palo Alto, where a recent cluster of suicides has caused much communitywide soul-searching, the district superintendent issued a decision in the spring, over the strenuous objections of some teachers, students and administrators, to eliminate "zero period" for academic classes—an optional period that begins at 7:20 a.m. and is generally offered for advanced studies.

Certainly, changing school start times is only part of the solution, experts say. More widespread education about sleep and more resources for students are needed. Parents and teachers need to trim back their expectations and minimize pressures that interfere with teen sleep. And there needs to be a cultural shift, including a move to discourage late-night electronic use, to help youngsters gain much-needed rest.

"At some point, we are going to have to confront this as a society," Carskadon says. "For the health and well-being of the nation, we should all be taking better care of our sleep, and we certainly should be taking better care of the sleep of our youth."

Critical Thinking

1. Why is sleep so essential to the human condition?
2. How do sleep patterns change in adolescence?

Internet References

Adolescent Sleep Patterns Biological, Social, and Psychological Influences
    http://assets.cambridge.org/97805216/42910/frontmatter/9780521642910_frontmatter.pdf
Adolescents and Sleep
    http://www.pbs.org/wgbh/pages/frontline/shows/teenbrain/from/sleep.html
Among teens, Sleep Deprivation an Epidemic
    https://med.stanford.edu/news/all-news/2015/10/among-teens-sleep-deprivation-an-epidemic.html
Create Central
    www.mhhe.com/createcentral
How We Can Help Teens Get Better Sleep
    https://journal.thriveglobal.com/amp/p/a8290067f5b3
Sleep Debt Cumulative, Not Totally Paid at Weekends in Teens
    http://www.medscape.com/viewarticle/846086

RUTHANN RICHTER is the director of media relations for the medical school's Office of Communication and Public Affairs.

Article   Prepared by: Claire N. Rubman, *Suffolk County Community College*

New Foundations of Adolescent Learning

Lessons from Behavioral Science, Social Science, and Neuroscience

LAURENCE STEINBERG

Learning Outcomes

After reading this article, you will be able to:

- Describe how 15 years of research on the adolescent brain has changed our approach to adolescence.

- Describe the effects of the limbic system on peer evaluation, peer pressure, and sensation seeking.

- Explain the outcome when an adolescent experiences greater interaction between the prefrontal cortex and the limbic system.

When country's adolescents trail much of the world on measures of school achievement but are among the world leaders in violence, unwanted pregnancy, STDs, abortion, binge drinking, marijuana use, obesity, and unhappiness, it is time to admit that something is wrong with the way that country is raising its young people.

That country is the United States.

We need to start thinking about adolescence differently. Fortunately, over the past two decades, there has been tremendous growth in the scientific study of adolescence. The good news is that the accumulated knowledge, which comes from behavioral science, social science, and neuroscience, provides a sensible foundation that can help parents, teachers, employers, health-care providers, and others who work with young people to be better at what they do. Parent more intelligently. Teach more effectively. Tapping into this accumulated knowledge will help

us supervise, mentor, and coach young people in ways that are more likely to succeed.

During the last 15 years, we've learned a great deal about adolescence as a stage of development, in part because of tremendous advances in our understanding of how the brain changes during this period. Whereas it was once thought that brain development was more or less complete by the end of childhood, because the brain reaches its full adult size by then, new research shows that the brain continues to mature well into one's twenties. But the changes that take place in the brain during adolescence are not so much about growth as they are about reorganization.

What distinguishes adolescence from other periods in brain development is not the fact that reorganization is taking place, but where it is happening. It occurs primarily in two regions—the prefrontal cortex and the limbic system. The prefrontal cortex sits immediately behind your forehead, and it is the main brain area responsible for self-regulation—it makes us rational. The limbic system is deep in the center of the brain, beneath the cortex. The limbic system plays an especially important role in generating emotions.

The story of adolescence is the story of how these regions learn to work together. It is a tale that unfolds in three overlapping phases.

Phase 1: Starting the Engines

Around the time of puberty, the limbic system becomes more easily aroused. This is the phase that has been described as "starting the engines." During this time, teenagers become more emotional (experiencing and displaying higher "highs" and lower "lows"), more sensitive to the opinions and evaluations of others (especially peers), and more determined to have exciting and intense experiences—something psychologists refer to as "sensation seeking." As a consequence, students are much more likely to engage in risky and reckless activity, because they pursue what they perceive as potentially rewarding experiences without paying sufficient attention to the risks these activities might expose them to. One reason it is so important to provide stimulating, structured, and supervised after-school activities for adolescents is that doing so limits the amount of time students are in situations where they are likely to experiment with alcohol, illicit drugs, and sex.

Phase 2: Developing a Better Braking System

The second phase of brain development is gradual, actually starting in preadolescence, but not complete until age 16 or so. During this phase, the prefrontal cortex slowly becomes better organized, a consequence of synaptic pruning and myelination (strengthening of neural pathways). As information begins to flow more rapidly across longer distances in the brain, advanced thinking abilities—so-called "executive functions"—strengthen, which improves decision-making, problem-solving, and planning. In this phase, adolescents' thinking becomes much more adultlike. During middle adolescence—say, from 14 to 17—parents and teachers often find that adolescents become much more reasonable and easier to discuss things with. A lot of the drama that had characterized the early adolescent years fades.

Phase 3: Putting a Skilled Driver behind the Wheel

Although a fine-tuned braking system is in place by the end of the second phase, the teenager can't always use the brakes effectively and consistently. In the third phase, which is not finished until the early twenties, the brain becomes more interconnected. This is especially true with respect to the connections between the prefrontal cortex and the limbic system. This increase in connectivity results in mature and more dependable self-regulation. During the late teens and early twenties, adolescents get better at controlling their impulses, thinking about the long-term consequences of their decisions, and resisting peer pressure. Their rational thought processes are less easily disrupted by fatigue, stress, or emotional arousal. Young people still have much to learn about life, but for all intents and

purposes, the intellectual machinery of adulthood is now fully in place.

As we mature into adulthood, the prefrontal cortex not only becomes more efficient, it also gets better at recruiting additional resources when a task demands more than this region can handle on its own. Compared with adolescents, adults are more likely to use multiple parts of the brain simultaneously. This is made possible by an increase in actual physical connections between nonneighboring brain regions. Compared with a child's brain, an adult's has many more thick white "cables" connecting widely dispersed brain regions. Generally speaking, children's brains have a lot of relatively "local" connections—links between nearby brain regions. As we mature through adolescence and into adulthood, more distant regions wire together. The brain continues to grow more interconnected until age 22 or so.

This interconnectivity doesn't develop overnight, however. As a result, during middle adolescence, mature self-control has a "now you see it, now you don't" quality. When circumstances are ideal—no distractions, no strong emotions—a 16-year-old performs just as well as an adult. But being upset, excited, or tired interferes more with prefrontal functioning during adolescence than during adulthood, because the relevant brain circuits aren't fully mature. Fatigue and stress can interfere with self-control at any age, but they have a particularly powerful impact when the skills they disrupt are still somewhat tenuous.

This is why it is important for teachers to understand that teenagers' capacities for self-control and good judgment can be bolstered or undermined by circumstances. High-school-aged adolescents make better decisions when they're calm, well rested, and aware that they'll be rewarded for making good choices. When they're emotionally or socially aroused, their judgment deteriorates. A student who appears to possess adult-like maturity in some situations may be surprisingly juvenile in others.

During the first half of adolescence, then, the prefrontal cortex improves by becoming more focused, which works fine as long as the challenges encountered are relatively simple and the environment doesn't weaken the adolescent's concentration (by fatigue or stress, for example). Self-regulation in early adolescence is stronger than it had been in childhood, but it is still somewhat tenuous and easily disrupted. During the second half of adolescence, self-control gradually becomes governed by a well-coordinated network of brain regions, which is helpful when we face a demanding task or distracting background conditions and we need additional brainpower. Part of becoming an adult is learning when we can do things on our own and when we need to ask for help. During this stage of life, brain maturation follows a parallel course.

Implications for Schools

The fact that there is extensive change in the prefrontal cortex during adolescence has important implications for educators. The prefrontal cortex is the brain's chief executive officer, responsible for higher-order cognitive skills such as thinking ahead, evaluating the costs and benefits of different choices, and coordinating emotions and thoughts. It is also the brain region most important for self-control, which is the foundation for critical "noncognitive skills," such as perseverance, determination, and the delay of gratification—a combination that some experts refer to as "grit." Studies have found that grit is more predictive of success in school and work than any other attribute, including intelligence or talent. If schools were to include activities that encourage prefrontal development, students would have additional strengths beyond those conveyed through conventional academic instruction. The need for schools to foster the development of capacities like perseverance and determination is especially great for socioeconomically disadvantaged adolescents, who are less likely to grow up in home environments that contribute to their growth.

There are many reasons to be enthusiastic about incorporating deliberate efforts to improve self-control into our middle and high school curricula. In the rapidly changing world in which we now live, schools cannot possibly anticipate the specific skills that will be needed to navigate the ever-evolving labor force. Many experts agree that schools should focus on fostering more general competencies that have value in many different work settings. These include, but are not limited to, being able to work effectively with others, developing and carrying out long-term strategic plans, acquiring and using new information, thinking flexibly and creatively, and, of course, self-regulation.

Fostering these capacities is not only important for success in higher education or the labor force. This supplement to conventional education would have the added advantage of cultivating the sorts of inner strengths that help protect against the development of problems such as depression, obesity, delinquency, and substance use. These problems stem in part from deficiencies in self-regulation, so anything schools can do to strengthen this capacity will have benefits that are likely to be far-reaching. Reorienting schools to help strengthen self-regulation in addition to teaching academic skills will not simply prevent problems from developing, it will actually help promote adolescents' physical and psychological well-being.

Strengthen Self-Regulation

At this point, no single approach to strengthening self-regulation warrants unequivocal endorsement, but some general principles can guide schools interested in fostering students' self-control.

Intellectual Engagement

First, because prefrontal development is stimulated by novelty and challenge, it is essential to expose students to demanding courses that push them intellectually. Many American high school students report that school is boring and unchallenging. I suspect this is not the situation in most independent schools (indeed, many parents choose to send their adolescents to independent schools for precisely this reason), but it is wise for educators to step back every so often and ask how well their school is faring in this respect. Schools that deliberately make academic life for students too easy, in order to ensure that they graduate with transcripts full of A's, are squandering an important opportunity to foster positive psychological development. It is through challenge—even if it means occasional failure—that students acquire the ability to manage themselves without parents looking over their shoulder and persevere in the face of obstacles, skills they will certainly need in college.

I saw the benefits of exposure to novelty and challenge firsthand when our son, Ben, was a student at Friends' Central School (Pennsylvania). The school's small seminars, in which the focus is on critical thinking, and its tolerance of a diverse array of viewpoints in class discussions exposed Ben to the sorts of demands necessary to promote the noncognitive skills that are so vital for subsequent success. When Ben entered Trinity College, he found himself far better prepared for the demands of a liberal arts education than many of his classmates whose grades might have been higher but whose high school experiences had been far less challenging.

Mindfulness

Second, there is increasing evidence that activities that promote mindfulness strengthen brain systems that regulate self-control. Mindfulness involves focusing one's attention on the present moment in a nonjudgmental fashion—really attending to what your senses are picking up, without trying to interpret or think about the experience. The most consistent evidence for the benefits of mindfulness training comes from studies of meditation, which has been shown to reduce stress and help alleviate many psychological disorders, especially those that involve anxiety, trauma, and addiction. One of the advantages of using meditation to improve self-control is that it has beneficial effects beyond this specific outcome. Because mindfulness meditation helps reduce stress, it also improves sleep, cardiovascular health, and immune function. There is also evidence in support of disciplined physical activity that combines focused exercise with mindfulness. These include, for example, activities like yoga and certain martial arts, like tae kwon do.

Aerobic Activity

Third, there is reason to think that aerobic exercise may also improve self-regulation. We know that aerobic exercise improves brain health in general by increasing blood flow. Schools need to make sure that all students—not just the athletic stars—have adequate time for exercise every day. And schools need to make parents aware of how important it is for adolescents to get adequate sleep each night; far too many American students are sleep-deprived.

The effects of aerobic activity on self-regulation in particular are more likely to be seen when the exercise demands challenging thinking as well as physical exertion, as in team sports that combine aerobic activity with strategy. Given this, it is not surprising that participation in school-sponsored organized athletics appears to help promote the development of self-regulation and initiative. In these cases, we can't say for sure whether the positive effects are due to the exercise, the cognitive demands, or, most likely, a combination of the two.

Social–Emotional Learning

Fourth, it appears that training in specific self-regulation strategies and skills (such as learning how to control anger) can also improve adolescents' capacity for self-regulation more generally. Some schools now incorporate "social and emotional learning" (SEL) into their curricula. SEL programs teach adolescents how to regulate their emotions, manage stress, and consider other peoples' feelings before acting. Although many of these programs were first intended to reduce problem behaviors such as aggression or delinquency (and have been evaluated with this goal in mind), they've also been shown to improve self-regulation in teenagers who don't suffer from these problems.

There are many different programs available for schools interested in SEL to choose among. A good source of information is the Collaborative for Academic, Social, and Emotional Learning (www.casel.org), a nonprofit organization that evaluates SEL program effectiveness.

Know the Brain Science

Finally, it is important that schools involve both students and parents in the conversation about how to draw on adolescent brain science to promote positive development. One way to do this is to incorporate information on adolescent brain development into the curriculum and into evening programs for parents. My experience is that teenagers find this information fascinating, as do their parents. And with this knowledge, parents parent more intelligently, and adolescents improve their ability to self-regulate.

These are just a few of the lessons from behavioral science, social science, and neuroscience as they pertain to adolescent development, education, and well-being. But they are essential lessons for both parents and educators. By paying attention to them, we can take advantage of and build on our new understanding of what young people need in order to develop into happy, well-adjusted, and successful adults.

Critical Thinking

1. Discuss why high schools should really challenge their students.
2. Explain the potential benefits of failure in high school.

Internet References

Adolescent Brain Development: Implications for Practice
   http://www.practicenotes.org/v17n3/brain.htm

All about Adolescence
   https://www.psychologytoday.com/basics/adolescence

Homepage: Lawrence Steinberg
   http://www.laurencesteinberg.com/

The Adolescent Brain
   https://www.ncbi.nlm.nih.gov/pmc/articles/PMC2475802/

The Adolescent Brain: Why Executive Functioning in Teens Is a Challenge
   https://www.beyondbooksmart.com/executive-functioning-strategies-blog/the-adolescent-brain-why-executive-functioning-in-teens-is-a-challenge

LAURENCE STEINBERG is a professor of psychology at Temple University and the author of Age of Opportunity: Lessons from the New Science of Adolescence (2014), from which this is adapted.

Unit 3

UNIT

Prepared by: Claire N. Rubman, *Suffolk County Community College*

The Self

Who are you? What are your greatest strengths and weaknesses? How do you view yourself? Thinking about self-image, read about how Instagram is trying to address self-image with a positive online campaign that targets adolescents. Read Andrea Stanley's (2016) discussion of self-acceptance through the eyes of five teenagers. Stanley details the confidence of an amputee who lost both of her legs and several fingers due to childhood illness. This is in stark contrast to another adolescent girl who can't decide if she is "too thin, too curvy, too tall or just right"! Another teen highlighted in this article experiences the self-realization that she cannot change how others see her but she can address her own "self-perception." This leads to her improved sense of self. Read about Shalom Blac who overcame a childhood accident that left her physically scarred and bald to become a fashion model. She reminds us of the pain of wishing to be "invisible." The final story highlights the harm that we can cause ourselves. Esmee describes how she tormented herself. She suffered from low self-esteem, always wishing she was prettier, thinner, or different. She admits that this led to self-harming, anorexia nervosa and hospitalization. Read about the positive outcomes for each of these adolescents and their stories of self-acceptance.

A strong "sense of self" allows an adolescent to successfully separate himself or herself and develop a sense of autonomy. Jim Pye's article, "Separation and Stuckness" (2015) looks at Erikson's crisis of identity versus role confusion (Erikson (1950, 1963). He explores how and why adolescents separate and form their own identity and sense of self.

How do we know, however, that we are developing a realistic and psychologically balanced sense of self? Jones (2016) explores the root causes of a distorted sense of self or a distorted body image in "Anorexia Nervosa and the Adolescent Self."

For some, it is not undereating, but over eating that has become a major issue. "The Obesity Challenge" by Adamaszwili (2016) looks at the food industry and its role in our daily diet. To what extent should we hold the food industry responsible for what we eat? Do labels on salt, caloric value or fat content actually change or eating habits? Where does personal accountability fit in to this discussion?

Article

Prepared by: Claire N. Rubman, *Suffolk County Community College*

The Obesity Challenge

Is reducing sugar in chocolate milk the ultimate solution?

KINGA ADAMASZWILI

Learning Outcomes

After reading this article, you will be able to:

- How sugar consumption in the EU differs from the United States.

- Explain the policy of the "added sugar annex."

The rising obesity prevalence among adults and children is a serious threat to public health systems and the future generations. The recent data show that public health policies have not been efficient to tackle this multifactorial challenge. We have seen that product reformulation and benchmarks on salt, fat, and sugar reduction per food category continue to be one of the preferred options discussed by the authorities. One may ask—is a single-nutrient approach an efficient and adequate measure to fight the obesity challenge? Are we aware of data showing that reformulated food makes people slimmer and healthier? And finally, should we focus on solutions without being certain of evident public health benefits? Maybe the time is ripe to look at the problem from another perspective.

The World Has an Obesity Problem

The recently published data of body-mass index trends in adults in 200 countries tell us that more people in the world are now obese as opposed to underweight.[1] According to the latest Lancet analysis, the number of obese people globally had increased from 105 million (1975) to 641 million (2014). At the same time, the number of underweight people had increased from 330 million (1975) to 462 million (2014). If post-2000 trends

continue, by 2025, the global obesity prevalence will reach 18 percent in men and surpass 21 percent in women; severe obesity will surpass 6 percent in men and 9 percent in women.

Trends in Europe are also not positive for the future generations—according to the latest WHO HBSC survey[2] on trends in adolescents, the prevalence of overweight and obesity has been growing in all EU regions with highest prevalence in the South (from 20.2 percent in 2002 to 22.5 percent in 2010) and the sharpest increase in the East (from 11.5 percent in 2002 to 18.5 percent in 2010). No doubt that these trends are alarming for health authorities in Europe and around the globe.

Product Formulation and Added Sugar on the EU Agenda

Since the beginning of 2016, we have seen an intensification of debates on how to combat the obesity challenge. It seems that policy makers tend to opt for reformulation and further reduction of "bad nutrients" in foods and drinks. After salt and saturated fat in the previous years, the main focus of 2016 is added sugar.

In January 2016, the European Commission and EU Member States experts (High Level Group on Nutrition and Physical activity[3]) have endorsed a strategy on reduction of added sugars in foods and drinks—including sweetened dairy products. The new policy (so called "Added Sugar Annex") aims at setting "general benchmarks for added sugar reduction of a minimum of 10 percent by 2020 in food products against the Member State baseline levels at the end of 2015 or to move towards 'best in class' levels." It is worth noting that the document suggests that reduced sugar should not be replaced by sweeteners as the overall aim is to reduce the sweet taste of foods.

In parallel, the Dutch Presidency has taken up product reformulation and reduction of fat, salt, and sugar as one of its priorities—the Dutch "Roadmap for action" widely presented in February 2016 called for "combined action to make food products healthier by gradually reducing the amount of salt, saturated fat and sugar (calories)." Interestingly, among the 22 Member States who have signed the Dutch Roadmap, we will not find neither Italy nor France—countries of undisputable rich culinary heritage.

Reflection on the Role of the Industry

The recent debates triggered further reflections around the duties of food and drink industry, including the products offered by dairy sector. EDA is fully engaged on nutrition and health topics with policy makers, industry groups, and other stakeholders to help make a positive impact on the overall public health.

The health and nutrition debate has always been very close to the dairy industry. Over the last years, the European dairy sector has put a lot of effort, research, and resources to ensure that consumers have access to a wide range of nutritious dairy products.

It is widely recognized that milk and dairy products are an important part of the dietary guidelines and recommendations across the EU. The health benefits of milk and dairy for school children has been continuously acknowledged in the recently evaluated European School Milk Scheme.[4] In a Western diet, dairy products provide between 40 percent and 70 percent of the recommended daily calcium intake. In some Member States, dairy is also one the main natural sources of iodine in diet—the intake of iodine from milk and dairy products is up to 37 percent. Milk and dairy products are also natural sources of high quality protein.

Are Dairy Products Really High in Sugars? Putting Facts into a Wider Perspective

Dairy products are low contributors to added sugar intakes in Europe while they are high contributors of essential nutrients in all population groups. The dietary surveys show that consumption of added sugars from dairy is low and ranges between 6 percent (UK) to 12 percent (NL). At the same time, dairy consumption contributes to 36 percent (UK) to 58 percent (NL) of calcium intake.[5] It should be considered that inadequate intakes of certain nutrients in the European diet may be partly a consequence of low dairy consumption. Adding sugar to dairy increases palatability and therefore may help consumers reach recommendations of dairy consumption. Flavored milks and yoghurts are a way to increase milk consumption and to boost the population's vitamin, mineral, and protein intake.

What Does the Science Say on Chocolate Milk and Health?

In many EU countries, sweetened dairy products such as flavored fruit yoghurt and fermented milks are consumed as desserts or snacks. A number of studies show that yoghurt consumption, including flavored ones, has a neutral or beneficial effect on weight status.[6,7,8] Consumption of flavored milk has been linked to better overall diet quality without any adverse impact on weight.[9,10,11] Recent science also shows a positive association between yoghurt consumption, including flavored ones, and diet quality and metabolic profile in children[12] and adults.[13] The latest science and dietary guidelines also suggest that higher intake of yoghurts, including flavored ones, is linked to a reduced risk of type 2 diabetes.[14,15]

Is the EU Food and Nutrition Policy Taking the Right Direction?

For many years, it has been challenging to explain to the policy makers that nutrients present in food exist in combination and there is a complex interplay which is not captured by a single nutrient approach. Our diets are not composed of isolated, single nutrients but of multiple, varied and complex foods.

The focus on "bad nutrients" in the EU food and nutrition policy might not bring the expected results. Consumers are expecting evidence-based advice on how to compose their daily diet and what products should find place on their plate. Do the policy makers take the right direction and use the best tools to tackle the obesity challenge? Is a nutrient-focused approach appropriate in the context of public health and nutrition policy? It seems that the reality is complex and this complexity needs to be adequately reflected in the health and nutrition strategy of the EU if the efficiency is at stake.

Dietary guidance and science increasingly recognize the importance of total nutrient content of food rather than of particular individual nutrients. Let's all make the effort to help the policy makers understand that a positive approach to nutritious wholesome foods such as milk and dairy products can play an important role in fighting the obesity challenge.

References

1. Trends in adult body-mass index in 200 countries from 1975 to 2014: a pooled analysis of 1698 population-based measurement studies with 19·2 million participants. The Lancet, Volume 387, Issue 10026, 1377–1396. Published 2 April 2016, doi
2. Unpublished data, HBSC (Health Behaviour in School-Aged Children), WHO Collaborative cross-national survey.
3. http://ec.europa.eu/health/nutrition_physical_activity/high_level_group/index_en.htm.
4. http://ec.europa.eu/agriculture/milk/school-milk-scheme/index_en.htm.
5. UK NDNS survey 2008/09-2011/12, NL Dutch National Food Consumption Survey 2007–2010, NL Kenniscentrum Factsheet on Sugar Consumption.
6. Mozzafarian D et al. (2011) Changes in diet and lifestyle and long-term weight gain in women and men. N Engl J Med 361: 2392–404.
7. Wang H et al. (2013) Longitudinal association between dairy consumption and changes of body weight and waist circumference: the Framingham Heart Study. International Journal of Obesity; 1–7.
8. M.A. Martinez-Gonzalez et al. (2014) Yogurt consumption, weight change and risk of overweight/obesity: The SUN cohort study. Nut, Met & Cardio Dis, dx.doi.org/10.1016/j.numecd.2014.05.015.
9. Nicklas TA et al. (2013). The nutritional role of flavored and white milk in the diets of children. J Sch Health: 83(10):728–33.
10. Fayet F et al. (2013). Australian children who drink milk (plain or flavored) have higher milk and micronutrient intakes but similar body mass index to those who do not drink milk. Nutr Res: 33: 95–102.
11. Murphy MM et al. (2008). Drinking flavored or plain milk is positively associated with nutrient intake and is not associated with adverse effects on weight status in US children and adolescents. J Am Diet Assoc: 108:631–639.
12. Zhu Y et al. (2014). The associations between yogurt consumption, diet quality, and metabolic profiles in children in the USA. Eur J Nutr.
13. Wang et al. (2013) Yogurt consumption is associated with better diet quality and metabolic profile in American men and women. Nutr Res; 33(1):18-–26
14. Chen M et al. (2014), Dairy consumption and risk of type 2 diabetes: 3 cohorts of US adults and an updated meta-analysis. BMC Med.12:215.
15. The Dutch Health Council published the most recent dietary guidelines in Europe. The Guidelines conclude that consuming 60 grams per day of yoghurt compared to 10 grams per day decreases diabetes risk by 15%.
16. Dutch dietary guidelines: http://www.gezondheidsraad.nl/sites/default/files/201524_richtlijnen_goede_voeding_2015.pdf (see page 32)

Critical Thinking

1. How does listing caloric intake and food labeling change eating habits?
2. Make three suggestions for encouraging American adolescents to eat more healthily.

Internet References

Adolescent Obesity in the United States
http://www.nccp.org/publications/pub_977.html

Childhood Obesity Facts
https://www.cdc.gov/healthyschools/obesity/facts.htm

How Much Sugar Should a Teen Have a Day
http://www.livestrong.com/article/478658-how-much-sugar-should-a-teen-have-a-day/

Obesity in Adolescence
https://www.urmc.rochester.edu/encyclopedia/content.aspx?contenttypeid=90&contentid=P01627

Teens Not Only Eat the Most Sugar—They're Affected More Intensely by It Too
http://www.takepart.com/article/2014/06/20/how-sugar-changes-teen-brain/

Article   Prepared by: Claire N. Rubman, *Suffolk County Community College*

Anorexia Nervosa and the Adolescent Self

Psychotherapy Can Help Patients with Anorexia Blossom into the Person They Really Are

WENDY JONES

Learning Outcomes

After reading this article, you will be able to:

- Explain why the adolescents are particularly vulnerable to eating disorders such as anorexia nervosa.

- Discuss why "perfectionist thinking" interferes with recovery from anorexia nervosa.

- Define "catastrophizing" and its role in the recovery process.

As an integrative child and adolescent psychotherapist, working predominantly with children and adolescents, I am particularly interested in how a sense of self develops, in attachment patterns and how these affect relationships with self and others, in habitual ways of managing stress and emotions, and in how all these are linked, in conjunction with individual temperament and societal and other factors, with disordered eating and the diagnosed eating disorders.

Anorexia nervosa is a psychiatric illness characterized by distorted body image and excessive dieting, leading to severe weight loss, with a pathological fear of becoming fat.[1] In the purging type, there is usually vomiting and/or laxative use. Sufferers often deny their illness, which frequently leads to malnutrition, semistarvation, and consequent medical complications, and, in some cases, death.

Recovery requires restoration of a healthy weight, and psychologically and emotionally outgrowing the illness so that it becomes superfluous. A full recovery may not be possible to achieve for those with more complex psychopathology and comorbidities than average, and for all sufferers, the illness may remain a kind of "Achilles heel," a way of being which is reverted to under stress.

In the psychotherapeutic processes of adolescents with anorexia with whom I have worked, there appear to be definite psychological stages which need to be satisfactorily negotiated and integrated for recovery. Many therapists have written extensively on the areas of psychological growth inherent in the psychotherapeutic processes of these patients, and I am merely adding to the melting pot my own personal "take" on this, in the hope that one day we will together find a more satisfactory way to facilitate these patients in achieving a truly sustainable recovery.

During psychotherapy, it appears that, despite individual idiosyncrasies, these patients intuitively move through broad categories of psychological development which are common to all and which generally appear centered around the development of a stronger sense of who they are/a core "sense of self." I wonder whether these patients are regaining a prior sense of self, or whether developing a healthy self outside the illness will actually be the first time they have had any real sense of self at all? I should perhaps add that, in the earlier years of life, psychological development is focused on the growth of a self which allows the person to function in the world (the ego), rather than in transpersonal dimensions of the self, and it is this so-called "egoic" self that I am concentrating on here.

Often, anorexia surfaces around puberty, which is of course when the young person is searching for self-identity; if the foundations of this are weak, for whatever reason, perhaps it is not surprising that this is when the illness develops. It seems likely, though, that all sorts of things are happening within the individual psyche prior to this, which could potentially be worked on earlier, with the aim of preventing the full-blown illness from developing.

The psychological steps which appear necessary for recovery are strikingly similar to those which the baby, then child, goes through while growing up within a secure primary attachment relationship, and additionally include stages connected with the illness itself. Although I have worked with inpatients who have made a good start on negotiating these steps, due to the way our services are set up, with a change of team after discharge, it is not possible to know if they could achieve a lasting recovery if their psychotherapeutic process was allowed to continue uninterrupted for as long as needed for psychological changes to become totally embedded in the psyche (several years, probably longer).

For ease of description, I have divided patients' psychological processes into three stages, described below, although there is much overlap between these. They are moved through, not in a linear fashion, but in a "spiraling forward" type of process, which integrates the various psychological developments into the psyche as it goes along. Some patients may need to negotiate other stages of growth and development in addition to those discussed here, and probably go round these stages several times in increasing depth before any lasting recovery can be achieved.

Early Stage of the Therapeutic Process

A crucial aspect of early work is to help the patient to at least tentatively connect with their innate life force or self-actualizing tendency,[2] so that they can begin to engage with their psychological journey toward recovery. Many hospitalized patients are not only completely disconnected from this, they are actually pulling strongly in the opposite direction toward death, by suicide or through medical complications of starvation. The irony of the illness is that, though unconsciously partly designed to protect the individual, it is pulling them toward the grave, and has the highest death rate of any mental illness.[3] Add to this that the illness brings a disconnection from the innate life force, and it is evident that it can be extremely hard to establish a therapeutic alliance in which both therapist and patient are alongside each other in their aims.

Initially, the patient may struggle to remain in the therapy room at all, perhaps due to a weak or practically non-existent sense of self, and therefore, with the fear of losing connection with themselves altogether within the context of a one-to-one relationship, so they have no "continuity of being."[4] Also, they are left without, or perhaps never "learnt," any way of managing what is inside—the internalization of the ability to regulate

emotions is one of the key processes of child development which occurs naturally in a secure primary attachment, and is part of the development of a sense of self. With an almost total lack of any means of self-regulation, what is inside is either pushed down hard and does not want to come out, or it spills out all over the place, completely uncontrolled. Emotions can appear too overwhelming to tolerate, and there may be panic, especially around mealtimes. There is often lots of "busy-ness" in the head, and a lack of awareness of the body or breathing. No wonder it is challenging to stay in therapy and begin daring to hope it may be possible to survive all this, let alone that there could be life beyond it; fear is an enormous obstacle to successful progress, both initially, and for much of the therapy.

Not being seen or heard is a common theme of early sessions, and is, I believe, interconnected with patients' lack of sense of self. They appear not to experience others as relating to them as if they have an identity; and losing so much weight that they physically almost disappear seems like an outward manifestation of their felt experience. At a deep level, could there be a connection between starving themselves and not having space for the self, both in early life and now therefore also in their own minds? And so, is the anorexia perhaps a sort of re-enactment of their early psychological experience?

Patients' perfectionistic thinking appears to be linked to their rock-bottom self-esteem, and sets them up to fail; in their eyes, they can never be good enough. They often completely identify with one way of being/thinking, and are not able to hold the opposite (or later on, the middle) position in mind at all, so are unable to inhabit the middle ground and are always at the extreme. They often habitually experience themselves as being at the "bad" end of the spectrum, while perhaps seeing others as being at the "good" end. Maybe they have to categorize people into good and bad in order to locate themselves at all?

Of course, perfectionistic tendencies may well be related to control issues too. It could be argued that the desperate need to gain control, which becomes focused on eating habits and body image, is related to weak self-identity, as well as the extremely turbulent and traumatic lives many have experienced. It is noticeable that, as these patients begin to develop some tenuous sense of identity outside the illness, they can start to gradually relinquish their iron grip on assorted aspects of their lives.

"Catastrophizing" is common, and is perhaps connected with a sense of futility and hopelessness, and also with their difficulty in allowing space for the positive, which I will return to later. They are experts at writing inner scripts with disastrous endings, making it very difficult, if not impossible, to be fully present in the here and now. There is a massive piece of work needed here, focused on helping them become aware of distortions in their thinking, both about themselves and others, and realizing that what they assume others think, may actually be a projection of their own negative views of themselves.

Middle Stage

Ambivalence is usually a major feature of this stage—patients may now want to recover, and they also do not want to, the latter being the stronger, immensely powerful driving force. For some, the illness is a way of getting attention (for which we could read "love"), but getting better would mean a move toward loving, or at least tentatively being kinder to, themselves, and of course they cannot do that, because in their eyes they are not good enough, and do not deserve to be well. Beyond that, it seems that to move from illness to wellness, they would have to experience losing themselves, as, by the time they are ill enough to be hospitalized, any sense of self they have is often totally bound up with how well they can be anorectic, this being the only way they feel they exist at all. Again, there can be tremendous fear and confusion—their very sense of who they are is being fundamentally challenged within the therapeutic process, and they have to relinquish their anorectic selves without having another sense of self to step into. Therapy involves a gradual process of building one, probably for the first time. Some, perhaps all, seem to have a fear of annihilation, which may be linked to early trauma—possibly as a result of abuse or neglect, but certainly, I suggest, as a result of a sense of annihilation of the self, which may be held in the unconscious mind even from the beginnings of life. This too can make it extremely difficult to negotiate the middle stage of therapy.

Working through ambivalence is partly about working through the experience of not moving forward in the therapeutic process. Despite the team's efforts, the patient may seem psychologically motionless; digging their heels in and, at some level, perhaps wanting their parent (the team in the patient's transference) to understand, know, and hear their pain. And yet, again, there is often ambivalence; they may not want to be seen or heard, as they do not know who they are, and, in any case, believe they are "bad" and so cannot be tolerated. They feel pulled both ways, toward recovery (once they are reconnected to their innate self-actualizing tendency),[2] and backward into the illness, with all that brings in terms of a sense of who they are and what they believe they deserve, in terms of a way of "managing" their emotions (albeit a dysfunctional way), and in terms of their habitual ways of being. They are stuck, pulled two ways, unable to move.

However, all is not lost if they start to develop a sense of agency and autonomy.[5] So often patients search for a sense of agency outside of themselves, and sometimes talk of remembering a wish to not be independent of their mothers before the onset of the illness—frequently encountered are enmeshed relationships with mothers, with no sense of a separate self having developed,[6] and also the "best friends" type of relationship, without clearly defined mother/daughter roles.[7] Sometimes,

mothers/parents do not want their offspring to grow up—there is no psychological space for the young person to develop a separate self in early life or during puberty—they are not seen or heard for who they are, and consequently do not know or experience who they are for themselves. In psychotherapy, there is a "potential space"[8] in which the patient can begin to search for, and gain, a sense of who they are. At this stage, I sometimes have a palpable sense of the patient struggling to "feel their edges," as it were—where do they stop and I start, at both an energetic and psychological level?

This connecting with who they are involves much work on tuning into emotions and thoughts, which may be habitually projected onto others; in therapy, there is a sense of reeling patients in to be with their own feelings and experiences. They can become aware of bodily sensations through mindfulness[9] and visualization; despite their obsession with body image, they are often totally disembodied psychologically and dissociated for much of the time. I sometimes wonder if, for some, a part of early trauma may be located in the anorexia, so there is a sense of the true self having died, and hence the felt sense of annihilation of the self, which seems to be lodged inside them.

In any case, many, maybe all, of these patients have been through experiences which have resulted in profound shame about who they are. Is it possible that they are unable to come near to their real self, as they are profoundly ashamed of it? Maybe we could think of the anorexia as a kind of false self?[8] The shame may well be constantly reinforced by their negative beliefs about themselves, and there is guilt about eating and regaining a healthy weight; about being nourished and loved, both physically and emotionally.

Patients' search for a sense of who they are may involve them swinging like a pendulum from one extreme to another, a bit like the polarized thinking, only this is in ways of being—for example, from wild "party-going"-type behaviour, at one extreme, to total withdrawal at the other. Again, there can be a struggle to find a balanced middle position, which perhaps is related to a weak ego, or disturbances to the ego–self axis, as described by some post-Jungian theorists—making a state of balance hard to maintain.[10,11]

Affect regulation usually continues to be a central part of the process, particularly now around food and eating. Commonly, there is fear of getting "fat"; is this perhaps partly linked to a profound psychological hunger for love and emotional holding which seems impossible to satisfy, causing a fear that if they start eating they will never stop?

The habit of getting stuck in the negative may partly be linked to a fear of change, and a sense of lack of control. Patients may have been unable to stop unwelcome changes which have happened in their lives. Additionally, as previously mentioned, the parent may not want the child to grow up, and this can become particularly apparent at puberty. So, fear of change and of the evolving cycle of life, may be held within the family and be taken in by the patient and made their own.

There appears also to be a huge problem in becoming flexible enough to allow space for the positive, perhaps due to patients seeing themselves as totally bad. However, at least they know who they are then—or so they think. Any move toward allowing space for the positive can be threatening to their sense of identity, sometimes to their very existence; a potentially huge stumbling block in moving through this stage. They may well be "people pleasers": with no psychological space to explore and develop a sense of who they were when babies and young children, they may attempt to become who they think others want them to be, so they have a sense of being someone at all, and also so they may just deserve to be loved.

Through the middle stages of therapy, there will hopefully be a very gradual increase in mental flexibility, and alongside this, in creativity, which is so closely linked with the development of a sense of self.[12] I find that as patients negotiate these middle stages, they usually become more able to think creatively, to occasionally use art materials or visualization and mindfulness techniques, and to begin to "play"—with words, with concepts, and eventually with developing an increasing sense of who they are.

Late Stage

By "late stage," I am here thinking of patients within an inpatient unit, and recognize that there will still be much work to do, probably for several years beyond discharge, in order to consolidate and build on psychological shifts already made.

One of the main strands of work now is helping the patient to develop a more compassionate and accepting attitude toward themselves. Patients so often struggle with their own self-loathing all along, and challenging extremely condemnatory self-concepts is part and parcel of the work from the start. By this stage of therapy, it is hoped that patients will be well engaged in the gradual process of gaining more self-acceptance, though for many this can be one of the most challenging aspects of their psychological journey, and will need to continue for a long time to come.

By now, hopefully they have some kind of internalized affect regulation system in place, and trust in themselves is growing. Mindfulness techniques can be helpful here in developing a sense of being able to stand firm and weather the emotional storm, and to know that their thoughts and emotions are just that—thoughts and emotions—and not the true essence of who they are, so they have a felt experience of the "ground" of being.[13]

Various things may happen in the patients' processes at this stage, triggered by the approaching discharge. Some may try to escape reality; for example, by sleeping all the time. They may not want to go home, perhaps associating this with the struggles which brought about, or at least triggered, the illness in the first place. There may be a pause in their forward momentum as they gather themselves in preparation for the next step, or they may slip back to earlier more dysregulated states, doubting they can manage their feelings once left alone to do this. While they may have fought against it for much of the time, the containing, "holding" environment of the unit can suddenly seem safer than the prospect of the outside world. They may attempt to sabotage discharge, for fear of psychological disintegration once they get home. They may not allow themselves to stay with the psychological shifts which have taken place. This testing time can be a measure of whether they have really embodied the shifts, or just made them at a cognitive level. As they gain an embodied sense of who they are, patients can begin to eat and allow themselves to be nourished by food and through relationship—they "fill out" in all ways into who they really are.

Whatever the individual manifestations of the reaction to the approaching discharge and the end of the work with a particular therapist, many patients may be unconsciously driven to ways of attempting not to feel; it is true, is it not, that a deeper connection with the self actually leads to increased awareness of all feelings, and so the fear and loss associated with leaving the unit, even if this is what the patient desires, may be felt all the more deeply after their therapy. And yet, of course, they will hopefully now be more fully connected with who they are, and, being more resilient emotionally and psychologically, may be better able to bear whatever they feel, and in time even come to embrace it as being part of their very humanness.

Patients' rigid views of themselves and of others often relax. Things no longer seem just "black and white"; it is possible to inhabit the grey area in between, and this in itself can help them to accept their understandable reactions to their imminent discharge. It is OK to feel anxious and to anticipate missing the unit, all their fellow patients and the staff who have been their surrogate family for all these months. It is understandable to feel nervous about stepping once more into the outside world, and it is possible to trust that they now have at least the real beginnings of a sense of who they are outside of the illness. This can bring with it the inner strength to begin to trust and support themselves as they continue to move forward on their journey of healing and psychological growth.

Relapse prevention work is an important part of the late stages of work prior to discharge, so that if life events again challenge their inner resources, they can recognize the warning signs within themselves, and have internalized within them ways of managing and pushing through these rocky patches. If the therapy has gone on long enough, and at a deep enough level, by this stage patients can have some internalized "good objects"[14] which will sustain them, although very stressful times may seriously challenge their ability to hang on to these. I do believe, however, that if a sense of self outside of the illness has really begun to develop, they now have the best chance of not reverting to anorectic ways of being. Therapy needs to continue post discharge so that permanent shifts are made and consolidated, and so that those areas in which progress has not been sufficient to prevent relapse can be worked on further.

Conclusion

I have provided the briefest overview of the psychological process which patients with anorexia appear to go through during recovery; usually, additional individual idiosyncrasies need to be tackled too. The factors which lead to the development of the illness are many, and are to some degree varied; some suggest there may even be a genetic component, which I have not considered here at all. However, whatever combination of factors has led to each individual case, it seems that the journey to recovery always involves the individual grappling with issues of self-identity and the development of a core sense of self. As a sense of self develops, brought about through the interactions within the psychotherapeutic relationship itself, so the extremely punishing "super-ego"[15] and disastrously negative self-concepts, which result in the perfectionistic and catastrophizing ways of thinking, can be relinquished. As emotions which were previously repressed or dissociated from are experienced, managed, and tolerated within the therapeutic relationship, so an internalized self-regulation system will develop. Consequently, the emotions themselves usually become less overwhelming, so that the extreme lengths which sufferers go to in an attempt to manage them (and the associated punishing thoughts), such as self-harm, the eating disorder itself, and even the contemplation of suicide, begin to become unnecessary. Over time, the patients' mental flexibility increases, so there can be a shift away from the "black and white" thinking toward the "middle ground." As psychological space for the positive grows, and a grounded sense of self develops, so the individual can develop self-acceptance and blossom into the person she/he really is, as both mind and body together can at last find a way of being which embraces healing and recovery, and ultimately life itself.

References

1. American Psychiatric Association. DSM-5. Washington, DC: American Psychiatric Association; 2013.
2. Maslow A. The farther reaches of human nature. New edition. London: Arkana; 1994.
3. Beat. Eating disorder statistics. [Online.] www.b-eat.co.uk/about-beat/media-centre/information-and-statistics-about-eating-disorders (accessed 16 March 2016).
4. Winnicott D. Human nature. London: Free Association Books; 1988.
5. Erikson E. Childhood and society. Reissue edition. New York: WW Norton & Company Ltd; 1993.
6. Mahler M. The psychological birth of the human infant: symbiosis and individuation. Later printing edition. New York: Basic Books; 2000.
7. Chernin K. The hungry self: women, eating and identity. New York; Harper Perennial reprint edition; 1994.
8. Winnicott D. Maturational processes and the facilitating environment: studies in the theory of emotional development. New edition. London: Hogarth Press; 1989.
9. Kabat-Zinn J. Full catastrophe living: how to cope with stress, pain and illness using mindfulness meditation. London: Piatkus; 2001.
10. Edinger E. Ego and archetype. London: Penguin Books; 1980.
11. Neumann E. The child: structure and dynamics of the nascent personality. Boston: Shambala Publications/CG Jung Foundation of Analytical Psychology; 1973.
12. Winnicott D. Playing and reality. Second edition. Hove: Routledge; 2005.
13. Washburn M. The ego and the dynamic ground: a transpersonal theory of human development. Albany: State University of New York Press; 1995.
14. The Melanie Klein Trust. Envy and gratitude and other works 1946–1963. New edition. London: Vintage Classics; 1997.
15. Freud S. The ego and the id. London: WW Norton & Company Ltd; 1962.

Critical Thinking

1. How could you support your friend if he or she lived with anorexia nervosa?

2. How does social media influence adolescent perceptions of body image?

3. How could we positively affect a change in adolescent perceptions of different body types?

Internet References

Adolescent Girls and Body Image
https://www.socialworkers.org/practice/adolescent_health/ah0204.asp

Anorexia and Bulimia Care
http://www.anorexiabulimiacare.org.uk/about/statistics

Anorexia Statistics
http://www.mirror-mirror.org/anorexia-statistics.htm

Eating Disorders Statistics and Research
https://www.eatingdisorderhope.com/information/statistics-studies

Get the Facts on Eating Disorders
https://www.nationaleatingdisorders.org/get-facts-eating-disorders

---

WENDY JONES is an integrative child and adolescent psychotherapist, with prior training as a play therapist. She has worked with children, adolescents, and some parents and adults, in a variety of settings, and is currently a member of the staff team at Ellern Mede service for eating disorders in London, which provides inpatient treatment for adolescents with severe and enduring eating disorders.

Article   Prepared by: Claire N. Rubman, *Suffolk County Community College*

Separation and Stuckness

JIM PYE

Learning Outcomes

After reading this article, you will be able to:

- Define the concept of "separation."
- Explain the need for separation during adolescence.
- Give two examples of separation rehearsal.

The process of separation in adolescents' lives is central and crucial. It is possible to think of the hectic experimentation, the acting out, the turbulence of adolescence as the outward and visible form of the internal business of separation, of turning into an individual. Who am I to be? Am I to follow the map given to me by my parents? Will I rip it up and set off chartless? Will I refuse to be the kind of person I know they long for me to be—and, what's more, do I believe in that person? Do I trust my parents and my teachers when they seem to know who I am and who I am becoming? And as for my parents, I don't need them anymore, do I? I wish they'd leave me alone; I wish they'd hurry up and die so I can get on with it. . . . Oh no, I don't really mean that.

Erikson's[1] characterization of the years 12 to 18 is that the adolescent task is to sort out "identity" from "role confusion." However, my memory of my reading when I researched the subject of "invisible children" in the 1980s[2] is that Goleman's empirical findings[3,4] question the notion that adolescence is always a time of identity crisis. Coleman's work showed that the process of separation tends more often to be relatively painless. So it's important to remember that adolescent development does not have to be stormy, and separation does not have to be arduous.

But it can be. I was preparing to present a workshop at the 2014 School Counsellors Conference in Didcot, Oxfordshire and my task would be to prompt participants to think about separation and its relevance for school counsellors—who are specialists and experts in adolescent storm damage and everything that can go awry in teenage development.

My thoughts then turned to parents, and teachers (their surrogates). Can they bear to let children go? Defending ourselves against the power of what we counsellors feel, we use distancing words like transference, and its awkward double, countertransference. But love—and its argument with hate—is our currency. As a teacher, I had been sad to say goodbye to pupils, even if I'd dreaded or abhorred them at times. And, as I pondered how best to design a workshop, it occurred to me that schools are in a difficult position when it comes to separation. Separation—calm or stormy—needs a certain ruthlessness: it's a triumph of the living over the soon to die. When my children tease me about my senescence, they're not just being affectionate, they're also practising the—usually benign—contempt that will make it easier to leave me behind.

Ruthless Separation Rehearsals

Schools are extraordinarily good at the tough business of loving their charges; but the corollary of their devotion is their vulnerability—to the many kinds of attack that adolescents will be compelled to mount as they flex their separation muscles. And because schools are also engines for the inculcation of civilized standards of behavior, teachers often, unavoidably, have to counter attack and squash teenagers' ruthless separation rehearsals. What an extraordinarily difficult trick to bring off: to accept the psychological necessity of intransigent behavior at the same time as containing it, and sometimes—with equal ruthlessness—imposing sanctions against its repeat. And all this must be achieved without giving in to the moments of hatred it is impossible not to feel while negotiating this complexity.

Adolescents' attacks, their so-called separation rehearsals, are likely to be more flagrant and demanding—or downright dangerous—if their family life is emotionally chaotic, neglectful, or abusive. And separation, as a process, is likely to be deeply compromised if this is the case. As a therapist in a university, I often worked with mature students whose return to education was part of an unconscious drive to start life again after very destructive early experiences. Many of these students had left home fairly young, having escaped or been thrown out. But, more often than not, separation had only happened externally: they brought with them to the psychological hard labour of their return the internal parents from whom they now, at last, were trying to free themselves.

Preparing further for my conference workshop, I dipped into the literature, most of it American and online, about "separation-individuation" in adolescence. The consensual notion in the literature is that it is a recapitulation of the task or stage that first takes place at toddler age. However Stern[5] contests this idea vigorously, claiming that a separate self exists from birth. As far as adolescence is concerned, I picked up a consensus, and an unsurprising one, that secure attachment predisposes toward successful separation. There was an interesting paper by Barrera and colleagues[6] that reports a study of 188 undergraduates and concludes that separation is likely to be more successful in families characterized by "extreme emotional connectedness," which I took to imply family "cohesion" rather than the adhesive parent-child relationships that, in my experience as a student counsellor, are liable to make for separation difficulty. This paper and others touched on the difficulty of generalising across cultures and ethnicities—let alone gender—when these matters are considered. But for the purposes of my workshop I decided to accept a rough-and-ready proposition about attachment, and I prepared a handout with quotes from Jeremy Holmes[7] that illustrated the three main attachment styles: avoidant, ambivalent and disorganised.

Cherished But Not Controlled

I did so because I decided to invite those attending the workshop to think about working with cases in which separation difficulty could already be discerned, or confidently predicted. My premise was that the "cohesion" noted in the paper I just mentioned is likely to be characterized by relationships based on what Holmes describes like this: "What I intend to convey . . . is . . . a nonpossessive, nonambivalent, autonomous, freely entered into attachment, in which the object is held and cherished but not controlled."[8] Holmes calls this, somewhat confusingly, 'nonattachment,' which, he says, "transcends detachment in that it implies a separation from the object based on respect rather than anger or avoidance."

I decided to invite my workshop participants to reflect on some cases in which the parental disposition was very far from being like this, because I had worked again and again with students in separation difficulty—or separation crises. They were

mature student clients such as I have quoted above, and younger students whose parents seemed incapable of letting their children go—who would ring and text them every day, for instance, out of their own need. They were clients who had been dealing for years with their parents' abdication, who had become pseudoparents to their younger siblings or had been forced to serve narcissistic parental demands.

A fictional example of such a person illustrates this idea. Let's call him Steven. His mother and father divorced when he was five-years old and he has been raised by his mother, a hospital administrator. Steven is now aged 20 and has two younger sisters aged 14 and 16. Steven loves and also deeply respects his mother, who has had to struggle against harsh odds. The father has been fickle, unable to offer much support of any kind and financially overstretched because he has two other children from his second marriage, also now ended.

Steven has always been a good boy, a hard worker. By the time, he was 15 he was his mother's best friend and helper. She never needed a babysitter because he always obliged—the boy whose sense of duty meant that he never finished his homework, was often late, seemed sleepy in lessons and a little depressed, and whose A level grades fell just short of expectations.

Nobody could accuse his mother of asking too much of him: circumstances made their relationship take a certain form. But when he leaves home for university his mother's task is to let him go and thrive in his own way. She wants to do this but she's desolate without him. She has neglected her own needs and has had only brief, unsuccessful relationships since the father's departure. Bringing up her two daughters without Steven suddenly feels completely different: different and daunting. His presence made the four of them a family. His absence frightens her.

She rings and texts every day. Some of the texts try to be jolly and light but there's often a reference to a problem with one of the sisters, and she signs off the same each time: Love you—miss you. The texts might appear on his phone at 11 in the morning or 10 at night; she's always, always there.

Meanwhile Steven has his first girlfriend. He's popular. He begins to have a social life. He dreads the texts and calls, and hates himself for dreading them. Guilt gathers. His mother—unconsciously—knows what he feels, but cannot stop herself contacting him. She feels guilty too.

They're stuck: inseparable, glued together with guilt.

Separation Fear

The opposite of separateness is so often "stuckness." At the workshop, I read aloud James Joyce's story "Eveline" from Dubliners.[9] I have loved this story for as long as I can remember. Eveline, 19, has a choice. Her mother is dead. Frank, her sailor boyfriend, is offering her marriage and a new life in South America. Will she accept him and escape her life as housekeeper to her controlling and sometimes violent father and surrogate mother to her younger siblings?

The father's power, his control, and the sense of duty that enforces her subjugation are very strong, yet "now she was about to leave it, she did not find it a wholly undesirable life." The other impulse is equally potent: "Escape, she must escape! Frank would save her. . ." She is in a separation crisis, and her development is in jeopardy. In the end, her courage fails her; terror takes hold of her: "All the seas of the world tumbled about her heart"—and the ship, with Frank aboard, leaves without her.

I asked the workshop participants to form groups and to transform Eveline into a case—a teenager who might appear in your room. Assume she's 15 or 16. Think of the critical features of her case—in particular, the nature of the relationship with the father.

What issues or problems might bring this girl to counselling? In particular, consider the possible transferences that might arise—with other staff or students—and not least with you as counsellor.

As far as technique is concerned, what in your practice might be particularly important? What would you probably need to do, and not do? What might be particularly difficult?

And, I added, the chief question I want you to discuss is this: in what ways does identifying separation as an issue help your thinking, your self-supervision in this case?

It might have been interesting to record the discussion. It was vivid and almost hectic—suggesting the rapidity with which people identified this configuration: the controlling parent, the suborned child. In the plenary, we discussed how difficult it can be to manage the strength of the relationship that might form with such a client. We acknowledged the need to recognize our own narcissism and to resist the seductive pleasure of being so dependably different from the parent in the case. We talked about the need for focus, for tight boundaries, and for strengthening the client's oppressed agency, ego strength and faltering ruthlessness.

Finally, I read aloud from Michael Balint's great book The Basic Fault.[10] have admired Balint ever since turning to counselling and psychotherapy in my 40s: his practicality, his wish for psychoanalytic ideas to be useful in the world beyond the consulting room. I also think his great distinction between useful and malignant regression is what I have needed to consider again and again in my work.

So I read my favourite passage. It's very short, about a young woman in her late 20s, still living with her parents. She is emblematically stuck: kept developmentally on permanent pause in the household of a "forceful, rather obsessional, but most reliable father . . . [and] a somewhat intimidated mother, whom she felt to be unreliable." She can't take a vital final examination; nor can she respond to any of the proposals from men who wish to marry her. We are told that "her inability to respond was linked with a crippling fear of uncertainty whenever she had to take any risk, that is, take a decision."

Balint has worked with her loyally for two years—loyal, perhaps, also to the primacy at that time of interpretation as the chief agent of change. When recalling this incident, he says: "At about this time, she was given the interpretation that apparently the most important thing for her was to keep her head safely up, with both feet firmly planted on the ground. In response, she mentioned that ever since her earliest childhood she could never do a somersault, although at various periods she tried desperately to do one. I then said: 'What about it now?' whereupon she got up from the couch and to her great amazement did a perfect somersault without any difficulty. This proved to be a real breakthrough."

And from then on all is well; her independent life begins.

I love the somersault for its transgressiveness, its cheekiness as an intervention. I am part of a local group of therapists who are at the moment contributing to a UKCP-supported study of so-called "moments of meeting": moments that transfigure a therapy suddenly and perhaps unexpectedly. Balint's impatience or frustration that prompted his manoeuvre possibly qualifies the somersault as just such a moment.

I also love the suggestion of such an enviably vast consulting room that it allows space for a full somersault. And—finally—I enjoy how typical the passage is of so much psychoanalytic literature in its neat deployment of a successful case that reads a little like a fable or fairy story, with the client left miraculously unstuck, in her rescued state, to live happily ever after. And with all such case histories, unverified by the patient, unsupported by other evidence, a voice always nags at me: "Can we really be sure things turned out as well as this?" But, even as an exemplary fable, it is brilliant, unforgettable.

This, on my handout, is how I asked for discussion in groups to proceed, again asking participants to translate Balint's client into an adolescent girl. Assuming that this girl's dilemma is that she cannot separate and that her stuckness is the issue, Balint's intervention liberated this girl's capacity to act freely for herself, to take risks, to express herself. The somersault can be read as a symbolic act of separation:

* what would the relationship with the father have been like?

* what might lead such a relationship to create problems, or even a crisis, that would bring the girl to counselling?

* assume she has been with you for two sessions. Then there is a crisis. Invent one that involves other students and members of staff. What role can you take—remembering that in your two sessions you have already created a relationship with this girl?

And/or:

* think of a "stuck" client—one whose story either does or might echo features of this girl's predicament. Briefly present the case to your group.

Again, I wish I had recorded the discussions in the groups and plenary because what became quickly clear is that school counsellors know stuckness as well as they know anything. It was as if stuckness is an adolescent condition, an ineluctable fact of adolescent life. What's more, everyone seemed familiar with predicaments like that of my invented Steven.

I sense now a further theme: of the embattled parent, struggling to keep financially afloat, perhaps depressed, perhaps dependent on alcohol . . . and unable to resist the temptation to rely on a teenage child. Such children flocked to the discussion: loyal, devoted, self-denying, dependable. Of course, their different cousins were present too: acting out, pushed to extremes to unstick themselves. But it was stuckness that we discussed.

If there is one presiding idea or mission informing the yearly School Counsellors Conference—two of which I've now attended—it's that counselling in schools must at all costs avoid being tucked away in a special corner. Counsellors must relate not only to individual clients but also to the school, its staff and its life. And it seemed so clear that those who attended my workshop were themselves guided by this idea. It was hard to imagine them sequestered in their consulting rooms. Still less was it possible to imagine them falling into the great error of our profession—the belief that all we need to do is sit and listen. Because what the discussion of stuckness revealed was the need in effective therapy to take risks, to be active, to be creative—and sometimes to trust that what's needed is a somersault.

But that doesn't mean that boundaries cease to be important: just make sure your walls are far enough apart.

This article is based on Jim's workshop on the theme of separation at the School Counsellors Conference, Didcot, September 2014. It was first published with the title "On Separation" in BACP Children & Young People 2015; March: 33–36.

References

1. Erikson EH. Childhood and society. London: Norton; 1950.
2. Pye J. Invisible children. Oxford: Oxford University Press; 1988.
3. Coleman JC. Relationships in adolescence. London: Routledge and Kegan Paul; 1974.
4. Coleman J. The nature of adolescence. In: Coleman J. Youth policies in the 1990s. London: Routledge; 1990 (pp. 8–27).
5. Stern D. The interpersonal world of the infant. London: Basic Books; 1985.
6. Barrera A, Blumer L, Soenksen S. Revisiting adolescent separation-individuation in the contexts of enmeshment and allocentrism. The New School Psychology Bulletin 2011; 8(2): 70–82.
7. Holmes J. The search for the secure base. London: Routledge; 2001.
8. Holmes J. Attachment, intimacy, autonomy. New York: Jason Aronson; 1996.
9. Joyce J. Dubliners. London: Paladin Books; 1989.
10. Balint M. The basic fault. New York: Brunner-Mazel; 1979.

Critical Thinking

1. Why is separation such an essential aspect of adolescence?
2. What are some of the potential obstacles that stand in the path of successful separation in adolescence?

Internet References

Adolescence: Developing Independence and Identity
http://open.lib.umn.edu/intropsyc/chapter/6-3-adolescence-developing-independence-and-identity/

Early Adolescence: The Point of No Return
http://www.thesuccessfulparent.com/categories/adolescence/item/early-adolescence-the-point-of-no-return-part-i#.WQuDsdIrKUk

Erik Erikson and Self Identity
https://www.mentalhelp.net/articles/erik-erikson-and-self-identity/

Understanding Early Adolescent Self and Identity: An Introduction
http://ahd1113.activehost.com/pdf/60549.pdf

JIM PYE was a student counsellor until he retired in August 2014. His first training as a counsellor was psychodynamic. He trained later at Metanoia as an integrative psychotherapist and is UKCP registered. He has a small private practice as a psychotherapist and supervisor.

Article Prepared by: Claire N. Rubman, *Suffolk County Community College*

The Young and the Riskless

Teens tend to make rash decisions, and it all comes down to the brain. Adults could learn a thing or two from them.

KAYT SUKEL

Learning Outcomes

After reading this article, you will be able to:

- Talk about the role of the amygdala and the insula in adolescence.

- Explain where rewards are processed in the brain and the function of the basal ganglia.

- Explain the role of dopamine and the "out-of-sync mesocortical limbic system."

If you came of age in the 1980s, as I did, you're likely familiar with the movie *Lethal Weapon*. Two mismatched police detectives unexpectedly find themselves partnered up: Martin Riggs, the loose cannon with revenge on his mind, and Roger Murtaugh, the older, wiser man of the force, counting the days until retirement. When I saw this film for the first time in high school, I identified with the loonier of the two, Riggs. He might be a little crazy, but man, he was fun. Also, easy on the eyes. When I watched the film recently, however, my sympathies had changed. Today, I'm more in Murtaugh's corner. Mostly because I find myself, as a middle-aged mom, inadvertently quoting his signature line, "I'm too old for this shit," on a regular basis.

I used to be a risk-taker. But now, I just feel too old to bother. The potential negative consequences of a risky decision, like the loss of financial or social stability, seem too great to bear. I have a mortgage to pay, for goodness' sake! I have a kid to raise. And the positive outcomes? Well, they just don't seem as compelling as they once did. But I can't help wondering why my approach has changed so much. Has my age and place in society somehow affected the way I'm perceiving

and pursuing risk? What's changed in me since my crazy, risk-taking teenage years?

The Teen Species

Jonathan is not the kid you think of when someone mentions your typical risk-taking teenager. At 18, he's an above-average student, secretary of the student council and a star player on his school's soccer team. He's friendly and well liked across his school's diverse social strata. Everyone in his life expects him to do great things. And he seems fairly unaffected by the weight of those expectations. He's the kind of kid who makes the teen years look good.

But even for Jonathan, adolescence isn't an easy process. It's a volatile time, both physically and emotionally. Abigail Baird, a brain researcher at Vassar College, says what you see on the outside is happening in the teenage brain as well.

"You see that explosive growth and the gawkiness that comes with it on the outside during adolescence—kids suddenly shooting up with long, clumsy arms and legs," she says. "What shouldn't be surprising, then, is that there's that same gawkiness when we're talking about the brain, too. It's not an exaggeration to say things are exploding in terms of brain growth."

And those changes, neuroscientists argue, make teenagers the ultimate risk-takers.

"The biggest source of morbidity and mortality in young people in industrialized countries isn't medical disease but problems with behavior and emotion," says Ronald Dahl, a researcher at the University of California, Berkeley's School of Public Health. "We're talking about suicide, homicide, car accidents, substance abuse and sexual risk-taking. There is something about the neurobiology of adolescents that makes them more likely to take risks than children or adults. We're only beginning to understand it."

That includes the so-called good kids like Jonathan. Dahl explains, "Eighty percent of adolescents don't do wild and crazy things. But even the shy, anxious kids tend to become more exploratory and more likely to experiment during mid- to late adolescence." Jonathan may have a good head on his shoulders, but, after a thorough talk, I learn he also has an unapologetic penchant for partying. Some of his and his friends' exploits include random (and sometimes unprotected) sex, drug use, fistfights, skipping school and home responsibilities, driving under the influence, and jumping off a second-story roof into a neighboring home's swimming pool.

A Brain Disconnect

Jonathan will be the first to admit he knows better. "I mean, I don't want to say any of that stuff is a good idea—it's not," he says. "But it's fun. Sometimes I think I should have just stayed home and worked on [soccer] drills or studied or something instead of going to the party. But I never think any of that [while I'm partying]."

As many of us remember from our adolescence, when it comes to risky business, it's not that teens don't know better. But knowledge isn't always the most important factor when you're making a decision in the moment. So, despite the known consequences, teens still often act unwisely. There seems to be some kind of disconnect between knowing and doing in the teenage brain—and new work in neuroscience suggests this disconnect is literal as well as figurative.

Laurence Steinberg, a social neuroscientist at Temple University, posits teens are more likely to indulge in risky business because of the way their brains are maturing. Right around puberty, when sex hormones are working their magic on our reproductive systems, they're also heralding some pretty dramatic changes in our brains. These alterations result in significant differences in how the brain processes dopamine—which not only affects the brain's risk-and-reward processing circuitry, but also mediates social and emotional behaviors.

At around age 10, spurred by sex steroids and other important growth hormones, the brain starts to prune dopamine receptors in the striatum, an important part of the basal ganglia, and in the prefrontal cortex. This pruning changes the relative density of receptors in the circuit linking the area of the brain involved with processing rewards (the basal ganglia) and the area of the brain implicated in inhibition and control (the prefrontal cortex). The changes in receptors mean that dopamine is flowing somewhat unencumbered. And the result is an out-of-sync mesocortical limbic system, which regulates emotion and motivation. So with emotion and motivation amped up and

inhibition and long-term planning capability dampened, basically, you see an increase in gas and a decrease in brakes. Looking back at my teen years, which were fraught with more than a bit of crazy, it makes sense to me.

These dramatic changes to the brain have led Baird to suggest adolescence is much like a second toddlerhood. When she first tells me this, I laugh. But on further reflection, I see her point. The toddler years are a sensitive period of growth in both the body and brain that helps babies transition into kids. And when I look closer at the behavior, I see the overlap. "That's not fair"-type tantrums? Check. Pushing boundaries? Of course. A proclivity for hyperbole? Sure. Sensation-seeking? Yep. A "me, me, me" mentality? Oh, yeah.

Studies out of Baird's lab and others suggest that those out-of-control emotions and bewildering motivations that so many parents wish they could quash are important to all that critical preadult learning. "The teen years require a lot of trial and error," Baird says. "If everything wasn't so dramatic and important and emotional, adolescents wouldn't have the motivation they need to get back up and do it again when they fail."

Processing Risk and Rewards

So why is everything so dramatic and important and emotional? It comes back to the neurotransmitter dopamine. A toned-down prefrontal cortex paired with an intensified emotion and motivation circuit is the perfect recipe for risk-taking. But while Dahl says it's easy to suggest hormones make teens temporarily crazy or unable to use their frontal cortices appropriately, those notions are incorrect. Jonathan, for the most part, thinks things through. For example, he has asked me to use a pseudonym. Despite that rationality, his teenage brain strengthens the power of rewards so that he's motivated to gain the experience required to grow and learn. And one way it's doing so is in how rewards are perceived.

Recent work by B. J. Casey and her colleagues at Cornell University suggests the teen brain processes risks the same way adult brains do, but with one important difference: Areas of the brain involved with reward processing are much more active in teens than in younger children or adults.

The implication is that this increased activity results in teens overestimating the value of rewards. When we consider Jonathan's decision to skip using a condom, his brain magnified the reward involved with a hookup. His brain was telling him that he couldn't pass up this encounter: This sex will be the sexiest sex of all time. It became a reward fantastic enough to outdo all other considerations, including the potential consequences of teenage pregnancy or venereal disease.

"Really wanting those rewards is to our advantage when learning," Baird notes. "One thing we do know about adolescence is that it's a really great time to learn new things. And having that incentive to get yourself up, dust yourself off and try it all over again is invaluable. Otherwise, we might not try again and get the experience we need to actually do that learning we need to move from childhood to adulthood."

Good Ideas and Bad Ideas

I first met Vassar's Baird at a neuroscience conference in Washington, DC, after hearing her present some research on the teen brain in a symposium about how neuroscience should shape the law. As part of her presentation, she queried the audience: "Tell me something," she said. "Do you think swimming with sharks is a good idea or a bad idea?"

The majority of the audience, mostly adults, instantly yelled back, "Bad idea!"

If any of the adult shark pooh-pooh-ers had been having their brains scanned at that moment, scientists would have seen increased activation in the amygdala and insula—two key parts of the brain's limbic system and important inputs to the meso-cortical limbic circuit.

You may know the amygdala as the seat of the fight-or-flight response. But Baird tells me that the amygdala is responsible for the four F's. "Fight and flight, everyone knows. The next F is feeding. And that last F stands for reproduction," she jokes.

The amygdala represents the things we need to stay upright, breathing and propagating the species. And, with the basal ganglia, it helps manage important rewards. But it's also involved in processing memory and emotional reactions and attaching social salience to objects and events. Baird likens it to the brain's "burglar alarm."

"This is a part of the brain that is very survival-oriented. It's all about keeping you alive," she says. "Not so much about thinking things through."

The insula, like the amygdala, is also implicated in emotion and decision-making. Like the amygdala, it plays a key role in survival. But it does so by helping you form visceral memories about experiences — both good and bad.

"The insula gives you those gut feelings about things—you know, those instant feelings that are critical to your decision-making, to your innate sense of right and wrong," Baird says. "But it is a highly developed structure. You aren't born with these gut feelings about things. You have to learn them."

Adults can rely both on the amygdala and the insula to help inform decision-making. But the teen brain reacts a little differently. When Baird and colleagues used fMRI to scan teenagers' brains as they were asked a variety of "good idea or bad idea" questions, including biting a lightbulb, eating a cockroach and jumping off a roof, they found their insulae weren't as active as the adults'. The majority of activation was occurring in the frontal lobes, where conscious thought occurs—and they were taking much, much longer to answer the questions.

"With adults, we get an answer that is very automatic and fast," Baird says. "But teens don't get that. Instead, they show a frontal lobe response. They actually think about it for a second. They don't have the experience to have built an automatic response. They have to work the idea through their frontal lobes, and it's just not as efficient."

In fact, they took roughly 300 milliseconds longer than adults to work the idea through. While 300 milliseconds may not seem long, Baird says it's significant. "People don't realize that 300 milliseconds gets people killed on a regular basis," she tells me. "That's a decision to run a red light when you're driving in your car. It's plenty of time to do damage when you're talking about a dangerous situation."

Old Climbers and Bold Climbers

It's clear teens have a neurobiological predisposition for pushing the envelope. And studies show that this increased risk-taking continues through the teen years and well into young adulthood. Around the age of 25, the prefrontal cortex matures to the point where one is better at applying the brakes when faced with a risky decision.

Radboud University risk researcher Bernd Figner says that studies consistently show that we take fewer risks as we get older. And the reason for that, he argues, is twofold.

"There is a maturation of the prefrontal cortex that is happening well into young adulthood that enables us to be better at inhibiting our most influential responses—that is one important thing," he says. "But you also see these changes because you are more experienced. You now have these experiences, and you start to realize that it's not always a good idea to take so many great risks. You understand the consequences better. You realize what's at stake."

So, it's not that I'm old and boring; it's just that I'm better experienced! My limbic system has picked up enough over the years to help guide good decision-making. And my frontal lobes have matured enough to actually do something with it all.

It would appear this effect is not limited to suburban moms. A study that looked at risky behaviors in experienced rock climbers found that they tend to scale back on riskier climbs as they age.

Gareth Jones, a researcher at Leeds Beckett University in England, in collaboration with researchers at the University of Cambridge, wondered why some rock climbers are so willing to engage in risky climbs like free soloing, or climbing without ropes, while others stick to ropes and familiar rock faces. What separated those risk-takers from your more play-it-safe types? They found that measures of self-efficacy—a personality trait that underlies how much you believe in your own abilities to accomplish a goal (as well as deal with the stresses that accompany working toward that goal)—were predictive of how risky a climber was willing to get.

The researchers recruited more than 200 active rock climbers, with one to 48 years of experience, from a variety of climbing venues in Great Britain. Participants completed a special questionnaire, called the Climbing Self-Efficacy Scale, to help researchers understand both the participants' self-efficacy levels and the kinds of climbing risks they usually undertook. The researchers found that self-efficacy was significantly correlated with experience, frequency of climbing and the difficulty of behaviors undertaken.

"Climbers who rated as high in self-efficacy engaged in riskier climbs—they do more climbing, too," Jones says. "And, yes, they do take additional risks, attempting harder climbs when they have that kind of confidence in their abilities."

"That almost makes it sound like a bad thing," I say.

"Not necessarily," he tells me. "What we've seen is that experienced rock climbers understand the inherent risks of the sport. And since they are well-practiced at performing this task, they manage them quite well—they have the experience to know what they can do and judge which kinds of climbs are within their capabilities."

But Jones and company also found another interesting trend in their data. Age impacted how confident the climbers were in their ability, regardless of experience. The older the climber, the less self-efficacy he or she showed. This was even observed in climbers who were, by all accounts, quite skilled.

"It would seem that self-efficacy is age-related," he says. "We saw that it reduces as you get older. There's an old saying in climbing, 'There's old climbers and bold climbers but no old, bold climbers.' And our research suggests that is probably quite accurate."

If there are no old, bold climbers, why would one expect there to be old, bold single moms? Even those of us who enjoy riskier hobbies seem to be laying off the gas as we transition from adolescence to adulthood. But is that necessarily a good thing? Figner, the risk researcher from Radboud University, says not always.

"For adults, when you look at these typical decision-making tasks we use in the lab, people are almost too risk-averse," he says. "We use lotteries [in the lab], typically, and we find that if participants would just be willing to take a few more risks, they would make a lot more money. Of course, whether or not it is a good thing to take a risk always will depend on the situation. But some of us might benefit from taking a few more risks every now and again."

I can't help thinking I am one of those people. Alas, it would appear that having fully developed frontal lobes, a few decades of experience and a finely tuned insula does more than just help us make more informed choices. It can also make our decision-making a bit too automatic. It can lead to us doubting our own self-efficacy, even in areas where we have ample skills and ability. And, perhaps, all that brain maturity will result in us going home with less—money, love, fun, know-how, whatever it is we value—because we can't muster up the same kind of motivation to try new things that we could when we were adolescents.

Critical Thinking

1. Knowing that adolescents like to take risks, describe the quintessential environment for adolescents to develop within—one that ideally protects them from themselves.

2. Suggest three ways that we can offer new sensations and rewards in a safer environment for our adolescent population.

Internet References

Adolescent Angst: 5 Facts about the Teen Brain
    http://www.livescience.com/21461-teen-brain-adolescence-facts.html
The Adolescent Brain: A Work in Progress
    http://patwolfe.com/2011/09/the-adolescent-brain-a-work-in-progress/
The Amygdala: An Agent of Change in Adolescent Neural Networks
    https://www.ncbi.nlm.nih.gov/pmc/articles/PMC3781589/
The Role of the Anterior Insula in Adolescent Decision Making
    http://www.cla.temple.edu/tunl/publications/documents/358918.pdf

Unit 4

UNIT

Prepared by: Claire N. Rubman, *Suffolk County Community College*

Parenting and Educational Issues

We have looked at the adolescent in the context of society, the adolescent's brain, and the perception of the self. Now, we turn our attention to parenting that adolescent child.

Should we parent an adolescent child differently from a younger child? How do discipline, trust and autonomy change as a child ages? Perhaps adolescents would choose "cool" parents like those described by Marybeth Hicks (2016). The truth is that in the long run, as the title of her article reveals, ". . .Cool Parenting Doesn't Help"!

Of course, there is also the other extreme—those parents who simply overparent. They hover over their children, hence the term "helicopter parents."

Caitlin Flanagan (2016) puts these parents under a microscope to examine their behavior. She labels them the "get real" parents and marvels at how they indulge their teens as they (jointly) pursue Ivy League or prestigious college acceptances. Flanagan describes how they engage in "social hosting" to allow their underage teens to drink—or worse. They collect care keys in an attempt to make the environment "safer." As these pampered and "helicoptered" teens go off to college,

Flanagan reflects on the impact that this "laissez-faire" parenting will have on their child's college experience or future employment.

Another parenting concern is how parents control their child's digital world. Do parents allow their adolescent children open access to the Internet? Do they consider supervision to be an invasion of their child's privacy? Should you read your child's texts in secret or ask them to share their browsing history with you? These issues are discussed in Hick's "Parenting Versus Teen's Digital Privacy."

Social media, college applications, and standardized tests all contribute to an extremely stressful experience for our adolescents. Read about how this stress has the potential to destabilize the developing brain. Read about the neurological research that links stress to delays in the limbi system and circuitry errors in the executive functioning of the adolescent brain. Are we, as Susan Roberts (2015) suggests, "collectively . . . like the frog in the beaker of water that adapts and adapts as the water gradually heats up . . . ?" Read more about the negative impact of stress in "First Do No Harm."

Article   Prepared by: Claire N. Rubman, *Suffolk County Community College*

How Helicopter Parents Cause Binge Drinking

The way some white professionals raise their children is exacerbating an alcohol problem on U.S. college campuses.

CAITLIN FLANAGAN

Learning Outcomes

After reading this article, you will be able to:

- Explain why parents are described as "the concierge at the Hyatt"!

- Discuss why some parents engage in "social hosting."

- Define a "get real parent."

I was a teenager in the 1970s. It was a different time. We did not drink—or do drugs or have sex—in captivity. We did those things in the wild, away from our parents, in the danger and thrill of the dark, sacred night. Our parents understood that it was the beginning of the end: We were leaving them. Some of us had curfews, others did not—but either way, you could get a lot done by midnight. Beyond us, on the other side of high school, was some sort of future, probably more or less in line with our parents' larger plans for us, but maybe not. The average middle-class kid (as we were called back then, meaning: a white kid whose parents owned a house and whose father was steadily employed) was not burnishing dreams of Princeton. Go to class, show up for the SAT, fill out the applications, and then enroll in the best, or the most interesting, or the farthest from home, or the cheapest college that lets you in. We didn't need much help from our parents to do those things. Which meant that at night, we were free. And we did many dangerous things. Mothers were not yet against drunk driving; cheerful ladies did not give you condoms at school. It wasn't an arcadia, and many times, things went terribly wrong. But most of us survived.

Today, of course, all of that is different: Professional-class parents and their children are tightly bound to each other in the relentless pursuit of admission to a fancy college. A kid on that track can't really separate from her parents, as their close involvement in this shared goal is essential. Replicating the social class across a generation is a joint project. That's why it's so hard to break into the professional stratum of society: The few available spots are being handed down within families. From this has flowed a benefit that parents love—deep emotional closeness throughout adolescence, with no shadow of a future parting. Kids don't rebel against their parents anymore; why would they? Would you rebel against the concierge at the Hyatt?

Which leaves only the problem of the dark, sacred night. What to do about it? It's full of everything parents fear the most: physical danger, unknown companions, illegal substances, and the development of a separate and secret life. And so, to keep their children close, to keep them safe, and to ensure that they do not escape into the wild freedom of an adolescence unfettered by constant monitoring, drinking in captivity has become a popular alternative. Drinking isn't like doing drugs—it's not something parents recoil from in horror. It's something they can make an accommodation for, and so they practice "social hosting," as the law refers to the custom: allowing teens to get hammered in the comfort and safety of the rec room. Let Charlotte and her pals suck down flavored vodka and giggle while watching Netflix; indulge Jack's desire to have a party in the backyard. Collect the car keys, make sure no one gets into trouble, peek out from an upstairs window, bustle into the TV room with a tray of alcohol-absorbent pizza bites, and then relax in the knowledge that the kids are all right. They have the freedom to experiment that they crave and the physical protection that your peace of mind requires.

Of course, not all parents are down with this approach, and so at high-school gatherings that include parents—sports events, back-to-school nights, college fairs—you can overhear the adults gingerly sounding out one another. They speak in a kind of code, but this is what they want to know: Are you a Good Parent or a Get-Real Parent?

Good Parents think that alcohol is dangerous for young people and that riotous drunkenness and its various consequences have nothing to recommend them. These parents enforce the law and create a family culture that supports their beliefs.

Get-Real Parents think that high-school kids have been drinking since Jesus left Chicago, and that it's folly to pretend the new generation won't as well. The horror stories (awful accidents, alcohol poisoning, lawsuits) tend to involve parents who didn't do it right—who neglected to provide some level of adult supervision, or who forgot to forbid anyone to get in a car after drinking.

Get-Real Parents understand that learning to drink takes a while and often starts with a baptism of fire. Better for Charlotte to barf her guts out on the new sectional than in the shadowy basement of a distant fraternity house. On the nights of big high-school events, Get-Real Parents pay for limos, party buses, Ubers—whatever it takes to ensure that their kids are safe. What is an Uber except a new kind of bike helmet?

In the beginning, everyone is a Good Parent. Bring up teen drinking among parents of elementary-school students and it will elicit the same shiver of horror as the word *adolescence* itself. But slowly people start defecting. At first, it's easy to demonize the ones who chuckle fondly about their kids' boozy misadventures. But by junior year, it feels as though everyone is telling these funny stories. The Good Parents comprise a smaller and smaller cohort, one that tends to stay quiet about its beliefs. Get-Real Parents can be bullies—they love to roll their eyes at the Good Parents, so it's best not to expose yourself.

Ridicule is not the only disappointment in store for the Good Parents. For one thing, high schools turn out to be more in the Get-Real business than they were a generation ago. Go to a parent meeting on some topic like "Teens and Drinking" and you're likely to get an earful about how to keep your teen drinker safe. Teach her to recognize signs of alcohol poisoning in her friends; tell her it's always okay to call 911; advise her to check in on conked-out partygoers every 15 minutes or so to make sure they're just sleeping it off and not unconscious. The message doesn't involve any moral or emotional imperatives; it has to do only with not ending up dead or in jail.

Furthermore, the Good Parent who naively assumes that preventing a teenager from drinking will help him or her in the college-admissions stakes is dead wrong. A teenager growing up in one of the success factories—the exceptional public high school in the fancy zip code, the prestigious private school—will oftentimes be a person whose life is composed of extremes: extreme studying, extreme athletics, extreme extracurricular pursuits, and extreme drinking. Binge drinking slots in neatly with the other, more obviously enhancing endeavors. Perhaps it is even, for some students, necessary. What 80-hour-a-week executive doesn't drop her handbag on the console table and head to the wine fridge the second she gets home? Her teenager can't loosen the pressure valve that way—he has hours of work ahead. A bump of Ritalin is what he needs, not a mellowing half bottle of Shiraz. But come Saturday night? He'll get his release.

The top colleges reward intensity, and binge drinking is a perfected form of that quality. Moreover, it's highly correlated with some of the activities admissions officers prize most, such as varsity sports: High-school athletes are less likely to use drugs and more likely to drink alcohol than their fellow students. Colleges complain like hell about binge drinking, but their admissions policies favor the kind of kids most likely to take part in it.

By 12th grade, parents have made their decisions, and made peace (more or less) with the decisions of their peers. The year grinds on, seeming to last forever, until, abruptly, it's over. After an oddly moving blast of "Pomp and Circumstance" on a hot morning, there it is: childhood's end. The summer is a strange, liminal time, and then, the cars are loaded up, the airplanes boarded, and the parents stand on green lawns in college towns and say goodbye. Now the teenagers are far from home, with only the remembered counsel of the people who love them most to help them negotiate what lies ahead.

College drinking, including extreme heavy drinking, has been a tradition since the 19th century. Because of this, it can be hard to convince middle-aged people that something has changed. But the consistent—at times urgent, at times resigned—report from college officials is that something has gone terribly awry and that huge numbers of students regularly transform the American campus into a college-themed spin-off of The Walking *Dead*. They vomit endlessly, destroy property, become the victims or perpetrators of sexual events ranging from the unpleasant to the criminal, get rushed off in ambulances, and join the ever-growing waiting lists for counseling. Depression and anxiety go hand in hand with heavy drinking, and both are at epidemic proportions on campus.

The National Minimum Drinking Age Act—the "21 law"— is often blamed for the college drinking problem, on the theory that it pitted students against campus authorities and drove drinking underground, where it became an extreme, ritualized behavior. But the truth is more complex. Overall drinking rates on campus have gone down since the law's passage in 1984, as they have among 18-to-21-year-olds not in college. The law's public-health benefits are undeniable. And yet, many of the students already primed to be heavy drinkers have begun consuming alcohol in the intense new manner, chasing not a high but oblivion.

How much are these students drinking? We don't know. In 1994, Harvard's College Alcohol Study established what is still the prevailing definition of a college binge: five or more drinks in a row for a man, and four or more for a woman. But while this measure may have been useful a quarter century ago, it's essentially useless today, when bingers often have 10 or more drinks in a night. The change on campuses may involve not the number of students drinking but the intensity with which they drink—by the traditional measure, fewer students are binge drinking, but of those who do, a sizable number are now doing so to the extreme. A study published in 2011 in the *American Journal of Health Education* found that 77 percent of college freshmen "drink to get drunk"—and what today's college student calls being "drunk" is oftentimes something an expert would define as being in a blackout.

Who are these students? By and large, they constitute the most privileged subset of undergraduates, and those who would (unwisely) emulate them. The students at the center of this culture are most likely to be the children of white, college-educated parents, young people whose free time is probably spent not working to help support themselves, but rather participating in certain activities, most notably Greek life and athletics. They are at the center of the most visible social scene on campus, and while their sorrows and travails unfold in private, their wild partying is a public spectacle.

Some less privileged students look on in disdain, while others gaze in envy, imagining that if they only pour enough booze down their throats, they will join the crowds of wealthy white sorority sisters, with their polished hair and bouncy cheerfulness. But for these kids, who lack the layers of protection and support that cocoon the richer and whiter kids, the consequences can be harsh.

Black students drink less than all other races on campus. Why? The question hardly merits an answer. Drinking while black can be downright dangerous, as local police officers tend to take a dim view of young black people breaking laws. Last year, a black University of Virginia student sustained head injuries requiring 10 stitches after he was arrested by three state law-enforcement officers for the outrageous act of trying to enter a student bar. "I go to UVA, you racists!" he yelled at the men, blood streaming down his face. Not long after the Ferguson riots, at a New Hampshire outfit named Keene State College (87 percent white), a local event called Pumpkin Fest turned the area around the campus into a kind of war zone in which young people—including students from Keene and other local colleges—took part in a massive drunken riot that included throwing billiard balls and full bottles of alcohol at cops, pulling street signs out of the ground, setting fires, overturning a car, and reportedly threatening to kill police officers. In the disappointed characterization of Keene State's president, the children failed to "pumpkin responsibly." How long would those behaviors be tolerated if they were committed by young black men?

This kind of spectacle, with its confusing mixture of misery and social power, encourages Good Parents and Get-Real Parents to make their very different decisions. Good Parents want their children to avoid the unhappiness that binge drinking can result in. They may also wish to transmit to their children larger values—of abiding the law, or of religious practice, or of aligning themselves with activities that will uplift rather than diminish a person. Intuitively, the Good Parent understands something public-health research confirms: that when it comes to alcohol use, adolescents take their parents' counsel into strong consideration. Today's young people—unlike members of my own, '70s generation—don't ignore their parents' guidance on important matters; they seek it. Even if the child of a Good Parent decides to drink, she has a lodestar that many of her peers do not. When she wakes up in the mess and humiliation of a morning after, she thinks: *This isn't what my parents want for me.*

What about the Get-Real Parents? Don't they love their children? Of course they do. Some of them even think they're helping their kids by teaching them to drink while they're still at home—like "the Europeans," or, more specifically, "the French." Leaving aside the fact that the French have their own burgeoning teen-drinking problem, the research shows that college binge drinking is a performative behavior, with its own customs and vocabulary and a high degree of intentionality. Kids don't binge instead of drinking moderately; they do it in addition—they perceive the two behaviors as distinct. You can teach a young person to enjoy a glass of good wine with dinner, but this will not be a protective factor when it comes to binge drinking. It will probably be irrelevant. Kids don't binge on pinot noir and braised lamb shanks. They binge on flavored vodka and cinnamon whiskey, and they do it until they puke. As for letting them drink heavily with their pals so they can "learn their limits"—the way parents did back in the day—that notion is out-of-date. The point of college binge drinking today is that there are no limits. Blacking out isn't a mistake; blacking out is the goal.

The real question about these parents (many of whom pay for their kids' alcohol, revel in their stories about the shit show, delight in e-mails from campus highlighting new services for the plastered, such as golf-cart rides back to the dorm by helpful safety officers) is this: Why have they so cheerfully handed over their children to this ugly and worthless experience?

To a large extent, what many Get-Real Parents are interested in is success. Ever since returning home from the maternity ward, they have been in the business of raising winners. Winners make varsity, winners take Advanced Placement classes, winners apply early decision to selective colleges, and winners are at the top of the social hierarchy at their competitive high schools—which means they boot and (more important) rally. Perhaps, for some of the more mercenary and lucrative professions—including stock trading, investment banking, and high-stakes sales—there are actually benefits to heavy drinking. A binge drinker emerges from college both elevated and coarsened: educated enough to compete in the market and sullied enough by the hard knocks of binge drinking that he won't be too shocked by what he finds there.

No wonder these young people keep drinking. The hollowness at the center of their lives—the increasing abandonment of religion, the untethering of sexuality not just from relationships but even from kindness, the race to jump aboard the stem express because that's where the money is, the understanding of eventual parenthood as something that will be subordinated to the management of two successful careers, and the understanding that their own parents care so little about them that they will happily allow them to sustain the kind of moral injuries that blackout behavior often engenders—would make too much consciousness hard for anyone to take.

What are these kids really vomiting up every weekend at their fancy colleges? Is it really just 12 shots of apple-flavored vodka? Or is it a set of values, an attitude toward the self and toward others, that has become increasingly hard for them to stomach?

Critical Thinking

1. What type of parent will you be (or are you currently)—the "good parent" or the "get real parent"?
2. What advice would you give to parents who are trying to prepare their young adolescent children for a future college experience?

Internet References

Dangers of Helicopter Parenting When Your Kids Are Teens
http://www.chicagotribune.com/lifestyles/sc-fam-0630-teen-helicopter-parent-20150623-story.html

Helicopter Parents: Hovering May Have Effect as Kids Transition to Adulthood
https://www.sciencedaily.com/releases/2016/06/160628110215.htm

Permissive Parenting
http://www.parentingscience.com/permissive-parenting.html

Social Host Fact Sheet
https://dbhdid.ky.gov/dbh/documents/sa/socialhost.pdf

Social Host: Your Role in Making a Difference
http://www.madd.org/underage-drinking/the-power-of-parents/high-school-parents/social-host/socialhostbroch.pdf

CAITLIN FLANAGAN is the author of *Girl Land* and *To Hell With All That.*

Article   Prepared by: Claire N. Rubman, *Suffolk County Community College*

Why Cool Parenting Doesn't Help

MARYBETH HICKS

Learning Outcomes

After reading this article, you will be able to:

- Explain why "buddy parents" can do more harm than good.

- Describe why the "they're going to do it anyway" argument is unsound.

Q. *This question might be filed under, "What are these people thinking?" My high school freshman got a ride home from a recent sporting event from a team-mate's parent. The conversation in the car turned to a high school party that took place a couple of weeks ago where teens were widely known to have been drinking and smoking weed. Rather than express any dismay or concern about this, the parent laughed, joked, and shared stories of his escapades in high school, and essentially said partying was a fun, normal part of growing up. We can't avoid sharing rides with this family. How should our son respond if this sort of conversation comes up again?*

A. A very wise mother once warned me, "The enemies of your child are the parents of his friends." At the time I thought, *Sheesh, that's harsh*. But my four children are all high school graduates, and during those years, I grew to understand exactly what that mom meant.

There was a time when parents were generally on the same page. We Baby Boomers could count on the moms and dads of our friends to pretty much echo the values and opinions of our parents, especially when it came to their expectations about appropriate behavior for high schoolers. This expectation was even greater if you sent your kids to a Catholic school, where the assumption of shared values and faith is reasonable.

But parents have changed. Many want to be perceived as the "cool parents" who are close to their teenagers. They think they'll achieve this closeness by revealing their past antics as a teen—or worse, by facilitating risky behavior for their children.

Versions of "buddy parents" can range from benignly embarrassing to outright dangerous. We've all seen the women who dress like their daughters (though the 50-something version is not a good look), or the dads who pull up to the high school parking lot blasting Journey songs through open windows. These folks are cringe-worthy, to be sure.

The parents we need to watch out for are the ones whose lack of judgment becomes an opportunity for our teenagers to engage in high-risk and illegal behaviors. Astonishingly, despite all the known perils and warnings from school administrators, public safety and law enforcement officers, and parent groups, there are parents who believe it's safer to provide alcohol for their teenagers as long as they collect everyone's car keys than it is to pressure kids not to drink, based on the theory, "They're going to do it anyway."

In fact, that theory is not true. Parental advice about teen drinking has a significant impact on teens' decisions to abstain during high school. Studies reveal that young adults whose parents had the strictest rules against teen drinking exhibited less binge drinking in college.

To be sure, a parent who tells a carful of teens that partying is a normal and expected part of growing up is not helping your cause. It's also not universally true. While statistics show a majority of teens will have experimented with alcohol by age 18, at least 30 percent haven't. So it's "everyone," but it's not everyone.

That dad did, however, offer you a teachable moment. Be sure to have a conversation with your son in which you state your feelings—bluntly—about the inappropriate nature of that parent's comments. I'd say something like, "Being an adult doesn't necessarily mean having good judgment. I don't think that a parent should joke about partying as a teenager, and I certainly don't think drinking or smoking pot is an expected part of growing up. I appreciate the shared transportation, but just know that we absolutely don't share those opinions."

Of course, thanks to that "buddy parent," you now know whose house party your son should avoid for the rest of high school!

Critical Thinking

1. Why do some parents want to act like their children's "buddy"?
2. If you were running a parenting workshop, what advice would you give to parents?

Internet References

Parental Friendship with Their Adolescent
https://www.psychologytoday.com/blog/surviving-your-childs-adolescence/201211/parental-friendship-their-adolescent

Should Parents Be "Friends" with Their Teenagers?
https://www.brainchildmag.com/2015/05/should-parents-be-friends-with-their-teenagers/

What Adolescents Really Need from Parents
http://greatergood.berkeley.edu/article/item/what_adolescents_really_need_from_parents

Why Adolescence Is More Brutal for Parents than Teenagers
http://nymag.com/news/features/adolescence-2014-1/index1.html

MARYBETH HICKS is a columnist, author, and speaker.

Article   Prepared by: Claire N. Rubman, *Suffolk County Community College*

Parenting Versus Teens' Digital Privacy

MARYBETH HICKS

Learning Outcomes

After reading this article, you will be able to:

- Describe how adolescents can build "trust" in the digital world.

- Explain how parents can respect their adolescent's privacy on social media while still protecting their child.

Q. *My daughter's smartphone buzzed when she was out of the room. I picked it up to see who was texting her and was puzzled by the message that previewed on the screen, so I read the entire exchange. What I discovered concerned me. When I talked to her about it, she turned the tables on me and said I'd invaded her privacy. The issue I discovered is important and I don't want to lose the chance to guide her behavior, but now we're only arguing about privacy and whether or not I trust her. How much privacy should I allow my daughter?*

A. Despite their insistence to the contrary, kids aren't entitled to privacy in the same way as adults, and how much privacy you allow depends on each child. If your children have built a record of trust, you might generally maintain a "hands off" approach to their use of technology and media. But privacy should never trump your concerns about any issue you feel needs your parental attention.

That said, the rule of thumb in the digital age is: There's no such thing as privacy.

That message wasn't meant for you, it's true. But there's nothing to prevent your daughter or her friend from taking a screenshot of it and forwarding it to others. This is why it's vital that kids understand how technology can be manipulated by anyone who wants to violate their intended privacy.

If you read the text exchange because you were already suspicious that something was up, say so and remind your daughter that you reserve the right to go looking for information when you believe she may be hiding something that could endanger her or someone else (think sex, drug use, covering for others, and so on). This means you may read her texts, see her social media pages, and check her phone records.

If you read her message inadvertently or out of curiosity, let her know you didn't go snooping intentionally because you were worried about her, but you are now. Your glimpse into her friendship raised an issue you can't ignore, even if the manner in which you learned of it annoys her.

Backing parents into a corner with an emotional outburst of "You don't trust me!" is a time-honored deflection technique employed by generations of teens. Don't fall for it! When she levels this accusation, your answer is, "Of course I trust you! I trust that you're a teenager and you'll make mistakes, and you need my guidance and instruction to grow up the way God intends."

This episode is an important reminder that parents should be vigilant, especially when we put the means to greater freedom into our kids' hands by way of a smartphone. Freedom is an important factor in developing responsibility, but it's also the avenue to poor, even risky, choices.

What your daughter calls invading her privacy I would call parenting, though progressive parenting specialists might disagree with me. Some say teens deserve privacy and the respect it conveys, just as an adult would. I believe that the risks of respecting a teen's privacy are greater than the risk of hurting her pride by inserting yourself into her life.

The key is to foster a relationship in which your teen knows she can talk to you about anything, even things that are difficult. When you respond to unsettling information calmly and demonstrate the maturity you want your teen to emulate, you create the environment for transparency.

Trust is earned and rewarded with freedom, responsibility, and yes—privacy. But it's not an entitlement until that teen is on her own and living as an independent adult.

Critical Thinking

1. How can you teach your child to use social media responsibly?
2. Would you (do you) check your child's digital footprint?

Internet References

13 Tips for Monitoring Kids' Social Media
http://www.parenting.com/gallery/social-media-monitoring-kids

Parent's Guide to Protecting Teens on Social Media
http://www.safesearchkids.com/parents-guide-to-protecting-teens-on-social-media/#.WQxzktIrKUk

Parents, Teens, and Digital Monitoring
http://www.pewinternet.org/2016/01/07/parents-teens-and-digital-monitoring/

Parents, Teens, and Online Privacy
https://cyber.harvard.edu/publications/2012/parents_teens_privacy

Article   Prepared by: Claire N. Rubman, *Suffolk County Community College*

First Do No Harm

What Neuroscience Tells Us about Stress in School

SUSAN C. ROBERTS

Learning Outcomes

After reading this article, you will be able to:

- Describe how stress affects the developing adolescent brain.

- Explain how the "fragile self" evolves.

If two decades of neuroscientific research have taught us anything, it's that stress is toxic to the brain. Images from functional magnetic resonance imaging and other such devices tell a sobering story: Neurons in the brains of healthy control subjects show many robust branches and connections while those in subjects exposed to chronic stress resemble frayed and broken threads. The cortexes of baboons at the top of the social ladder light up with a rainbow of colors while those of harassed baboons lower down the hierarchy are dim and dull from inactivity. Other studies show how stress shrinks the brain while it expands the belly, causes inflammation throughout the body, and generally makes us fat, dumb, and depressed.

In the face of these findings, you'd expect to see stress declared Public Health Enemy No. 1, like smoking or obesity before it. And yet for most of us in 21st-century America, stress remains a silent killer that we seem unwilling or unable to acknowledge. Collectively, we are like the frog in the beaker of water that adapts and adapts as the water gradually heats up until it is finally boiled to death. Indeed, according to Bessel van der Kolk, a professor of psychiatry at Boston University Medical School, the denial of our situation seems to go with the territory. "We know all this and yet we continue to load on the stress," he says. "This is the definition of insanity."

But as educators we need to break through this wall of denial, especially because we know stress is more harmful to children and adolescents than it is to adults, possibly setting them up for

a lifetime of physical and psychological problems. Those of us in independent schools have a second wall of denial to break through—the "it-can't-happen-here" syndrome that leads us to believe overwhelming stress is something reserved for people living in grinding poverty, in the midst of war, or in the wake of natural catastrophe. In fact, children growing up in privileged circumstances may suffer a different kind of stress—one linked more to psychological than material pressures and to fears of failure rather than of physical annihilation. It's easy to dismiss such suffering as a "first-world problem" or a case of "poor little rich kids" until one considers the very real damage excessive stress does to a young person's brain and nervous system. If, as teachers and administrators, we cannot end the stress in our students' lives, at least we can avoid adding to it, perhaps taking an educator's Hippocratic oath to "First do no harm." We can also make time in the school day to help students understand stress and learn to protect themselves from its most ravaging effects.

How Stress Affects the Adolescent Brain

To understand how stress can be so harmful to young people, it helps to know some basic neuroscience. Despite the brain's capacity for creativity and higher-order thinking, it is essentially a primitive instrument. Shaped by ancient evolutionary forces, our brains and nervous systems are wired for survival and thus hyperattuned to potential threats to our safety. It's the limbic system, or emotional brain, that registers such threats, triggering a cascade of physiological responses known as the fight-or-flight response. Stress hormones flood the body, preparing it to do battle or run like hell, while the cortical regions of our brains where higher-order thinking takes place go offline altogether. Once the emergency has passed and we feel safe again, we can return to reflecting on and evaluating our experience. But in the moment of stress, all that is beside the point.

While the fight-or-flight response helped our primal ancestors escape from saber-toothed tigers and other predators, an identical process may be set off in our students by events that seem far less harrowing: an upcoming SAT upon which they believe their future hangs or being called on in class when they don't know the answer. The nervous system makes no distinction between physical or psychological threats. Thus, on any given day, we should expect a certain number of our students to show up to class in a state of nervous system hyperarousal. Such students may appear disruptive, distracted, or just plain checked out. Whatever the presentation, the result is the same—students who are not available for learning.

In general, adolescents are more prone than adults to such "hijackings" of the conscious mind because their limbic centers have not yet been brought under the modulating influence of the higher cortical areas of their brains. Thus, teenagers are quicker than adults to react to stimuli and to perceive events as threats. This same developmental vulnerability makes adolescent brains more susceptible to the long-term damage stress can cause. Beginning around the time of puberty, a large-scale remodeling process takes place in the teenage brain in which lesser-used neurons are pruned back while those that are used more often are built up and strengthened. In a process called myelination, fatty sheaths form around these neurons, acting like insulation around electrical wires to speed up transmission of the electrical impulses by which brain cells communicate with one another.

In this way, the different areas in the brain of the young adolescent become more efficient at performing their particular functions. But the circuits that would connect these specialized brain regions and get them working together are still lacking. Thus, while young adolescents are capable of great feats of artistry, athleticism, and intellect, they tend to be reactive and impulsive, requiring adults to supply guidance, supervision, and other "executive functions." As adolescence progresses, the brain builds more connections between the lower limbic or "mammalian" centers and the higher "executive" centers such as the prefrontal cortex. By the time, a young person reaches the early to mid-twenties, his or her emotions, sensations, intuitions, logic, and memories should be working together more or less harmoniously. A person possessed of such an "integrated" brain is able to tolerate difficult feelings, rely upon a fairly solid sense of self, sustain trusting relationships, and plan and problem-solve in a flexible way. In other words, he or she has matured into a stable young adult.

But the integration process does not always go so well. In the face of prolonged or overwhelming stress, the limbic brain gets stuck in fight-or-flight mode, the executive brain shuts down, and construction of neural circuitry between the two regions is forestalled. In such individuals, the prefrontal cortex is not able to assume its proper role as captain of the ship or CEO of the personality. Instead, the brain becomes hypervigilant, perceiving danger even in neutral or positive situations. While all adolescents are prone to a certain "negativity bias"—overreacting to criticism and reading anger or disapproval even on emotionally neutral faces—negativity becomes a default setting for those exposed to chronic stress. As psychologist Rick Hanson puts it, their brains become "Velcro for bad experiences and Teflon for good ones."

It Can't Happen Here

We expect to see this kind of nervous system arousal in survivors of combat, accidents, natural disasters, or terrorist attacks, as well as those living in neighborhoods plagued by poverty and violence. We don't expect to see it in middle- and upper-middle-class children who have been raised in relative comfort and security.

But even if they are not subjected to the most horrendous traumas, many young people do experience distressing events. The Centers for Disease Control asked 17,000 Americans about stressors they had experienced early in life, including emotional or physical abuse or neglect, sexual abuse, substance abuse or mental illness in a family member, parental divorce or separation, or parental incarceration. According to the survey, 67 percent of respondents had undergone at least one of these "Adverse Childhood Experiences" (ACEs) and 12 percent had experienced four or more. Far beyond any other variable including race, educational level, or household income, such "ACEs" were found to predict social, emotional, and cognitive impairment, disease, disability, and early death, with the severity of impacts rising with the number of adverse events.

In a TED Talk about the study's implications, Dr. Nadine Burke Harris cautions individuals from privileged circumstances against the tendency to disavow the trauma in their histories. "We marginalize the issue because it does apply to us. Maybe it's easier to see in other ZIP codes because we don't want to look at it" in ourselves, she says. "We'd rather be sick."

In short, a certain amount of trauma goes with the human condition regardless of one's station in life. As educators, we need to be better informed about the lasting physical and psychological repercussions of traumatic events and how to respond to students who may be affected by them. We also need a better understanding of the physiological or genetic factors that make certain individuals more sensitive than usual to seemingly ordinary stressors.

But we should also acknowledge a significant layer of stress generated by the very conditions of affluence and privilege, which we as independent school educators may unwittingly perpetuate. Psychologist Suniya S. Luthar has studied young people growing up in such conditions and found rates of anxiety, depression, and somatic disorders to be twice as high among them as in the general population of high school students. Rates of alcohol use, binge drinking, and marijuana use were also found to be far above the norm. "Education and money may once have served as buffers against distress, but that is no longer the case," she reports in *Psychology Today*. "Something fundamental has changed: the evidence suggests that the privileged young are much more vulnerable today than in previous generations." She goes on to enumerate a variety of causes, beginning with the unrealistically high expectations placed upon privileged young people by parents, schools, and even their fellow students. From all quarters, these young people receive the message that, in light of all the advantages they've been given, failure—and even ordinariness—is not an option. "Maintaining the mantle of success is a special imperative for the affluent," she writes. "Achievement of their lofty goals is tantalizingly within reach, which renders it all the more obligatory."

According to psychologist Madeline Levine, author of *The Price of Privilege*, it's not just the academic workload that stresses students out but what success or failure means in terms of their parents' love and approval. Young people growing up in the culture of affluence do not feel unconditionally loved, she writes, but believe they must earn their parents' positive regard through achievements in school or outside activities. This excessive focus on accomplishment leads the children to develop "false" or "fragile" selves, driven by the need for external recognition rather than intrinsic motivation. "It is hard to develop an authentic sense of self when there is constant pressure to adopt a socially facile, highly competitive, performance-oriented, unblemished 'self' that is promoted by omnipresent adults," she writes.

What is driving these inordinate demands for achievement? Certainly heightened competition from a global economy has something to do with it, along with the disappearance of the American middle class. Even if they are financially secure, many parents worry that their children will lose their footing on the increasingly slippery slope between haves and have-nots. Stuck on a treadmill of work-and-spend consumerism, such parents may model for their children a way of life that values rewards in the future over satisfaction in the present and material goods and status over relationships. This mindset extends to the children in the form of an obsession with grades, SAT scores, Advanced Placement classes, and admission to prestigious colleges. Young people caught up in this "race to nowhere" are overburdened by schoolwork, deprived of sleep, and cheated of the opportunity to explore the world on their own terms and discover their own sources of meaning and passion. One high school senior expressed the agony of such a life in response to a recent *New York Times* column about a rash of suicides among teenagers in Palo Alto, California, one of the country's "epicenters of overachievement": "My junior year was one of the most depressing years of my life, especially because each day I was telling myself, 'I'll never be 17 again and I spend every day, every night, and every weekend doing a mind-numbing amount of endless work.' It tore me apart."

To add to the problem, young people feel it's taboo to complain. They are led to believe that, because of all they've been given, their suffering is not legitimate. As the student cited above goes on to write, "I know I am SO PRIVILEGED to be getting this education, and this awareness [makes] me even more ashamed of the sadness."

Nor is the peer group a reliable refuge from adult demands; too often, it is a source of yet more pressure and shame. After all, one's classmates are also caught up in the quest for academic achievement, attractiveness, athletic prowess, popularity, and—for girls, at least—"effortless perfection." As it is, adolescents are constantly comparing themselves with others; such a competitive atmosphere only intensifies their anxiety and self-consciousness.

In this Darwinian universe, students who can't keep up with the fast-moving herd feel ashamed. To cry uncle, admit that it's too much, would be to admit failure and risk being labeled a loser. And so they redouble their defensive armoring and seek solace and self-soothing on the side—in the form of marijuana or alcohol, compulsive Internet or video game usage, procrastination, and myriad other forms of avoidance and distraction. Their anxiety and depression also take the form of somatic complaints such as chronic headaches, insomnia, or digestive disorders. Indeed, these are some of the most common presentations, as they can be easily dismissed as purely physical in nature by both the ashamed young person and the adults in her world who don't wish to acknowledge the existence of stress or the very real damage it can do.

What to Do?

The first step is to stop denying the stress in our own lives, to take ownership of our anxiety, and to stop inflicting it on the kids. Next, we can stop denying the stress in our students' lives. Rather than admonishing and shaming them for their dysfunctional behaviors, we can recognize what's behind those behaviors: namely, a need to alleviate intolerable stress. Finally, we can educate students about the neurobiology of stress, teach them ways to cope with it, and provide opportunities for building healthier brains . . . and selves.

Fortunately, along with what we've learned about the damage caused by an always-turned-on fight-or-flight response, neuroscience has confirmed the efficacy of some fairly simple practices that quiet dysregulated nervous systems and repair broken brains. The secret lies in shutting out the external world with its expectations, judgments, and overstimulation and tuning in to the world inside through practices such as mindfulness, meditation, and yoga. After years of controlled studies and clinical experience, van der Kolk and others have come to regard such mind-body approaches as the gold standard for treating toxic stress. The question we should be asking ourselves, he says, is "How do you get people to notice themselves . . . to feel their bodies and to feel what goes on inside themselves? Only after you know your interiority can you begin to have a life."

Psychiatrist Daniel Siegel urges schools to incorporate such practices into their daily routines. Through his "Mindsight" program, he offers a handful of breathing, relaxation, mindfulness, and journaling exercises designed to help students increase awareness of their emotions, physical sensations, intuitions, and thoughts. By learning to focus on the present moment, letting go of worry about the future and regret about the past, students strengthen their prefrontal cortexes and other higher-level brain centers, Siegel reports. At the same time, they build neural connections between those executive areas and the limbic brain, thus enhancing their ability to regulate their emotions and navigate their way in the world with greater flexibility and wisdom.

Another approach to putting on the brakes on stress involves activating not the brain itself but what neuroscientist Stephen Porges calls "a part of the brain that migrated south." He is referring to the heart and the vagus nerve to which it is connected, which together make up our "social-engagement system." If our primitive limbic centers respond to stress by sending us into fight-or-flight mode, this more sophisticated survival mechanism counteracts stress by activating our instincts to "tend and befriend."

"We have a whole neural circuit to make us feel safe," Porges says. "The potential of an individual will only emerge in a situation of safety." The social engagement system can be switched on in any number of ways, most of them as old as human culture itself: by a reassuring tone of voice, or face-to-face interaction with someone who likes and encourages us, by singing, and by all forms of creative play. It comes alive in situations in which we feel a sense of belonging and can let down our defenses enough to share with others in open and honest ways.

The above approaches can be integrated into the school schedule via social–emotional programs, advisory periods, or, for schools that are ready to undertake a fundamental shift in values and culture, any number of other situations throughout the day. The point is not the delivery of specific content or organized activities. What matters is providing the time and space for students to slow down and turn off the stress response, to hit the pause button on incessant thinking and get grounded in the body, to observe and process their experiences and feelings, and to connect with others in genuine, caring ways.

It's a sad commentary on the present state of affairs that in order to advocate for adding such humane elements to the school day you have to resort to MRI scans and other laboratory studies showing the toxic effects of stress on the brain. And even then it's a hard sell. In the face of the hundred-and-one mandates schools are trying to fulfill, such things as emotions, the inner life, and relationships seem touchy-feely and a waste of time. Many teachers and administrators are near-boiled frogs themselves, numb to stress or addicted to it, and unable to imagine any other way. In independent schools, as in privileged groups generally, the rewards for winning may seem too great and the penalties for losing too severe for stakeholders to want to change the status quo. Thus, while many public school educators are turning to a model of "trauma-informed care" to guide them in dealing with students overwhelmed by stress, the moat of privilege that surrounds private schools keeps many of us ignorant about such innovations.

Though schools may be slow to pick up on it, the findings from neuroscience make one thing clear: the social–emotional dimension of students' lives is not tangential to academic success but foundational. Considering how vulnerable the young people in our charge are to stress—whether in its physical or psychological form—we need to attend more closely to the emotional climate of our schools and the psychic burdens attached to our expectations and demands.

References

Frank Bruni, "Best, Brightest and Saddest?" *New York Times*, April 22, 2015.

Rich Hanson, "What's Next for Brain Science and Psychotherapy?" *Psychotherapy Networker*, January/February 2014.

Nadine Burke Harris, "How Childhood Trauma Affects Health Across a Lifetime," TED Talk, February 17, 2015. Web, July 17, 2014. www.youtube.com/watch?v=95ovIJ3dsNk.

Daniel J. Siegel, *Brainstorm: The Power and Purpose of the Teenage Brain*, New York: Tarcher, 2014.

Bessel van der Kolk, "The Body Keeps the Score: Brain, Mind, and Body in the Healing of Trauma," *YouTube*, Center for Healthy Communities, May 22, 2015. Web, July 17, 2015, www.youtube.com/watch?v=53RX2ESIqsM.

Critical Thinking

1. Thinking about the high school life and culture, which stressors contribute to the "social-emotional dimension" in our adolescents' lives?

2. In an effort to reduce stress, how would you address the college application process for high school students?

Internet References

Adolescent Stress and Depression

http://www.extension.umn.edu/youth/research/youth-issues/adolescent-stress-and-depression/

School Stress Takes a Toll on Health, Teens, and Parents Say

http://www.npr.org/sections/health-shots/2013/12/02/246599742/school-stress-takes-a-toll-on-health-teens-and-parents-say

Stress, College Admissions, and the Parent's Role

https://www.healthychildren.org/English/ages-stages/young-adult/Pages/Stress-College-Admissions-and-the-Parents-Role.aspx

Stress Management and Teens

https://www.aacap.org/AACAP/Families_and_Youth/Facts_for_Families/FFF-Guide/Helping-Teenagers-With-Stress-066.aspx

Stressors and Child and Adolescent Psychopathology: Evidence of Moderating and Mediating Effects

http://vkc.mc.vanderbilt.edu/stressandcoping/wp-content/uploads/2014/11/Grant-et-al-2006.pdf

The Stress of College Applications

http://www.nytimes.com/2008/04/29/health/29well.html

The Teenage Brain: The Stress Response and the Adolescent Brain

https://www.ncbi.nlm.nih.gov/pmc/articles/PMC4274618/

SUSAN C. ROBERTS, a licensed clinical social worker in Washington, DC, has worked as a school counselor in independent schools for 17 years.

Unit 5

UNIT

Prepared by: Claire N. Rubman, *Suffolk County Community College*

Sexuality

Since Romeo and Juliet teens have been falling in love! Is "adolescent love" the same today as it was when Shakespeare wrote about it in the 1590s? We certainly know more about the effects of dopamine, serotonin, and oxytocin during puberty. We also know that physical development often precedes emotional maturity in adolescents. Their slow developing "executive function" contributes to poor impulse control, faulty decision-making, and risky behavioral choices. Added to this is an adolescent's freedom of expression on the Internet with online dating apps and numerous sites devoted to love such as "girls ask guys.com" or "quora.com." Dating apps, sexting, and social media sites make dating more public but do they help our adolescents to better navigate their emotions or make better choices? Read about "Teenagers in Love" by Susan Moore (2016) and decide for yourself.

One aspect of teenage relationships is teen pregnancy. One teen in the United States becomes pregnant every minute according to Nichalos Kirshof (2014). This is 5 times the rate of teenage pregnancy in France and 15 times the rate of Swiss teenagers. What could possibly be contributing to this staggering teen pregnancy rate in our culture? To what extent does technology play a role in our teens' lives? Does social media contribute to these staggeringly high pregnancy rates? As the title of Wallace's article suggests; "It's Complicated"! How have casual and anonymous sexual encounters changed our behavior? Read about our "hook up culture" and decide for yourself.

What about teens who are not comfortable with their gender, those who do not identify with the gender that they were assigned at birth? It is a road fraught with difficulties. Statistics show that 40 percent of our transgender community will attempt suicide in their teenage years. They seem to be plagued by high levels of homelessness, depression and substance abuse. Read about Breland's gender clinic and follow the story of Jordan as he makes a life changing decision after a surgical procedure.

To what extent does television play a role in an adolescent's perception of gender, sex, or pregnancy? The TV show "16 and Pregnant" or "Teen Mom" were reported as an excellent way to put teens off parenthood! As a result of watching these shows, teens reported misconceptions about free time, access to health care, perceived wealth and realistic educational goals for teen mothers. Women's Health Weekly magazine (2014) reported that these show actually encourage unrealistic views of teen motherhood.

Article Prepared by: Claire N. Rubman, *Suffolk County Community College*

Teenagers in Love

SUSAN MOORE

Learning Outcomes

After reading this article, you will be able to:

- Discuss the negative outcomes that adolescents might experience such as aggression or sexual coercion.

- Describe the hormonal changes that puberty triggers and their effect on mood and the libido.

The singer of a plaintive hit song from the 1950s croons "Each night I ask the stars up above, Why must I be a teenager in love?," as he bemoans the ups and downs of his romance, one minute on top of the world, next minute in the deepest slough of despondency. Such angst!

Has anything changed? In modern pop songs, young people still sing about their crushes, unrequited loves, and romantic breakups; about feeling awkward, unsure, in despair, overwhelmed, joyous and inspired, although these days the sexual imagery is much more obvious. And it can appear that the tender feelings of first love are at odds with today's world of "out there" sexuality. Adolescents are heavy consumers of online pornography, they are sexting, and using "apps" to meet partners for casual sex hook-ups. They may post on Facebook about their sexual and romantic successes and failures. Research has not yet caught up with the long-term implications of these new ways of courting, but it does seem that falling in love and romantic relationships are still part of the developmental timetable for many adolescents.

Let's look at what is known. The US-based National Longitudinal Study of Adolescent Health (Add Health), involving a representative sample of thousands of school children in Grades 7 to 12, found that over 80 percent of those aged 14 years and older were or had been in a romantic relationship, including a small number (2–3 percent) in same-sex relationships (Carver et al., 2003; Grieger et al., 2014). Many of these relationships were short term, especially among younger adolescents, but a significant number were a year or more in duration. Evidence that these relationships were socially normative was shown by the finding that in most cases, parents had met their child's romantic partner and the couples had told others of their romantic status. There is limited data on romantic relationships in other developed countries, but existing research suggests similar percentages to the US data, although with somewhat older age groups (e.g., Moore et al., 2012).

The normative nature of adolescent romantic relationships means that those young people without a girlfriend or boyfriend can feel stressed or "different" (Scanlan et al., 2012). Given that adolescence is a time when there is a great deal of pressure to conform to peer norms, young people who are not linking up romantically can feel lonely and out of step with their peers. For example, on the Internet site girlsaskguys.com, an anonymous young woman asks:

I've never had a boyfriend or girlfriend. Would you assume that there is something bad or wrong with that person that makes people not want to go out with them? I think it's because I am ugly. I am not fat however. What is wrong with me?

On a different advice site (quora.com), this young man similarly questions why he is different:

I am 21 and never had a girlfriend. Most of my friends are in a relationship. I feel kind of depressed and that I would never have a girlfriend. What should I do? I've asked a couple of girls whom I like to go out with me in the past and they declined.

Of course, not every young person is interested in romantic relationships. Some feel they are not ready, some want to concentrate on their studies or sport, and others are more tempted by the casual sex culture of temporary "hook-ups." Nevertheless, most adolescents begin their sexual lives within the context of a romantic relationship, and generally, involvement in romantic relationships in adolescence is developmentally appropriate and healthy (Collins et al., 2009).

What Happens When Teenagers Fall in Love?

Falling in love is an emotional upheaval at any age, but for adolescents, the feelings are likely to be even more difficult to manage. Teenage bodies and brains are maturing at a rate not experienced since infancy. There is a growth spurt, development of secondary sex characteristics and young people change in appearance from child to adult. Physical awkwardness often results from growth asynchronies; young people can feel embarrassed and self-conscious about the sexualization of their bodies or their perceived inadequacies in terms of often-unrealistic body ideals. As well, the adolescent brain has been described as "a work in progress," with certain areas maturing more quickly than others, leading to potential mismatches between physical, emotional, and cognitive development. For example, there can be incongruities between adult bodily appearance, increasing sex drive and the brain development required for mature decision-making and self-regulation of behaviour and emotions. The "executive functioning" area of the brain—the prefrontal cortex—is among the last areas of the brain to fully mature, usually sometime in the 20s (Petanjek et al., 2011). Adolescence therefore becomes a time of diminished prefrontal cortical control, with the heightened possibility of risk-taking and poor judgment decisions, especially in environments described as "reward-sensitive," where the temptations of immediate feel-good experiences are high, such as in romantic and sexual situations (Braams et al., 2015; Suleiman & Harden, 2016).

Hormonal changes, triggered by brain and body developments, are strongly implicated in the intense feelings of sexual attraction and falling in love. Testosterone and oestrogen—male and female sex hormones—are associated with heightened sexual urges, while the hormones oxytocin and vasopressin are implicated in attachment and bonding. During puberty, the volume of these circulating sex hormones in the body rises dramatically. In girls, the ovaries increase their production of oestrogen sixfold and in boys, the testes produce 20 times the amount of testosterone. Both sexes have male and female hormones circulating in the bloodstream, but during adolescence, a boy's testosterone level becomes 20 to 60 percent higher than that of a girl, while her oestrogen level becomes 20 to 30 percent higher than his. These hormones have strong effects on mood and libido. Young people are hormonally "primed" toward being sexually attracted to others but, especially in early adolescence, they are not used to the feelings associated with the rapid increases and fluctuations in their hormone levels. High concentrations of certain hormones for one's age, or rapid fluctuations of hormone levels may trigger more negative moods and greater mood variability (Buchanan et al., 1992).

Emotions associated with being "in love" or "in lust" are likely to be confused and confusing, even overwhelming for some (Temple-Smith et al., 2016).

It's not only the sex hormones that are involved in falling in love. Ortigue and his colleagues (2010) used brain imaging to show that when a person falls in love, 12 areas of the brain work in tandem to release euphoria-inducing chemicals such as dopamine, adrenaline, and serotonin. Adrenaline is a stress hormone, causing sweating, heart palpitations, and dry mouth—just catching a glimpse of the new love can trigger these bodily sensations. Dopamine stimulates desire and pleasurable feelings and has been described as a "feel good" hormone with similar effects to the drug cocaine. Fisher et al. (2006) found heightened levels of dopamine in the brains of couples newly in love. Further, Marazziti and Canale (2004) examined levels of serotonin in the bloodstreams of couples in love and people with obsessive-compulsive disorders. Their finding that levels were similarly heightened in the two groups led these researchers to conclude that serotonin level is associated with those constant thoughts about the loved one that are part of being "love struck."

In another illustration of how some of these effects are manifest, a study by Brand and colleagues (2007) compared newly "in love" adolescents with a control group who were unpartnered. The "in love" group scored higher than the controls on hypomania, a mood state (with accompanying thoughts and behaviors) in which emotions are more labile: euphoric one minute, in despair the next. The diary entries of the adolescent lovebirds showed they had more positive morning and evening moods than the controls, shorter sleep times but better quality sleep, lowered daytime sleepiness, and better concentration during the day.

Falling in love takes some getting used to, all those different emotions, mood swings, needs, and desires. Nevertheless, through their romantic relationships, adolescents have the potential for psychological growth as they learn about themselves and other people, gain experience in how to manage these feelings, and develop the skills of intimacy. They also face new risks and challenges. These positive and negative aspects of adolescent romantic relationships are discussed below.

Psychosocial Development

Lifespan developmental theorist Erik Erikson (1968) viewed crushes and youthful romances as important contributors to adolescent self-understanding and identity formation. He described teenage "falling in love" as a form of self-development rather than true intimacy. Adolescents, becoming more self-aware as their cognitive powers develop, can try out their "grown-up" identities with romantic partners and through feedback from the partners' responses and behaviors, gradually clarify self-image. The endless talking (and now texting) that often accompanies teen romances is a way of experimenting with different forms of "self" and testing their effect on the other person.

As well as aiding identity development, adolescent romantic relationships—both short term and longer term—can provide positive learning experiences about the self, for example, through influencing self-esteem and beliefs about attractiveness and self-worth, and raising status in the peer group (Zimmer-Gembeck et al., 2001, 2004). They can assist young people in renegotiating and developing more mature and less emotionally dependent relationships with their parents, as a precursor for independent living. When there is good will and warmth between the partners, romantic relationships offer a safe environment for learning about and experimenting with sexuality and sexual orientation (Collins et al., 2009). Teenage romantic relationships are, in a sense, a training ground for adult intimacy, providing an opportunity for learning to manage strong emotions, to negotiate conflict, to communicate needs, and to respond to a partner's needs (Scanlan et al., 2012).

Challenges and Problems

On the downside, romantic relationships can sometimes lead to unhealthy outcomes. Young people can become too exclusive when they pair up, cutting themselves off from friendship, and support networks in ways that do not advance optimal development. Identity formation may be compromised if a teenager closes off developmental options through a partnership in which unhealthy living choices are made, or through early, unplanned parenthood.

Adolescents can be exposed to abusive and violent interactions or unwanted or coerced sexual activity within their romantic relationships (Mulford & Giordano, 2008). Aggression between romantic partners is common, with boys as likely to report abuse behaviour as girls. Collins et al.'s (2009) review indicates that, depending on the sample surveyed, 10–48 percent of adolescents experience physical aggression and 25–50 percent report psychological aggression from their romantic partner, including being sworn at, insulted, and threatened. These days, aggression and bullying also occur online, for example, vengeful ex-partners have been known to share private photos or information on social media, causing embarrassment, humiliation, or worse to the victim. Some teens appear to be more accepting of these situations than is healthy, for example, interpreting jealousy and overly possessive behaviors as reflections of love.

Sexual coercion within romantic relationships is relatively common. A national survey of over 2,000 Australian secondary students in Years 10, 11, and 12 found that among those who were sexually active, one-quarter had experienced unwanted sex (Mitchell et al., 2014). Reasons given for having sex when they did not want to included being too drunk to say no (49 percent), frightened (28 percent), or pressured by their partner (53 percent). A US study of over 750 female students found almost 50 percent had had at least one experience of unwanted sex, 70 percent as part of a casual "hook-up," and 57 percent in a committed romantic relationship (Garcia et al., 2012). Regretted sex is also not an uncommon phenomenon among teenagers (e.g., Skinner et al., 2008).

Other challenges facing young people seeking or participating in romantic relationships include unrequited love and breaking up. In the case of unrequited love, fantasies about the other can be intense and obsessional, sometimes leading to misinterpretations that the feelings are reciprocated. In extreme cases, this may result in maladjusted acting-out behaviors, such as aggression and stalking (Leitz & Theriot, 2005), but more commonly the distress is turned inward, contributing to depression and low self-esteem, sometimes with the risk of self-harm.

Breakups are a very common feature of adolescent romantic relationships, some of which last only a few weeks. Among a large sample of young people in their early twenties in Australia and Hong Kong, 80 percent had experienced a breakup (Moore et al., 2012). The impact of splitting up may not be particularly severe or long-lasting, especially in the case of short-term liaisons. Nevertheless, some teenagers are more vulnerable than others. Several studies have shown romantic breakups associated with depression, particularly among those who have already experienced mood disorders (Davila, 2008; Welsh et al., 2003). In our 2012 study, 40 percent of participants felt very hurt following their relationship breakup, even though the majority of these dissolutions were self- or mutually initiated. Breakups were more distressing if they were partner-initiated, and among adolescents with more "clingy" relationship styles and greater tendencies toward negative mood.

Usually, time heals and experience teaches. Connolly and McIsaac (2009) researched breakups among Canadian adolescents and found that the most common reasons given for ending a relationship related to unmet affiliation, intimacy, sexual, or interdependence needs. In other words, young people were "moving on" when their relationships were not fulfilling, and in the process, hopefully, were learning more about themselves and others. Over time, and through talking with others, including parents, peers and partners, adolescents can develop cognitive frameworks for better understanding the nature of intimate relationships and learn to cope with their ups and downs. One example comes from a study by Montgomery (2005) of nearly 500 young people aged 12 to 24 years, in which it was shown that older adolescents were less prone to romantic idealization than younger ones. They were more realistic in their expectations of a romantic partner, so less liable to be disappointed. With experience, if all goes well, love becomes a little less blind.

Protective Factors

With age and maturity come more realistic expectations and, hopefully, stronger capacities to make discerning partner choices, communicate and negotiate with partners and recover from relationship set backs and breakups. "Hopefully" is the operative word here, because we know that people of any age can be undone by their heartbreaks and poor romantic choices. Nevertheless, there are some protective factors likely to assist young people to negotiate first romantic relationships and survive breakups.

Early sex education is important, ideally emanating from the home and supported by the school curriculum. It's a bit late for "the talk" on the eve of a young person's first date. Education that goes beyond the mechanics of sex and emphasizes mutual respect, decision-making, and the meaning of consent should help young people to resist relationship bullying and sexual coercion. School and community-based programmes that focus on teaching the characteristics of healthy romantic relationships, recognizing gender-based stereotypes, improving conflict-management and communication skills, and decreasing acceptance of partner violence can effectively reduce dating violence in adolescent relationships (Foshee et al., 1998). In addition, parental modeling of respectful interrelationships sets a pattern for young people to aim for in their own interactions.

Family and peer discussions that normalize teenage romantic relations—and breaking up—also help young people to frame their expectations and experiences in context. Some teenagers may need extra encouragement to maintain links with their friends and peer group and to keep up their sports and hobbies when they are in the throes of an intense romance. But it is important that they do maintain these support links in order to help them resist the kinds of relationships that are too interdependent and have an obsessional quality. When this kind of relationship breaks up, there is a greater risk of distress and depression. Maintaining links with friends provides a distraction from troubles and a sounding board for adolescents to discuss their romantic successes, failures, and hopes.

In today's world, cyber safety is a key issue for all of us, but especially young people. Education about topics such as the potential dangers of sexting, online sexual predators, and the distortion of romantic relationships depicted on pornography sites is essential for adolescents. Parental monitoring of online activity, especially among children and younger teenagers, may be advisable, and this requires that parents too become educated in new media—savvy about Facebook, Instagram, Tinder,

and the like. While adolescents need their privacy, it is important for parents to be watchful for warning signs of obsessive and secretive Internet use. The heady emotions of falling in love can lead teenagers into unwise activity; the problem with the Internet is that sexts and social media posts can come back to haunt them well after a relationship is over.

In summary, adolescent romantic relationships—with all their ups and downs—have the capacity to be growth-promoting, confidence-boosting, and healthy experiences that teach young people about the give and take of intimacy. They also provide traps for young players. And while we cannot (and should not) shield the adolescents in our care from all the hurts and disappointments that life throws up, there are protective factors that limit the likelihood of serious harm from toxic partnerships or distressing breakups. Watchful, kindly and respectful parenting, strong friendship networks and relationship-oriented sex education can all play their part in helping adolescents enjoy their romantic adventures and learn from them.

References

Braams, B.R., van Duijvenvoorde, A.C.K., Peper, J.S. & Crone, E.A. (2015). Longitudinal changes in adolescent risk-taking. *Journal of Neuroscience, 35*, 7226–7238.

Brand, S., Luethi, M., von Planta, A. et al. (2007). Romantic love, hypomania, and sleep pattern in adolescents. Journal of *Adolescent Health, 41*(1), 69–76.

Buchanan, C.M., Eccles, J.S. & Becker, J.B. (1992). Are adolescents the victims of raging hormones: Evidence for activational effects of hormones on moods and behavior at adolescence. *Psychological Bulletin, 111*(1), 62–107.

Carver, K., Joyner, K. & Udry, J.R. (2003). National estimates of adolescent romantic relationships. In P. Florsheim (Ed.) *Adolescent romantic relations and sexual behavior: Theory, research and practical implications* (pp. 23–56). Mahwah, NJ: Lawrence Erlbaum Associates.

Collins, W.A., Welsh, D.P. & Furman, W. (2009). Adolescent romantic relationships. *Annual Review of Psychology, 60,* 631.

Connolly, J. & McIsaac, C. (2009). Adolescents' explanations for romantic dissolutions: A developmental perspective. *Journal of Adolescence, 32*(5), 1209–1223.

Davila, J. (2008). Depressive symptoms and adolescent romance. *Child Development and Personality, 2*(1), 26–31.

Erikson, E. (1968). *Identity, youth and crisis.* New York: Norton.

Fisher, H.E., Aron, A. & Brown, L.L. (2006). Romantic love: A mammalian brain system for mate choice. *Philosophical Transactions of the Royal Society B: Biological Sciences, 361 (1476)*, 2173–2186.

Foshee, V.A., Bauman, K.E., Arriaga, X.B. et al. (1998). An evaluation of safe dates, an adolescent dating violence prevention program. *American Journal of Public Health, 88*(1), 45–50.

Garcia, J.R., Reiber, C., Massey, S. & Merriwether, A. (2012). Sexual hookup culture: A review. *Review of General Psychology, 16*(2), 161–176.

Grieger, L.D., Kusunoki, Y. & Harding, D.J. (2014). The social contexts of adolescent romantic relationships. *Focus, 31*(1), 15–17.

Leitz, M.A. & Theriot, M.T. (2005). Adolescent stalking: A review. *Journal of Evidence-Based Social Work, 2*(3), 97–112.

Marazziti, D. & Canale, D. (2004). Hormonal changes when falling in love. *Psychoneuroendocrinology 29*, 931–936.

Mitchell, A., Patrick, K., Heywood, W. et al. (2014). *Fifth National Survey of Australian Secondary Students and Sexual Health 2013*. ARCSHS Monograph Series No. 97. Australian Research Centre in Sex, Health and Society, La Trobe University, Melbourne, Australia.

Montgomery, M.J. (2005). Psychosocial intimacy and identity: From early adolescence to emerging adulthood. *Journal of Adolescent Research, 20*(3), 346–374.

Moore, S., Leung, C., Karnilowicz, W. & Lung, C.L. (2012). Characteristics and predictors of romantic relationships in late adolescence and young adulthood in Hong Kong and Australia. *Australian Psychologist, 47*(2), 108–117.

Mulford, C. & Giordano, P.C. (2008). Teen dating violence: A closer look at adolescent romantic relationships. *National Institute of Justice Journal*, No. 261, pp.34–40. Available via www.nij.gov/journals/261

Ortigue, S., Bianchi-Demicheli, F., Patel, N. et al. (2010). Neuroimaging of love: fMRI meta-analysis evidence toward new perspectives in sexual medicine. *Journal of Sexual Medicine, 7*, 3541–3552.

Petanjek, Z., Judaš, M., Šimić, G. et al. (2011). Extraordinary neoteny of synaptic spines in the human prefrontal cortex. *Proceedings of the National Academy of Sciences of the United States of America, 108*(32), 13281–13286.

Scanlan, F., Bailey, A. & Parker, A. (2012). *Adolescent romantic relationships – Why are they important? And should they be encouraged or avoided?* Headspace, Orygen Youth Health Research Centre: Australian Government Department of Health and Ageing. Retrieved 6 February, 2016 from tinyurl.com/hósóprg.

Skinner, S.R., Smith, J., Fenwick, J. et al. (2008). Perceptions and experiences of first sexual intercourse in Australian adolescent females. *Journal of Adolescent Health, 43*(6), 593–599.

Suleiman, A.B. & Harden, K.P. (2016). The importance of sexual and romantic development in understanding the developmental neuroscience of adolescence. *Developmental Cognitive Neuroscience, 7*, 145–147.

Temple-Smith, M., Moore, S. & Rosenthal, D. (2016). *Sexuality in adolescence: The digital generation*. London: Routledge.

Welsh, D.P., Grello, C.P. & Harper, M.S. (2003). When love hurts: Depression and adolescent romantic relationships. In P. Florsheim (Ed.) *Adolescent romantic relations and sexual behavior: Theory, research and practical implications* (pp.185–212). Mahwah, NJ: Lawrence Erlbaum Associates.

Zimmer-Gembeck, M.J., Siebenbruner, J. & Collins, W.A. (2001). Diverse aspects of dating: Associations with psychosocial functioning from early to middle adolescence. *Journal of Adolescence*, 24(3), 313–336.

Zimmer-Gembeck, M., Siebenbruner, J. & Collins, W.A. (2004). A prospective study of intraindividual and peer influences on adolescents' heterosexual romantic and sexual behavior. *Archives of Sexual Behavior, 33*(4), 381–394.

Critical Thinking

1. Explain how romantic relationships help identity development in adolescence.

2. Design a sex education course for adolescents that goes beyond the "mechanics of sex." What else would you include in this educational opportunity, that is, online dating sites, sexting, coercion, alcohol, and loss of inhibitions or risk taking behavior?

Internet References

Addressing Teen Dating Violence
https://www.pinerest.org/addressing-teen-dating-violence/

Adolescents and Online Dating Attitudes
http://www.irma-international.org/viewtitle/50701/

Sexting and Sexual Behavior in At-Risk Adolescents
https://www.ncbi.nlm.nih.gov/pmc/articles/PMC3904272/

Teen Sexting
What Messages Should We Be Sending Our Teens about Sexting?
https://www.psychologytoday.com/blog/teen-angst/201502/teen-sexting

Teens, Technology, and Romantic Relationships
http://www.pewinternet.org/2015/10/01/teens-technology-and-romantic-relationships/

Susan Moore is an emeritus professor of psychology at the Swinburne University of Technology in Melbourne, Australia.

Article   Prepared by: Claire N. Rubman, *Suffolk County Community College*

It's Complicated

Beyond the Hookup Culture: Taking Initiative and Mitigating Risk

STEPHEN GRAY WALLACE

Learning Outcomes

After reading this article, you will be able to:

- Explain "hook-up" culture.

- Describe why teens today might be less prepared for sex and relationships.

- Discuss the relative dangers of letting adolescents learn about sex, love, and relationships from the media.

Navigating what has become known as the "hookup culture" is no easy task for young people of all ages and both sexes. Although it has now been popularized in song (including pop star Katy Perry's "Last Friday Night" [Perry et al., 2010] and country musician Blake Shelton's "Lonely Tonight" [Anderson and Howard, 2014]), for years researchers could only guess at the longer-term consequences of the advent of casual, intimate, and sometimes even anonymous sexual behavior among teens and young adults.

Indeed, eight years ago this month, my *Camping Magazine* article "Hooking Up, Losing Out?" (Wallace, 2007) explored that very issue while casting light on what was considered a seismic shift in sexual attitudes and practices of youth.

Changes on that scale have been few, starting with the advent of the automobile in the 1920s, which facilitated unsupervised dating, followed by the "sexual revolution" of the 1960s (which by today's standards seems rather tame) and the one taking place now (Garcia et al., 2012).

Does it matter? It very well might.

Sexual decision-making may have important implications for you and your camp this summer. Thus, it's a critical time to consider what your camp's expectations are for your behavior and how it could impact your campers' development.

At many camps, discussions with campers about sex, if they occur at all, are led by trained professionals. Most likely, any guiding you do will be in the form of role modeling and how you might respond to questions from the children.

One thing is clear: Times have changed. And, fortunately, new data have arrived. Unfortunately, it's, well, complicated—as the ubiquitous Facebook® relationship status so often reveals.

Puberty: A Changing Landscape

Earlier onset of puberty in children only accelerates the process of preparing for impending change and, when it occurs, harnessing, processing and, in some cases, acting on complicated biological and psychological forces.

While earlier puberty in girls (defined as beginning of breast development) has been acknowledged for years, in 2012, the narrative began to shift with new research from the American Academy of Pediatrics revealing that American boys are showing signs of puberty six months to two years earlier than they did 30 to 40 years ago (Herman-Giddens et al., 2012). In that study, puberty was defined as genital and pubic hair growth and early testicular development, which on average was age ten for white and Hispanic boys and about nine for black boys.

As children of both sexes move through puberty and into their adolescence, hormones surge, bringing about well-known physical manifestations of maturity.

But supercharged doses of hormones influence more than just physicality—they also engender changes in mood and emotion. During this time, a massive reorganization of the brain ensues. Sleep cycles switch, making young people more nocturnal. And cognitive advancement makes them more inclined to think abstractly. Thus, these youth are better able to see the nuances of a host of life situations, including, perhaps, their first romantic relationships with members of the opposite, same sex, or both.

Temple University professor Laurence Steinberg, PhD, in his book *Age of Opportunity—Lessons from the New Science of Adolescence*, offers some warning signs, stating, "Early-maturing adolescents experience a greater gap between when they mature physically and when they mature in other ways. This discrepancy can cause problems, as when an adolescent develops an interest in sex before he can think ahead well enough to carry condoms, or when a girl starts to attract boys before she has the emotional wherewithal to decline their advances" (Steinberg, 2014).

Like I said, it's complicated.

Puberty can be a confusing time not only for children but also increasingly for their parents and other caregivers, including their camp counselors.

Most girls at least seem prepared. Boys, on the other hand, may not be.

In his book *Challenging Casanova*, psychologist Andrew Smiler shares that only about half of American high school and college students have talked with their parents about sex, and the majority of them are girls (Smiler, 2012).

With parents avoiding "the talk" and mandatory sex education in schools still somewhat limited, too many children are left shortchanged in preparedness for the developmental milestone that is puberty. But that doesn't mean that they're steering clear of sex. According to the Centers for Disease Control and Prevention, almost half (46.8 percent) of high school students have had intercourse (CDC, 2015). And, according to a 2014 *TIME* magazine article, nearly 80 percent of them had no formal sex education in advance (Sifferlin, 2014).

In his April 2013 piece in *The Huffington Post*, "It's Time to Make Sex Education Mandatory in Our Nation's Schools," author Steve Siebold said, "The average teenager has been exposed to more sexually explicit movies, games, magazines, and other materials than we have in our entire lives. They're learning lovemaking through porn" (Siebold, 2013).

Sex in America Today

Indeed, your technology-infused generation may be learning about sex, and sexuality, in ways foreign even to your parents.

A 2010 article in *Pediatrics* reported that early sexual activity among American adolescents presents risk of pregnancy and sexually transmitted infections. No surprise there.

It also points to the media, including television, music, movies, magazines, and the Internet, as motivating factors for initiating intercourse. "There is a major disconnect between what mainstream media portray—casual sex and sexuality with no consequences—and what children and teenagers need—straightforward information about human sexuality and the need for contraception when having sex" (Strasburger, 2010).

An opinion editorial by Nicholas Kristof for *The New York Times*, "Politicians, Teens, and Birth Control," similarly bemoans our failure to adequately prepare young people for sex, stating that American teenagers become pregnant at a rate of about one a minute, three times the rate in Spain, five times the rate in France, and 15 times the rate in Switzerland. Kristof argues, ". . . states and schools should embrace comprehensive sex education, teaching contraception, the benefits of delaying sex, and, also, the responsibility of boys" (Kristof, 2014).

Getting in the Game: The Hookup Culture

According to *Teens Today* research from Students Against Destructive Decisions (SADD), while older teens are more likely to report being sexually active than are younger teens, nearly one-quarter (24 percent) of sixth graders report some type of sexual activity other than kissing (Wallace, 2008).

In her book *You're Teaching My Child What?*, psychiatrist Miriam Grossman states that 34 percent of girls are sexually active by age 15 and by ninth grade 20 percent of teens have had oral sex (Grossman, 2009).

As we have seen, in our society sex is hard to escape, even for young people. And all that exposure may create a sense of urgency for them to become sexually active, often before they want to be.

Eighteen-year-old John says he felt that pressure because "My friend kept saying, 'Come on, man, get in the game!'"

Fourteen-year-old Alex felt pressure earlier, after his dorm mates at prep school taunted him for being a virgin in ninth grade.

Ellen said, "I turned 17 and it was like, 'Well, I have to have sex now.' So I did."

Peter, 15, had sex with a girl at a party because she handed him a condom and told him they were going to. Feeling he couldn't return to his friends with the deed undone and risk ridicule, he complied—and he wasn't happy he did.

He is not alone. The National Campaign to Prevent Teen and Unplanned Pregnancy states that the majority of teens who have had intercourse wish they had waited (stayteen.org, 2015).

Historically boys have been painted as the aggressors. However, recent research from the Center for Adolescent Research and Education (CARE), in collaboration with SADD (CARE/SADD, 2012), points to changing gender roles in sexual behavior, with teen girls 16- to 19-years old more likely than boys the same age to say they have ever participated in sexual intercourse (31–22 percent) and other intimate sexual behavior (40–29 percent).

Downsides of Casual Sex

"Sexual Hookup Culture: A Review," published by the American Psychological Association, tells us that hooking up (defined by the authors as brief uncommitted sexual encounters among individuals who are not romantic partners or dating each other) has "taken root within the sociocultural milieu" of adolescents and emerging adults, with 70 percent of sexually active 12- to 21-year-olds reported having uncommitted sex within the last year (Garcia et al., 2012).

It further reports that the negative consequences of hooking up can include emotional and psychological injury and sexual violence.

While reviewing the data, researchers found evidence of "hookup regret" in a web-based study of undergraduate students reporting embarrassment (27.1 percent) and emotional difficulties (24.7 percent). Conversely, on average, both men and women seem to have a "higher positive affect" than a negative one following a casual sexual experience.

Odd.

Ironically, while a majority of both men and women are inclined to engage in such behavior, they often say they desire a more romantic relationship.

Perhaps most disturbing are links from this cultural phenomenon to sexual violence.

Landslide—Sexual Assault on Campus

Facing a landslide of sexual assault allegations on college campuses across the country, the White House in January 2013 issued a memorandum establishing a task force to protect students from sexual assault (The White House, 2014a).

Despite the fact that some have challenged a definition of sexual assault that includes "verbal, visual, or anything that forces a person to join in unwanted sexual activity or attention" (Contorno, 2014), a report from the White House Council on Women and Girls paints a rather grim picture of the problems faced by young people of both genders and differing ages, especially college students (The White House, 2014b).

- Women and girls are the vast majority of victims: nearly one in five women—or nearly 22 million—have been raped in their lifetimes.
- Men and boys, however, are also at risk: one in 71 men—or almost 1.6 million—have been raped during their lives.

Tellingly, most victims know their assailants.

The report also discusses the psychological fallout and economic repercussions ($87,000 to $240,776 per rape) of what can really only be called an epidemic. Finally, it identifies some contributing factors, including "the dynamics of college life" in which "many victims are abused while they're drunk, under the influence of drugs, passed out, or otherwise incapacitated" (The White House, 2014b).

The link between intoxication and sexual assault is hard to deny, even if some brave college presidents have been criticized for pointing it out (Svokos, 2014).

A "Campus Sexual Assault (CSA) Study" conducted for the Justice Department's National Institute of Justice states that the majority of sexual assaults occur when women are incapacitated due to their use of substances, primarily alcohol (Krebs et al., 2007).

On that point, the National Institute on Alcohol Abuse and Alcoholism states that "more than 97,000 students between the ages of 18 and 24 are victims of alcohol-related sexual assault or date rape" (NIAAA, 2013).

Some other potential factors include the hookup culture—something controversially referred to by columnist George Will (2014) and discussed by the Kinsey Institute (Garcia et al., 2012).

While causes and effects are important, so, too, are solutions. To that end, the federal government has called for far-reaching action, including changing the culture (The White House, 2014b).

Perhaps that offers an opportunity to take a closer look at the common cultures of camp.

Creating a New Normal

The prolific nature of sexual assaults on college campuses raises the question: Are camps safer than schools? While the obvious answer seems to be yes, the less obvious is why.

Partly because summer camps have a unique ability to create campus cultures qualitatively different than those elsewhere.

Yes, we need to be prepared for the worst. Michael Shelton made this point in his 2004 *Camping Magazine* article, "Staff Sexual Assault: Prevention and Intervention," which takes camp directors on a cautionary tour through definitions of sexual assault, gender differences in perceptions and communication, and the handling of allegations (Shelton, 2004).

In truth, sexual assaults can be an issue anywhere. Denying that fact would be counterproductive, for it would leave your camp—and all the others—at risk, if for no other reason than for failing to follow federal laws relating to sexual harassment and assaults.

What *is* productive is to reflect on what makes camps the physically and emotionally safe places that parents, teens, and children say they are. These important nuances, such as respect for the individual, freedom to try new things without fear of failure, and an emphasis on individuality, community, and teamwork are all critical components of caring, compassionate camp communities.

Together, we can create a "new normal" for cohabitating adolescents and emerging adults—not only by what we say, but also by what we do.

In an environment removed from the college culture and from broader societal norms, summer camps remain some of the last, best places on earth for the development and maintenance of safe, nurturing relationships among counselors and campers alike.

It's time to look beyond the hookup culture and take initiative for mitigating risk.

Maybe it's not so complicated after all.

References

Anderson, B., & Hurd, R. (2014). Lonely tonight. Performed by Blake Shelton. *Bringing Back the Sunshine*. Retrieved from www.lyrics.com/lonely-tonight-lyrics-blake-shelton.html

CARE/SADD. (2012, May 29). CARE/SADD survey investigates risky behaviors by teens on college visits. Retrieved from http://sadd.org/press/presspdfs/FINAL_CARE_052912.pdf

Centers for Disease Control and Prevention. (2015). Sexual risk behavior: HIV, STD, & teen pregnancy prevention. Adolescent and School Health. Retrieved from www.cdc.gov/healthyyouth/sexualbehaviors/index.htm

Contorno, S. (2014, Dec. 7). In light of UVA story, pundits ask: are 1 in 5 college women sexually assaulted? *Tampa Bay Times*. Politifact.com. Retrieved from www.politifact.com/punditfact/article/2014/dec/07/light-uva-story-pundits-ask-are-1-5-college-women-

Garcia, J., Reiber, C., Massey, S., & Merriwether, A. (2012). Sexual hookup culture: A review. *Review of General Psychology*. American Psychological Association. Retrieved from www.apa.org/monitor/2013/02/sexual-hookup-culture.pdf

Grossman, M. (2009). *You're teaching my child WHAT?* Washington, D.C. Regnery Publishing. Retrieved from www.miriamgrossmanmd.com/books

Herman-Giddens, M., Steffes, J., Harris, D., Slora, E., Hussey, M., Dowshen, S., Wasserman, R., Serwint, J., Smitherman, L., & Reiter, E. (2012, October 20). Secondary sexual characteristics in boys: Data from the pediatric research in office settings network. *Pediatrics*. American Academy of Pediatrics. Retrieved from http://pediatrics.aappublications.org/content/early/2012/10/15/peds.2011-3291.abstract

Krebs, C., Lindquist, C., Warner, T., Fisher, B., & Martin, S. (2007, October). The campus sexual assault (CSA) study final report. Prepared for National Institute of Justice. Retrieved from www.ncjrs.gov/pdffiles1/nij/grants/221153.pdf

Kristof, N. (2014, November 12). Politicians, teens and birth control. *The New York Times*. Retrieved from www.nytimes.com/2014/11/13/opinion/nicholas-kristof-politicians-teens-and-birth-control.html

National Institute on Alcohol Abuse and Alcoholism. (2013, July). College drinking. National Institutes of Health.

Retrieved from www.niaaa.nih.gov/alcohol-health/special-populations-co-occurring-disorders/college-drinking

Perry, K., Gottwald, L., Martin, M., & McKee, B. (2010, August). Last Friday night. Performed by Katy Perry. *Teenage Dream*. Retrieved from www.metrolyrics.com/last-friday-night-lyrics-katy-perry.html

Shelton, M. (2004, May/June). Staff sexual assault: Prevention and intervention. *Camping Magazine*. Retrieved from www.ACAohio.org/members/knowledge/risk/cm/045assault

Siebold, S. (2013, April 9). It's time to make sex education mandatory in our nation's schools. *The Huffington Post*. Retrieved from www.huffingtonpost.com/steve-siebold/sex-education-schools_b_3006483.html

Sifferlin, A. (2014, November 13). Why schools can't teach sex ed. *TIME*. Retrieved from http://time.com/why-schools-cant-teach-sex-ed

Smiler, A. (2012). *Challenging Casanova: Beyond the stereotype of the promiscuous young male*. San Francisco: Jossey-Bass. Retrieved from http://challengingcasanova.com

Stayteen.org (2015). Waiting. Stay informed. The National Campaign to Prevent Teen and Unplanned Pregnancy. Retrieved from http://stayteen.org/waiting

Steinberg, L. (2014). *Age of opportunity—lessons from the new science of adolescence*. New York, NY: Eamon Dolan/Houghton Mifflin Harcourt.

Strasburger, V. (2010, August 30). Sexuality, contraception and the media. *Pediatrics*. Retrieved from http://pediatrics.aappublications.org/content/126/3/576.full

Svokos, A. (2014, November 25). Eckerd College president: You can stop rape by not drinking or having casual sex. *The Huffington Post*. Retrieved from www.huffingtonpost.com/2014/11/25/eckerd-college-president-rape_n_6221136.html

The White House. (2014a, January 22). Memorandum—establishing a White House task force to protect students from sexual assault. Office of the Press Secretary. Retrieved from www.whitehouse.gov/the-press-office/2014/01/22/memorandum-establishing-white-house-task-force-protect-students-sexual-a

The White House. (2014b). Rape and sexual assault: A renewed call to action. The White House Council on Women and Girls and the Office of the Vice President. Retrieved from www.whitehouse.gov/sites/default/files/docs/sexual_assault_report_1-21-14.pdf

Wallace, S. (2007, March/April). Healthy teens: hooking up, losing out? *Camping Magazine*. Retrieved from www.ACAcamps.org/campmag/0703wallace

Wallace, S. (2008). *Reality gap: Alcohol, drugs and sex—what parents don't know and teens aren't telling*. New York, NY: Sterling Publishing/Union Square Press.

Will, G. (2014, June 6). Colleges become the victims of progressivism. *The Washington Post*. Retrieved from www.washingtonpost.com/opinions/george-will-college-become-the-victims-of-progressivism/2014/06/06/e90e73b4-eb50-11e3-9f5c-9075d5508f0a_story.html

Critical Thinking

1. Who do adolescents ask when they have questions about sex or relationships?

2. Why do more American teenagers get pregnant than teens other countries such as Spain, France, or Switzerland?

Internet References

Adolescent Pregnancy, Birth, and Abortion Rates across Countries: Levels and Recent Trends

https://www.ncbi.nlm.nih.gov/pmc/articles/PMC4852976/

Adolescent Sexuality and the Media a Review of Current Knowledge and Implications

https://www.ncbi.nlm.nih.gov/pmc/articles/PMC1070813/

Adolescent Sexuality: Talk the Talk before They Walk the Walk

https://www.healthychildren.org/English/ages-stages/teen/dating-sex/Pages/Adolescent-Sexuality-Talk-the-Talk-Before-They-Walk-the-Walk.aspx

Sexual Hookup Culture: A Review

https://www.ncbi.nlm.nih.gov/pmc/articles/PMC3613286/

Social Media, The Secret Lives of Teenagers, and Hook-up Culture

http://thefederalist.com/2016/03/10/social-media-the-secret-lives-of-teenagers-and-hook-up-culture/

STEPHEN GRAY WALLACE, MS Ed, is the director of the Center for Adolescent Research and Education, a national collaborative of institutions and organizations committed to increasing positive youth outcomes and reducing risk. He has broad experience as a school psychologist and adolescent/family counselor and serves as a senior advisor to Students Against Destructive Decisions, a director of counseling and counselor training at Cape Cod Sea Camps, a member of the professional development faculty at the American Academy of Family Physicians and American Camp Association, and a parenting expert at kidsinthehouse.com and NBC Universal s parenttoolkit.com. For more information about Stephens work, please visit StephenGrayWallace.com.

Article   Prepared by: Claire N. Rubman, *Suffolk County Community College*

A Second Puberty

More and more clinics are offering transgender protocols for children, which critics say is dangerous.

JESSICA FIRGER

Learning Outcomes

After reading this article, you will be able to:

- Explain what Breland meant by ". . . a new kind of puberty."

- Describe how GnRH agonists work in the body to delay puberty.

- Describe the issues that Breland uncovered through his research on patient care.

WHEN TAI JORDAN was a child, he would visit the local swimming pool and puzzle over why boys were allowed to splash about without their shirts on, while he was forced to wear a bathing suit that covered most of his body. And when he daydreamed about his wedding day in the faraway future, Jordan didn't envision himself walking down the aisle in a poufy white gown, as his family hoped he would do one day. Jordan wanted to be the groom, waiting at the very end of that aisle for his bride.

"I've never really identified with the body I was born in," says Jordan, an 18-year-old student at Evergreen State College in Olympia, Washington. "The way I decided to carry myself, the way I acted, was always more masculine."

Jordan initially identified as a lesbian in 2013, but even after coming out about his sexual orientation, he still didn't feel "complete." Confused about his body and his orientation, he became an avid triathlete and threw himself into sports, which led him to an epiphany. During a soccer competition in his junior year of high school, he tore both quad muscles and needed surgery. When doctors performed an MRI of his lower body to diagnose the injury, they spotted something else much more serious. Next to Jordan's ovaries was a rare type of benign tumors, known as teratomas. Jordan underwent a surgical procedure to remove both ovaries. With that, the doctors took away Jordan's ability to have biological children. The surgery also left him searching for answers to even more complex questions about who he was. That quest helped Jordan realize he wasn't gay. He wanted to become a man.

Announcing to the world—or just your family—that you want to transition to the opposite sex is almost never easy, and making that transitions always a long ordeal, physically and psychologically. Though it's a procedure that's slowly becoming much more accepted by the public and the medical community, the prospects are still fraught for a young person who may have been chided by adults for feeling trapped in the wrong body, or ignored. Families and pediatricians may insist it's just a symptom of the undignified phase of life known as puberty, or another bit of self-indulgent behavior typical for angsty teens.

Jordan's experience was much more positive. He came out to his mother a second time (first as a lesbian, now as transgender) and watched her tear up (again). "She wasn't crying because she was sad, she was crying because she knows the statistics, and she knows the reality of what happens to people in the LGBTQ community the unprecedented rates of suicide, the ability to fall into depression, the lack of resources," says Jordan, who knows that around 40 percent of people who identify as transgender will attempt suicide as teenagers. These young people also have significantly higher rates of homelessness, substance abuse, and depression, compared with the general population.

Jordan is one of approximately 700,000 people in the United States who identify as transgender, according to the Williams Institute, an independent organization dedicated to research on sexual orientation and gender identity. Thanks to greater awareness and acceptance, transitioning is now an option at an increasingly younger age. However, the medical interventions used—hormone treatments, drugs to halt puberty—are highly controversial. Critics argue that the treatments are unethical and that young people are not psychologically or emotionally equipped to make such momentous decisions.

Others in the medical community vehemently disagree, and they are working hard to normalize the process by providing these treatments at children's hospitals.

Jordan connected with Dr. David Breland, a physician of pediatric and adolescent medicine at Seattle Children's Hospital and director of its new Gender Clinic. Soon after meeting with Breland, Jordan began testosterone therapy to trick his body into developing certain characteristics associated with a man. Breland specializes in working with transgender teens, and he has seen at least 200 young patients like Jordan. He helps families make sense of the process. He calls it a new kind of puberty, through which young people can grow into the adult they want to be. Advocates say going through this transition process early minimizes stigma and improves both the medical and cosmetic outcomes.

Seattle Children's Hospital is the fifth to open a clinic dedicated to the complex needs of this young patient population. Breland and his colleagues will see children and adolescents ages 8 to 21, offering a high level of care that include specialists in endocrinology and behavioral medicine. At the Seattle clinic, children will also have access to psychological counseling. And they may be provided with pubertal blockers to "buy the family some time" before starting on cross-sex hormones at the onset of puberty, says Breland. Though the hospital isn't doing reconstructive surgery to alter the appearance of genitals or the chest, it does provide guidance and referrals if a patient wants to undergo surgery later, most likely after reaching 18. Experts in this specialized field say it's clear that transitioning earlier in life can result in fewer medical procedures as an adult. Hormones administered in early puberty can prevent a person's features from becoming too masculine or feminine, and the process is much less painful than the often drastic and costly cosmetic surgery some patients require to look the way they see themselves. Early transition, some say, also results in improved mental health.

But Breland knows the timing is different for every patient. "There's a lot of risk factors that happen with these people, and they just want to be themselves," he says. "That's why we think it should be a team effort, with a medical provider and a mental health provider so they can use psychotherapy and mental health evaluation to make sure it's the right decision for them."

Better to Have Cancer?

Most doctors in this growing specialty follow established protocols for early transition. The World Professional Association for Transgender Health, a nonprofit, provides education and

training for physicians to learn about caring for this patient population. It also advises the growing number of children's hospitals offering these services on standards of care for transgender patients.

Other, more mainstream medical organizations have also weighed in. The American Academy of Pediatrics, for example, recommends physicians and adults have the first discussion about transitioning when the child is 12, but the organization believes the process should start at 18.

Though advocates in the field have their own ideas about when to start the process, not enough is known about the factors that prevent transgender patients from receiving the right kind of care. Breland recognized this and conducted some research before starting his clinic. For the study, published in the *Journal of Adolescent Health*, he and his colleagues interviewed 15 transgender patients and 50 caregivers to learn more about the challenges they faced when seeking care. They identified several big issues. Some participants said it was hard to find pediatricians trained to provide "gender-affirming health care." Others reported a lack of consistently applied protocols for handling these patients. Some said they encountered clinicians who failed to coordinate care or limited and delayed access to pubertal blockers and hormones. It was common for doctors to inconsistently use chosen names and pronouns. Breland says his research proved "it's easier to have a chronic medical condition" than to be transgender.

When treating his youngest patients, he prescribes pubertal blockers that halt puberty altogether and prevent the development of biological sex characteristics. These Food and Drug Administration-approved medications, known as GnRH agonists, were initially created to treat precocious puberty (when a child begins puberty before 8 or 9). The hormone in the drug overstimulates the gonadotropin-releasing hormone receptors in the brain, and "it just shuts these receptors down," says Breland. The effects are mostly reversible if a patient stops taking the agonists.

When the patient and family feel ready, the clinic will move forward with the transition. Breland says most decide to, and he then prescribes the cross-sex hormone—testosterone for transmales and estrogen for transfemales. This usually begins at around age 12. Adding these drugs allows patients to begin developing into an adult of the reassigned sex. "Just like someone going through puberty, their testosterone or estrogen will gradually increase, and that's what changes the body and voice and hair growth and breast development," says Breland. He prescribes a gradual increase in dosage so levels of estrogen or testosterone will rise in the body, as they normally would for an adult who is biologically female or male.

Taking the hormones affects a number of the person's physical traits. Boys transitioning to girls won't develop biological sex characteristics such as bigger stature, a broad face, larger hands, an Adam's apple and a deeper voice. Girls transitioning to boys will develop some traditionally male characteristics, such as facial hair. A biological female in this protocol usually stops menstruating after six months. Transitioning to a male will cause the patient's voice to become deeper, and that's likely to be a permanent change. The hormones don't change the overall appearance and function of a patient's genitals, but testosterone may cause an enlargement of the clitoris, which can be useful should the patient want to have genital reconstruction later in life, says Breland.

Jordan began taking testosterone to transition from female to male in 2014, during his junior year of high school. He now administers his own testosterone shots every other week, and it will be something he does for the rest of his life. He says the process feels like a "second puberty." The difference this time is that he welcomes the changes in his body. "You've got the acne, the facial hair, the voice cracking at weird points in the day," he says. "These are the secondary sex characteristics I would have liked to have happened initially."

Dissing Dysphoria

Up until 2012, the American Psychiatric Association listed "gender identity disorder" in the Diagnostics Statistical Manual of Mental Disorders, which suggested that patients who questioned or felt troubled by their biological gender were abnormal. In 2012, after decades of classifying transgender people as mentally ill, the APA replaced the term with "gender dysphoria," which is used to describe the distress felt by some patients about this aspect of their identity. It essentially affirms that gender nonconformity isn't a psychiatric illness.

Many LGBT advocates hail that change, but some doctors think it's dangerous to make it easier for young people to rush into transitioning. Dr. Lawrence Mayer, a resident in the department of psychiatry at the Johns Hopkins University School of Medicine and a professor of statistics and biostatistics at Arizona State University, argues that young people aren't equipped to make these judgments for themselves. Kenneth Zucker, a researcher at the University of Toronto and a therapist, suggests in several journal articles based on studies he conducted that early traumatic experiences with family, such as an absentee parent, can bring out gender-nonconforming behavior—but these feelings eventually go away. His research suggests that as much as 90 percent of the children who identify as transgender eventually accept their biological sex after puberty. In a follow-up study of 25 transgender biological females, he found that only three still identified as transgender in adulthood.

Zucker used his research to formulate his own approach to treating these patients. His treatment is controversial because he focused on helping a child become more comfortable in his or her body, rather than getting the care needed to transition early.

Mayer and others believe early intervention shouldn't include drugs. Instead, it should focus on encouraging young people to experiment with their gender in ways that are more mutable. This may include changing hairstyle and clothing and using a different name. "I would be happy if these children would be sent to general child psychiatrists and followed for a period of time without their parents being there and see what they believe and how persistent it is," he says. "If it's persistent enough, I would be supportive of them because I care about patients."

Mayer co-authored a report that argues more data are needed to understand the outcomes of early transition. The problem, he says, is that very few balanced studies have been conducted, especially on early intervention. His paper cites one study, published in *Pediatrics*, that found that reassignment surgery in young adulthood alleviated gender dysphoria, and that the well-being of these patients was similar or better than young adults in the general population. But Mayer says this study wasn't well-designed—it was based on only 55 transgender young people and didn't have a matched group of transgender patients who didn't undergo medical treatment.

Jordan doesn't feel as if he needs studies to affirm his experience. He's adamantly against Mayer's watch-and-wait approach, which he believes simply reflects a misunderstanding of the situation. "If it's going to take a little poke or a pinch or some soreness to feel better, to feel happy and to be able to move on with my life, then it's a mere hiccup in the rest of my life," he says. "Nobody knows your body better than you do."

Even if it turns out to be the wrong one.

Critical Thinking

1. What is gender dysphoria?
2. At what age should children be allowed to opt for hormonal or surgical procedures for gender reassignment?
3. How does society assign gender roles and how does society react when those gender roles are in question?

Internet References

Care for Transgender Adolescents

http://www.acog.org/Resources-And-Publications/Committee-Opinions/Committee-on-Adolescent-Health-Care/Care-for-Transgender-Adolescents

Health Considerations for Gender Non-conforming Children and Transgender Adolescents

http://transhealth.ucsf.edu/trans?page=guidelines-youth

Largest Ever Study of Transgender Teenagers Set to Kick Off

http://www.nature.com/news/largest-ever-study-of-transgender-teenagers-set-to-kick-off-1.19637

"Psychology Works" Fact Sheet: Gender Dysphoria in Adolescents and Adults

http://www.cpa.ca/docs/File/Publications/FactSheets/Psychology WorksFactSheet_GenderDysphoriaInAdolescentsAndAdults.pdf

Serving Transgender Youth: Challenges, Dilemmas, and Clinical Examples

https://www.apa.org/pubs/journals/features/pro-a0037490.pdf

Transgender Children and Youth: Understanding the Basics

http://www.hrc.org/resources/transgender-children-and-youth-understanding-the-basics

Article   Prepared by: Claire N. Rubman, *Suffolk County Community College*

Study: Heavy Viewers of "Teen Mom" and "16 and Pregnant" Have Unrealistic Views of Teen Pregnancy

Learning Outcomes

After reading this article, you will be able to:

- Explain why people's perceptions of the impact of reality shows have changed.

- Describe what heavy viewers of teen shows believe about pregnancy and parenting.

The creator of MTV's "16 and Pregnant" and "Teen Mom" said the shows have been called "one of the best public service campaigns to prevent teen pregnancy." A new Indiana University research study finds the opposite to be true.

The paper accepted for publication in the journal *Mass Communication and Society* presents findings that such teen mom shows actually lead heavy viewers to believe that teen mothers have an enviable quality of life, a high income and involved fathers.

Teens who perceived reality television as realistic were most likely to hold these perceptions.

The paper's authors are Nicole Martins, an assistant professor of telecommunications in the College of Arts and Sciences at IU Bloomington, and Robin Jensen, an assistant professor of communication at the University of Utah.

"Heavy viewers of teen mom reality programs were more likely to think that teen moms have a lot of time to themselves, can easily find child care so that they can go to work or school and can complete high school than were lighter viewers of such shows," Martins and Jensen wrote.

Frequent viewers of the programs also were more likely to believe that teen moms have affordable access to health care, finished college and lived on their own.

"Our data call into question the content of teen mom reality programming," they added. "Heavy viewing of teen mom reality programming positively predicted unrealistic perceptions of what it is like to be a teen mother."

Martins, the lead author, and Jensen were unable to ask the 185 high school students surveyed about sexual behavior. But they were able to ask about their perceptions of reality TV and teen pregnancy.

"The fact that teens in the study seemed to think that being a teen parent was easy might increase the likelihood that they'll engage in unsafe sexual practices," Martins said, "because that's not a real consequence to them."

MTV recently announced that "Teen Mom 3" will not be renewed for next season. However, the more successful franchise sequel, "Teen Mom 2," will return with a fifth season January 20. Both programs spun off from an earlier series, "16 and Pregnant." They have been among the network's highest rated shows.

"As you study reality television with younger populations, you're going to find that younger children are going to have a harder time understanding that this is something that is scripted, edited, and put together in a purposeful way to create a narrative and a drama," Martins said.

"Indeed, there are some individuals who believe that this reality TV show is like real life. For them, they were the most likely ones to hold unrealistic perception about teen parenthood."

The professors were somewhat surprised by the findings. Martins said the initial program, "16 and Pregnant," seemed to do a better job of focusing on the harsh realities faced by the teen moms. But the subsequent series, "Teen Mom," turned some of the young women into celebrities who end up on the cover of tabloid magazines.

"Maybe that's what's drawing viewers' attention: the fact that one of the teen moms, Farrah Abraham, repeatedly is on the cover of Us Weekly for all the plastic surgery that she's had. Well, a teen mom living in this country can't afford that; most unmarried teen mothers are on welfare," Martins said.

It is possible that teens desire the celebrity status afforded to the shows' teen mothers, which makes a larger impression on their perceptions of the teen mom experience than does the real-life narratives being broadcast.

"In other words, the attention and opportunities seemingly thrown at these teen parents may appear so appealing to viewers that no amount of horror stories from the reality shows themselves can override them," the professors wrote.

Industry estimates have suggested that the primary stars of "Teen Mom" received more than $60,000, as well as other commercial considerations. In contrast, nearly half of all teen mothers fail to earn a high school diploma and earn an average of $6,500 annually over their first 15 years of parenthood.

Students in the study attended schools that were chosen because demographically, the median annual household income and racial makeup of each school was consistent with the national average: $52,000 and 80 percent white. Participants ranged in age from 14 to 18. There were nearly even numbers of boys and girls.

Eighty percent of the young men said they never watched "16 and Pregnant" or "Teen Mom," but 58 percent of the young women reported they sometimes or always watched the shows.

Interestingly, the impact of exposure to these programs affected young men and women similarly. Even though more young women than men watched the shows, the effect between exposure and perceptions remained significant when gender was statistically controlled.

"This study makes a valuable contribution because it links exposure to specific content—teen mom reality programming—to teens' perceptions of teen motherhood," the professors concluded. "While it would be inappropriate to suggest that viewing these programs is the cause of teen pregnancy, one might consider it a contributing factor."

Critical Thinking

1. How has reality TV changed our lives?
2. To what extent could reality TV contribute to an adolescent choosing to become pregnant?

Internet References

Does Reality TV Misrepresent Teen Parenthood?
http://www.npr.org/2011/08/16/139676173/does-reality-tv-misrepresent-teen-parenthood

How MTV's "16 and Pregnant" Led to Declining Teen Birth Rates
https://www.washingtonpost.com/news/arts-and-entertainment/wp/2014/04/09/how-mtvs-16-and-pregnant-led-to-declining-teen-birth-rates/?utm_term=.952329aa8ca7

How "Teen Mom" Affects Teen Pregnancy
http://www.livescience.com/42535-teen-mom-pregnancy-reality-tv.html

Reality Television and Teenage Pregnancy Tuned in, Turned Off
http://www.economist.com/blogs/democracyinamerica/2014/01/reality-television-and-teenage-pregnancy

The Price of Teen Pregnancy and the Influence of Reality TV
http://jjie.org/2011/09/21/price-of-teen-pregnancy-reality-shows-influence-teen-pregnancy-rates/

Unit 6

UNIT

Prepared by: Claire N. Rubman, *Suffolk County Community College*

The Context of Adolescence in Society

How do our adolescents interact in society? As they begin to enter the work force and drive on our roads, they get a taste of adult life. Perhaps it depends on how we have taught them. Gary and Kimberly Embree (2016) offer suggestions in their article "Training Teens to Drive." My mother-in-law always used to say to me "little children, little problems—big children, big problems." This was made crystal clear to me the day my son turned 16 and the keys to the family car became a major focus in our lives. How do you prepare your child to be safe on the roads and highways? Read the advice that the Embree parents give about teaching your teen to drive. They suggest that you begin with a personal inventory of your own good and bad habits in the car. They remind us that, like so much in life, we are our child's first, and most often inadvertent, teacher. Do we demonstrate good driving habits, for example, do we wait patiently at intersections and keep our hands on the steering wheel as we were taught? Where is our cell phone when we drive? What is our emotional state? Bandura's Social Learning Theory (1977) suggests that our children learn vicariously form us. The power of observational learning suggests that we should model good driving habits for our children long before they apply

for their driver's permit. Read the Embree's other road tips in "Training Teens to Drive."

Driving can be expensive between the cost of a car, gas, and insurance, so who should pay those bills? Some parents expect their adolescent children to work and pay for their own costs. According to Harrington and Khatiwada (2016), while most teens want to work, only about 27 percent were actually employed in 2014.

If you are one of the lucky teens who found employment, what should you expect to earn? Should you earn the same as an adult who is doing the same job? Would lowering adolescent pay, as Battles and Watkins (2016) suggest, increase potential employment opportunities for teens?

When teens are not gainfully employed they have a great deal more free time. Some choose to spend much of that time online. According to Strom and Strom (2012), this can have potentially negative outcomes including excessive or hypertexting, that is, more than 120 messages per day. If you could eve's drop on those texts and online conversations, what would you hear? Nancy Jo Sales (2016) did exactly that! She listened to over 200 teens talk about their social issues. Read about what she learned in her interviews titled "Peggy Sue Got Sexted."

Article   Prepared by: Claire N. Rubman, *Suffolk County Community College*

Training Teens to Drive

Parents are the single most important teachers in training teens to be safe, responsible drivers.

GARY EMBREE AND KIMBERLY EMBREE

Learning Outcomes

After reading this article, you will be able to:

- Describe how to look for a good driving instructor.
- Check your personal driving habits to ensure that you are a good role model for an adolescent driver.

Few things strike fear into parents' hearts like handing the car keys to their teens for the first time. In the interest of giving home-educating parents the tools they need to purposefully prepare their teens for the enormous responsibility of driving, we offer the following advice gleaned from our experience as parents, home-educators, and driving school operators. Knowing that God has not given us a spirit of fear, but of power and of love and of a sound mind (2 Timothy 1:7), we hope to provide you with practical ideas that will help you and your teen faithfully travel the road to responsible driving.

Given the enormous lifestyle differences across the United States, we acknowledge that not all of the tips presented will be applicable for every family. Children from farming families have likely been introduced to driving trucks and tractors from an early age, while children residing in densely populated cities may rely on public transit and not have the option of driving as teens. That said, this article most closely addresses the situation of suburban families, with guidance for preparing future drivers during the early years of childhood, training teen drivers, assessing professional instruction, and incorporating driver education into a homeschool curriculum.

Preparation in the Early Years

As with all aspects of child development, driving skills are heavily influenced by parental role models. Our children have been soaking up our good and bad driving habits all their lives.

Take an honest inventory of yourself as a driver. Are you familiar with the rules of the road? Do you stop behind the limit line and come to a full, complete stop at stop signs or do you coast? Are you looking over your shoulder and signaling every time you change lanes or merge into traffic? Is your cell phone safely stowed away or are you glancing at text messages? Do you have a habit of speeding or of accelerating through intersections when the light is yellow? Do you drive when you're tired or overly emotional? Do you keep both hands on the wheel at 10:00 and 2:00 and make careful, hand-over-hand turns? Time and again, we observe the habits of parents in the default driving behavior of the teens that come to our driving school for behind-the-wheel lessons. As you identify areas of personal weakness, be mindful to make corrections and communicate with your children about the Lord's conviction and your desire to model safe driving practices. As Paul admonishes in Philippians 3:17, let us lead our children in Christ-like behavior in this endeavor.

Another way to prepare your children for success as drivers is to limit screen time for young teens while they are passengers in the car. The ubiquitous nature of handheld electronic devices and in-car entertainment systems has undermined development of observation skills. Are your young teens aware of their surroundings? Can they navigate between familiar landmarks and locations in your hometown by memory? During driving lessons, Gary often asks teens to drive to their homes from a point within a mile of their address. Many teens have no idea where they are within this mile radius and cannot drive to, or give directions to, their homes. You may consider creating a game to develop neighborhood and regional awareness by asking your child to serve as your in-car navigational system and give you turn-by-turn directions the next time you are headed to the local market.

Finally, throughout childhood, promote activities that develop gross motor skills, hand-eye coordination, and observation abilities. Generally speaking, in 20 years of training teen drivers, we have observed that student athletes swiftly acquire safe driving skills while those exclusively dedicated to video gaming and other more screen intensive or tunnel-vision pursuits (reading, sewing, etc.) struggle with basic driving skills. Although this is a completely anecdotal observation, it has been a consistent one among teens from all kinds of family and educational backgrounds and across age and gender variables. There is something about identifying where you are in space during a game and interacting with moving teammates, as well as objects that are flung or kicked about you that translates to handling a motor vehicle well.

Training Teens

Depending on your teen's maturity level, several years to several months before your teen is eligible to obtain a driver's license, you can begin training them to be defensive drivers. To begin with, when you and your teen are traveling in the car together, narrate the drive. What potential hazards are around you? Are there pedestrians nearby? Are children or animals playing in the area? Is a distracted driver in the lane near you? Is there road construction or repairs up ahead? Do you hear sirens blaring from approaching emergency vehicles? As time goes on, ask your teen to narrate. Gently point out the hazards your teen fails to notice, compliment correct identification, and discuss the appropriate response to various scenarios. What should you do if the child you saw at the end of the street darted into the road to chase a pet or toy? What route should you take to remove yourself from the vicinity of a distracted driver who may rear end you or swerve into your lane? How can you best maneuver to the side of the road to allow emergency vehicles to pass? Keep in mind that your responses to these hazards are largely ingrained after years of driving experience, but your teen lacks the subconscious autopilot function you have developed. Observation is the first step in the process of building defensive driving skills.

When your teen obtains a learner's permit from your state and is ready to take the wheel of your family car with you as a passenger, designate your teen as your personal chauffer. Build extra time allotments into your scheduled errands and commutes to church, co-op classes, or extracurricular activities so that you and your teen are not pressured to beat the clock to arrive on time. Make sure that you are giving your teen valuable behind the wheel practice in every possible situation: heavy traffic during commute times, in the dark and in all sorts of weather conditions, and traveling both familiar and unknown routes to destinations. Avoid limiting your teen, such as only allowing driving back and forth to church in the early morning, and be wary of falling into the rut of driving the same routes at the same times. If possible, incorporate training into a family road trip or vacation to give your teen extended time driving on the freeway with semis roaring by, or on curvy mountain, dirt, or gravel roads. The idea is to create as many experiences as possible for your teen while you are in the car to guide and encourage. Over time, encountering and working through diverse and challenging experiences will develop your teen's knowledge and confidence and build the stamina necessary to remain alert and aware behind the wheel.

When Your Teen Obtains a Driver's License

Part of the process of letting our fledglings fly from the nest in our modern culture is allowing them to drive unsupervised once they have passed their driver's license examination and demonstrated sufficient maturity for the responsibility. When that time arrives, sit down with your teen for an adult conversation about the obligations that accompany the privilege of driving a motor vehicle. Each family possesses its own set of values and expectations for teens. Some parents draw up a contract with driving privileges awarded for completion of household duties or withheld for misbehavior. Others require teens to earn money to contribute financially for car maintenance, registration, insurance, and fuel costs. Some teens take on the task of building or buying their own car, while others simply learn how to check tire pressure, change a car engine's oil, or replace a flat tire.

Plan for the time when your teen will drive away from your home alone. Pray, seeking the Lord for protection of your teen and peace for your heart. Establish a protocol that will grant you peace of mind, by instructing your teen to call or text you when they have safely arrived at their destination and/or when they are headed back home, so that you may estimate a reasonable time frame for their return. Discuss with your teen how to handle an unfortunate accident, even role playing as another driver involved in a collision or as a peace officer taking a statement at the scene of an accident. What should your teen do if the other driver is angry or obviously impaired? What if there are injuries? Does your teen know where the vehicle registration and proof of insurance are stored in your vehicle? Help your teen be savvy about how to trade insurance information after a minor fender bender, what to say—and not say—at the scene of an accident, and proper conduct if there are injuries and/or property damage.

If your teen is involved in an accident, whether minor or major, it is important to acknowledge and empathize with their fears, trepidation, and any other associated emotions. At the same time, it is vital to give any warranted correction or additional training while getting your teen "back in the saddle" as soon as possible. While it may be necessary to take a step back and ride shotgun with your teen for a bit, make sure you build their confidence back up and demonstrate by your words and behavior that accidents are exceptions, not the rule, so that your teen does not become paralyzed by a mistake or frightening experience. Remind them that their Heavenly Father goes before them and is hemming them in just as He did Joshua: *"And the Lord, He it is that doth go before thee; He will be with thee, He will not fail thee, neither forsake thee: fear not, neither be dismayed"* (Deuteronomy 31:8).

Professional Instruction: What to Look For

While parents are the single most important teachers in training teens to be safe, responsible drivers, professional instruction is helpful to parents in guiding their teens and is often required by state law. For instance, professional driving instructors in the State of California are required to pursue ongoing education annually to maintain their state-issued licenses. Licensed California driving schools are also notified by the Department of Motor Vehicles about any new laws or changes to required paperwork and bureaucratic processes for new drivers, which are not always known by the general public. Aligning yourself with a professional school may gain you tips for teaching and save you a lot of aggravation as your teen applies for a license. When searching for a professional driving school, first ask your friends and acquaintances who are also parents of teens for referrals. Develop a list of options, and make sure the schools are licensed by your state's Department of Motor Vehicles. Speak with a school's representative not only to determine pricing and availability of lessons, but to discover the philosophy of instruction.

Beware of schools that focus on quantity over quality, trying to move teens through the training program solely for the sake of satisfying state requirements with little regard for teens' actual development as safe drivers. For instance, some schools have no qualms about booking several lessons within a week or month's span. Cramming lessons into such a limited period is equivalent to repeating the first lesson multiple times. It is essential that teens be practicing in between their lessons, in order to solidify skills as they are introduced. Ask the school about the age and experience of the driving instructor who will work with your teen as well as the age and condition of the training vehicle. If for any reason you feel uncomfortable or pressured, look for another alternative. If you are unable to find an instructor with sterling references and are concerned about risk to your teen's well-being, ask the school if they will allow you to ride in the back seat as a quiet observer while your teen receives instruction, at least for the first lesson.

Incorporating Drivers' Ed into Your Curriculum

As with so many other life skills, it is a simple matter of recording and documenting studies and hours spent practicing to grant high school credit for teen driver education and training. In California, teens younger than the age of 17.5 are required to complete a 30-hour driver education class in order to obtain a certificate required when applying for a learner's permit. Our school, like many others, offers an online course for teens to easily meet this requirement. Time spent on each class unit is electronically stamped, and quiz scores are recorded, a helpful resource for home-educating parents in particular. Upon receiving a learner's permit, California teens then must take six hours of training with a professional driving instructor and log 50 hours of driving practice with a licensed driver age 25 or older, ten of those hours at night. You can determine your state's requirements by obtaining a driver handbook from your local DMV branch or by visiting your state's DMV website. Beyond actual driver education and training as a high school homeschool course, depending on your resources, you could certainly expand studies to include an auto shop course or incorporate driver's education into a Life Skills course and require your teen to obtain auto insurance quotes, create auto maintenance logs, shop for a used car, etc.

Throughout the process of training your teen to be a safe, responsible driver, relax. Trust your heavenly Father to guide you and your teen through the process. Speaking from experience, as the frequency of white-knuckled excursions down the street subside and your teens grow in skill and confidence, driver training will give you sweet times together. Enjoy the fleeting time before they drive away into adulthood, knowing that you have done your best to equip them as skilled, defensive drivers.

Critical Thinking

1. Suggest three other "life skills" associated with driving that are not required but that might be useful for adolescents, that is, insurance quotes or autoshop education.

2. If you could reinvent driver's ed.—what would you do differently?

3. Develop a list of 10 tips for parents of younger children to encourage more awareness of the road and driving.

Internet References

CDC Teen Drivers
https://www.cdc.gov/motorvehiclesafety/teen_drivers/

Expert Advice for Parents about Teen Driving
https://www.edmunds.com/car-safety/expert-advice-for-parents-about-teen-driving.html

Parents Are the Key to Safe Teen Drivers
https://www.cdc.gov/parentsarethekey/

Teen Driving—Tips for New Drivers
http://teendriving.com/

Teens' Biggest Safety Threat Is Sitting on the Driveway
http://www.nsc.org/learn/NSC-Initiatives/Pages/teen-driving.aspx

GARY EMBREE AND KIMBERLY EMBREE reside in the Sacramento suburbs of Northern California, where they own and operate Freedom Driving School. This home-based business supplements Gary's salary as a public school teacher, allowing Kimberly the privilege of home educating their three middle and high school aged children. Gary has been training teens to drive since their oldest son, now a college sophomore, was an infant. Both spend a lot of time guiding teens, Gary as the faculty advisor to his school's Bible Club and as a leader of their church's annual youth mission trip to Mexico, and Kimberly as a coach for a competitive speech and debate club. In rare moments of spare time, Gary is an avid golfer and fly-fisherman while Kimberly enjoys reading and experiencing the arts.

Article   Prepared by: Claire N. Rubman, *Suffolk County Community College*

Is It Fair to Pay Teens Less Than Adults

BOB BATTLES AND MARILYN WATKINS

Learning Outcomes

After reading this article, you will be able to:

- Give three reasons why teens should earn the same as adults for the same job.
- Give three reasons why lower teen pay would be beneficial to society.

Young people face the highest unemployment rate of all age groups in the United States. The Bureau of Labor Statistics reports that 15 percent of 16- to 19-year-olds who are actively looking for work can't find jobs. Some lawmakers believe they have a fix: lowering the minimum wage for teens, to encourage businesses to hire them. In Washington state, lawmakers are debating a bill that would lower the minimum wage for anyone under 20 to $8.05 an hour, compared with $9.47 an hour for adults. A similar measure is in effect in Michigan, and another is being considered in South Dakota.

Yes

You need experience to get hired, but unless you get hired, you can't get experience.

Many young people across the country face this dilemma. A lower minimum wage for teens would encourage businesses to hire them. That would give teens more opportunities to gain work experience and learn valuable life and career skills, such as the importance of showing up to work on time and how to be professional and reliable.

Federal law limits what teens can do while on the job. At grocery stores, for example, teens under 18 can bag goods, but they aren't allowed to operate a cardboard-box compactor.

When young people can't do parts of the job, employers have to hire someone else to do those tasks. If there are going to be legal restrictions on what teens can do, then it makes sense that their pay is lower as well.

Plus, your average teen doesn't have the same kinds of skills that workers in, say, their 20s have. When employers have to pay everyone the same starting wage, it often makes more sense for them to hire older, more-skilled workers instead of teens.

But a high youth unemployment rate is bad for society. Research shows that unemployed teens are more likely to drop out of high school and become involved with the criminal justice system. Studies have also found that students with part-time jobs are more likely to earn higher wages in the future compared with their classmates who don't work.

The bottom line is that lowering the minimum wage for teens makes it easier for them to find jobs. And putting all Americans back to work will ultimately help improve our nation's economy.

No

Why should a worker get paid less simply because he or she happens to be a teenager? If they're performing the same tasks as a 20-year-old, they should earn the same amount of money.

Teens often need jobs as much as any other workers. Many have to work to help support their families. Others live on their own or are trying to save money for college. In recent years, the cost of higher education has skyrocketed. According to the College Board, average tuition and fees at four-year public colleges and universities has increased by 40 percent–or nearly $3,000–since 2006. If teens are forced to accept lower wages, it will be even harder for them to afford college. And research shows that people who have graduated from college typically earn higher wages.

Young people aren't the only ones who would be affected by creating a lower teen wage. It could also displace older workers. Employers might prefer to hire a rotating series of teens because it would be cheaper.

There's already a lot of pay inequality in the United States. For example, the Bureau of Labor Statistics estimates that women earn on average about 78 cents for every dollar a man makes. We shouldn't pass laws that reinforce wage discrimination—especially when there's little evidence to suggest that businesses would be more likely to hire teens if they could pay them less than adults.

There's also a broader economic reason not to pay teens less. The health of the U.S. economy depends heavily on consumer spending, and teens spend more than $250 billion a year. If young people earn less money, they won't spend as much. That's bad for the economy.

Every hardworking American deserves fair compensation, and that includes teens. After all, isn't paying people an honest wage for honest work a fundamental American value?

Teen Workers by the Numbers

31 Percent
PERCENTAGE of 16- to 19-year-olds who worked during the summer of 2014, down from 63 percent in 2000. Teen employment peaks in the summer and falls the rest of the year.
Source: PEW RESEARCH CENTER

24 Percent
PERCENTAGE of 16- to 19-year-old workers who had full-time jobs in 2014. Most teen workers have part-time jobs.
Source: BUREAU OF LABOR STATISTICS

3.5 Million
NUMBER of jobs held by 14- to 18-year-olds in 2014, down from 5.2 million in 2001.
Source: CAREERBUILDER

Critical Thinking

1. Imagine that you are an employer; describe two advantages and two disadvantages of hiring adolescents at your company.

2. Imagine that you are a U.S. lawmaker. Make the case for lowering teen wages.

Internet References

First Job Means First Bills: 4 Expenses Your Teen Can Pay For
http://www.doughmain.com/pub/first-job-means-first-bills-4-expenses-your-teen-can-pay-for/

How Much Money Does the Average Teen Earn Through Summer Jobs?
http://work.chron.com/much-money-average-teen-earn-through-summer-jobs-3446.html

Should Teens Earn Less Than Adults?
http://choices.scholastic.com/story/should-teens-earn-less-adults

What Every Teen Needs to Know about Getting Paid at Work
https://www.aol.com/article/2014/05/27/what-every-teen-needs-to-know-about-getting-paid-at-work/20875851/

Article   Prepared by: Claire N. Rubman, *Suffolk County Community College*

The Benefits and Limitations of Social Networking

PARIS STROM AND ROBERT STROM

Learning Outcomes

After reading this article, you will be able to:

- Explain the term "hypertexters."

- Describe some of the potential benefits of spending more time with adults instead of social media.

Studies that evaluate the influence of blogs on student attitudes, behaviors, and motivation have yet to emerge. However, these benefits can be anticipated:

- When children share their impressions, reciprocal learning can occur.
- There may be a sense of assurance in confirming personal views are shared.
- Dialogues and debates are welcomed by teens whose conversations with adults may offer little opportunity to express opinions and challenge logic.
- Communicating with age mates from other backgrounds yields appreciation for cultural diversity that may not be represented at the school students attend.

The following guidelines for online users support civil dialogue and safety:

1. Do not share personal or private information.
2. Do not harass or threaten others.
3. Do not cyberstalk, spam, or send unwanted messages.
4. Do not insult other races, cultures, genders, sexual lifestyles, or religions.
5. Do not post, transmit, or distribute obscene, sexually explicit, vulgar, pornographic, ethnically offensive, or untrue content.
6. Do not solicit sexually explicit photos or text.
7. Do not post or transmit photographic violent images of youth.
8. Do not disrupt flow of blogs with abuse, repetitive posts, and off-topic content.
9. Do not impersonate anyone.
10. Do not steal a password, account data, or other information.
11. Do not post material created by others without direct permission and authorization.
12. Do not post advertising for goods and services.
13. Do not include URLs for sites that violate any of these rules.
14. Do not post anything inappropriate.

The Center for the Digital Future at the University of Southern California surveys 2,000 households each year to find out how online technology affects Internet users. Findings in the latest report show social networks are increasing and a majority of users report feeling as strongly about their communities online as their real-world communities. In fact, 75 percent report participating in communities related to social causes on the Internet. Nearly 90 percent are involved in social causes new to them since their involvement with online communities. The growth of online communities is creating a range of new sources for positive social change.

Some disadvantages of social networks deserve consideration. A majority of parents expressed discomfort about the increasing amount of time their children spent in online communities because it takes away from time spent with the family.

Excessive Texting

Texting while driving is seen as a dangerous form of multitasking for teenagers. Additional hazards may be related to excessive involvement with texting. Researchers at Case Western

Reserve School of Medicine surveyed 4,200 high school students to determine the association between use of communications technology and health behaviors. Results indicated excessive users of texting and social networking are much more likely to engage in unhealthy behaviors.

Being hypertexters, defined as texting 120 or more messages a day, was reported by 20 percent of the teenagers, many of whom were female, minority, low income, and did not have a father present at home. Survey outcomes showed that hypertexters are 40 percent more likely to have tried cigarettes than those who spend less time texting; 43 percent more likely to be binge drinkers; 41 percent more likely to engage in substance abuse; 55 percent more likely to have been in a physical fight; 3.5 times more likely to have had sex; and 90 percent more likely to report having had four or more sexual partners.

These findings suggest that, when texting and other forms of staying connected are not monitored by adults, there could be adverse health effects.

Excessive Social Networking

Hypernetworking adolescents, defined as spending three hours or more each day on social networking sites, is also risky. Of teens surveyed, about 12 percent reported spending over three hours a day social networking. This subpopulation was found to be 62 percent more likely to have tried cigarettes; 70 percent more likely to have tried alcohol; 69 percent more likely to have used illicit drugs; 94 percent more likely to have been in a physical fight; 69 percent more likely to have had sex; and 60 percent more likely to report having had four or more sexual partners.

Social Network Improvement

Robert Epstein, in *The Case Against Adolescence*, argues against blaming brain development as the primary cause for foolish risks taken by adolescents. Instead of tracing poor judgment to a delayed rate of brain growth in the frontal cortex, he suggests placing more attention on the 24/7 immersion within a peer culture facilitated by cell phones and the Internet. Many youth are in contact with friends 70 hours a week but may lack meaningful contact with important adults in their lives. Some spend only brief periods with parents and often it is time watching television, eating, or checking in by phone. Epstein argues that adolescents are infantilized by our culture, causing isolation from adults and motivating them to communicate almost entirely with their peers.

A potentially powerful solution is to increase the amount of time students spend with relatives, allowing them to join the adult world in as many ways as possible. This requires adults to

have a different way of looking at youth, recognizing their capabilities and nurturing talents. More contact with trustworthy adults online and in person along with increasing responsibility is necessary to replace a strictly peer-driven communication environment. The trajectory for mutually beneficial relationships between adults and adolescents requires sustained interaction rather than permitting the Internet social sites limited to peers to substitute for dialogue within families. This need is illustrated by a three-generational study in Taiwan. A sample of 116 grandmothers were asked how often they communicated with their 116 adolescent granddaughters using any electronic medium. The answer given by 95 percent was "Never."

Finding ways to improve social networking of children should be assigned high priority. Here are some possibilities:

- Partnerships between schools and businesses to help explore careers.
- Students post recreational reading reactions for classmate consideration.
- Indigenous mentors answer student questions on aspects of their culture.
- A question and answer site on using the Internet to improve schoolwork.
- Enabling students learning a language to practice interacting with others.
- Having parents help children create profiles to go on social networks.
- Peer counseling as a source of guidance regarding concerns at school.
- A polling site where students inform adults about their concerns.
- Pen pals across national boundaries through matching mutual interests.
- A support group for children facing similar challenges led by counselors.
- School chat rooms by grade level for students monitored by counselors.
- A site with volunteer options for children often excluded because of age.
- A place for children to display drawings or pictures and obtain feedback.
- An online book club where children share literature they read.

Critical Thinking

1. Suggest three ways to encourage adolescents to spend less time on social media.

2. Explain why teens are so attracted to the Internet and social media.

Internet References

Just One Hour a Day on Social Media Makes Teens Miserable

http://www.nbcnews.com/business/consumer/just-one-hour-day-social-media-makes-teens-miserable-n700786

Teens Addicted to Social Media

http://www.huffingtonpost.com/judith-johnson/teens-addicted-to-social-_b_9696378.html

Social Networking for Teens

https://www.commonsensemedia.org/lists/social-networking-for-teens

Teens, Social Media & Technology Overview 2015

http://www.pewinternet.org/2015/04/09/teens-social-media-technology-2015/

Teens: This is how social media affects your brain

http://www.cnn.com/2016/07/12/health/social-media-brain/

PARIS STROM is a professor at Auburn (AL) University.

ROBERT STROM is a professor at Arizona State University, Tempe. Condensed, with permission, from the Child Research Network. Read the article in its entirety at www.childresearch.net.

Article   Prepared by: Claire N. Rubman, *Suffolk County Community College*

Peggy Sue Got Sexted

For her new book, Nancy Jo Sales spoke to 200 teen girls. The takeaway: Many of them feel constantly harassed about sex.

NINA BURLEIGH

Learning Outcomes

After reading this article, you will be able to:

- Explain the term "moral panic" in the context of online communications.

- Explain the "harassment" that teens sense from social media.

Nancy Jo Sales has a special gift: the ability to talk—really talk—to teenagers. From New York City rap hipsters to the notorious, fame-obsessed teen burglars that Sales dubbed "the Bling Ring," the author and veteran journalist can get teenagers to open up about almost anything.

For her new book, *American Girls: Social Media and the Secret Lives of Teenagers*, Sales spent two years on the road listening to over 200 teenage girls talk about what plagues them today. Sales, the mother of a high school freshman, has delivered a harrowing compendium of anecdotes about coming of age in an era of mainstream sexualization, slut shaming, online porn, and cyberbullying. She spoke to *Newsweek* about why she wrote the book and what she learned about preparing teen girls—including her own—to grow up female online.

Q. Where did you grow up, and what kind of a teenage life did you have?
A. I grew up in Miami in the 1970s. I loved my parents; my parents loved me. I went to a good public high school. I grew up in this unusually diverse atmosphere, all sexual orientations and all colors—people who followed gurus, hippies. It was good, but what I remember was that my mother always had this very strong sense of what was age-appropriate for children. I really was schooled in that concept from her: Certain things are OK at certain times.

Q. What is the biggest difference between Female American Teenage-hood in the 1970s and now?
A. Nobody is saying kids haven't always been interested in sex—we all were—but I think what's different is that access to pornography has changed how kids view sex in a big way. If you had asked me two years ago, "What do you think of porn?" I would have said, "Whatever, live and let live." I really have a different view now that I have looked at it. Gonzo porn is the most popular version, and it's very degrading to women.

We know from studies that porn influences girls' views of themselves and their bodies. This is a huge, huge change. The way this relates to social media is that online culture is influenced by this porn aesthetic—Tumblr is almost like a porn site. Also, iPhones. My book is about porn-plus-iPhone. It is changing childhood and teenage life.

Q. Are you sure you don't just feel the same generational difference that parents in the 1960s felt about their kids and free love, or their grandparents felt about making out in cars?
A. I hear that all the time. "Oh, it's always been that way, it's just *moral panic.*" I am sorry, but there should be a word for the opposite impulse of moral panic—maybe there's a German word for it. It's denial. Sure, the car was once considered a dangerous thing because kids could drive off and neck. Well, now you can be doing an approximation of that in math class. You can be sexting at school, [watching] porn at school. It used to be that Saturday night, you might have an experience. Now, it can happen all the time. It happens when you open your eyes in the morning and get sexted. The constancy of it—we can ask, Is it healthy?

Q. You have a daughter. Do you monitor her social media life and phone?
A. I feel really lucky because when I started doing the first story on this for *Vanity Fair*, she was only 12 and didn't have

a phone yet. I was able to learn about all these things and start having this ongoing conversation with her. We talk about this every day. She tells me about things that are going on in her peer group. It's something you have to talk to them about. Like, what happened in school today? What happened on social media today?

Q. Will you talk about how social media affects consent and body image?
A. A lot of social media is posting provocative pictures. These girls are styling themselves to a porn aesthetic, and there are sexual comments. It's all about likes; it's all about the validation. The one thing that's different from when we were kids is there's a number on your popularity and everyone knows it. What gets a lot of likes is you in a bikini. And then so-called "slutpages" are in every school I went to [during reporting], and there's a sexting ring in every school. These are amateur porn sites. There's a whole minimizing thing that goes on, like, "It's just a prank." But it leads to terrible cyberbullying and sometimes suicide. The pictures are like Pokémon cards to the boys, who use them to jerk off or as a trophy.

This is a cultural phenomenon. I began to see how deeply entrenched this is in the lives of teenage girls. I was not aware of it, and I felt so bad for them, that they were trying to deal with this. And the boys too, because "bro" culture is boy culture, and boys are overwhelmed. It's also really homophobic. It's not just sexist.

So What's the Takeaway?

More than 200 girls in my book agree that there is a lot of harassment. They are pressured into sexualizing themselves; they are more vulnerable to cyberbullying. People need to know that these girls are concerned. More than half of the book is in their voices—it's one thing to hear an adult say it; it's another thing to hear a kid say it.

We have to change this culture. We cannot have a generation of girls growing up like this. We have to have a conversation about porn—parents can't be afraid to say, "Nope, you are not doing that." Schools can institute sessions where kids can talk to each other about this, so it's not like an adult telling you what to think. It might be useful for sessions to be single-sex and then join them together. Some of the best conversations I had were when the girls started talking to each other. They said, "We never talk about this." The law hasn't caught up to the technology. Girls are so vulnerable to having these pictures passed around. They know this is out there, and they have this incredible feeling of threat that has got to be addressed. Only a small percentage of boys will rape, but a lot more will press a button and send a picture. It's e-rape.

Critical Thinking

1. Thinking about adolescents and social media, what can be done to reduce harassment and cyberbullying?

2. Develop three ways to help adolescent girls to avoid the social pressure of oversexualizing themselves on social media.

Internet References

Cyberbullying
http://kidshealth.org/en/teens/cyberbullying.html
Pew Research Center Cyberbullying
http://www.pewinternet.org/2007/06/27/cyberbullying/
Teen Cyberbullying and Harassment
http://www.criminaldefenselawyer.com/resources/teen-cyberbullying-and-harassment.htm
Teenagers in America: Oversexualized and Undervalued
http://www.all.org/teenagers-in-america-oversexualized-and-undervalued/
The Sexualization of Women and Girls
https://www.psychologytoday.com/blog/overcoming-child-abuse/201203/the-sexualization-women-and-girls

Unit 7

UNIT

Prepared by: Claire N. Rubman, *Suffolk County Community College*

Behaviors and Challenges Associated with Adolescence

As we encourage our adolescents to interact in society, so we see problems emerging. How does the developing adolescent brain cope with challenging situations and peer pressure?

Firger (2016) looks at Internet challenges such as "#Fire-SprayChallenge" and discusses why adolescents would even consider setting themselves on fire. She also looks at other dangerous Internet challenges that have resulted in poisonings or worse such as eating a spoon of cinnamon or pouring vodka into your open eyes.

Firger looks at the role of peer pressure, the hormone dopamine, and the developing adolescent brain in "#No Dare Too Stupid."

It is not just the Internet that poses a problem for sensation seeking adolescents, read about the increase in "pill parties" and the dangers that they create. Read about the tragic death of Corey Suazo after a "pharm party." Known as the "Ritalin generation," these teens bring their own supply of prescription or OTC pills to "skittle parties." Research suggests that over 70 percent of these pills are from friends or relatives.

Smoking is also an issue in adolescence. Although cigarette use is on the decline, e-cigarettes, hookahs, and the use of other nicotine products are on the rise. Read about the effects of these products on the developing adolescent brain. Learn about pending FDA legislation that would restrict the use of nicotine related products to persons over 18-years old.

The same adolescent brain that craves e-cigarettes, online dares, or pharm parties is often susceptible to extreme ideologies. Unfortunately, a small percentage of our adolescents fall prey to radicalization. Whether they are lonely, disenfranchised, or disengaged, they can become enamored with the idea of martyrdom. Read about three Muslim teenagers who flew from England to Turkey to join ISIS in "What Are They Looking For?" by Catherine Jackson (2015). How do we identify our most

vulnerable adolescents in our community who may be seeking attention, affection, romance, or validation? Read about the climate that is most likely to breed extremists according to Professor Bhui at the University of London, England. Learn about successful interventions. Read an alternative point of view on adolescent vulnerability as Vicki Coppock warns of the dangers of "problematizing" normal adolescent behaviors.

Radicalization is extreme and rare but what happens to our disenfranchised students who don't play by society's rules? Who are these teens and what are their crimes? Read about poor, often minority or learning-disabled students who sometimes end up in jail if they misbehave in school. In the Meridian Public School District, this is known as the "school to prison pipeline." This "taxi service" was for offenses that were as minor as uniform infractions or chewing gum. Delinquent high school students were labeled as potential "superpredators." They were characterized in William Bennett's 1996 book titled "Body Count" as "criminalized and radically impulsive, brutally remorseless youngster with little regard for human life." It appears that the mass shooting at Columbine high school in 1999 fueled a fear of students and an escalation of punishment. It would appear, however, according to Owens (2015), that African American and minority students were suspended or expelled at three times the rate of their white counterparts. Even at the preschool level, more African American 4- and 5-year olds were suspended—48 percent of all African American preschool children were suspended but they only accounted for 18 percent of the total preschool population according to the U.S. Department of Education's Office for Civil Rights. Read more about the criminalization of students in Owen's article titled "How Prison Stints Replaced Study Hall" (2015). Learn about her gentler approach to discipline within our educational system.

Article   Prepared by: Claire N. Rubman, *Suffolk County Community College*

#NODARETOOSTUPID

The teenage brain is primed to take any social media challenge, no matter how half-baked or dangerous.

JESSICA FIRGER

Learning Outcomes

After reading this article, you will be able to:

- Discuss what is happening in the adolescent brain that encourages such risky and dangerous behavior.

- Explain the concept of "social maturity."

What would happen if you took a can of aerosol hairspray or air freshener and sprayed it directly at a cigarette lighter's flame? Any rational adult is likely to say, *Nothing good.* But if you're a teen, you might think, *Great snap!*

Since mid-March, social media outlets have been flooded with videos of young people creating blowtorch-size dragon-breath puffs of fire by putting flame into contact with flammable liquid (usually while indoors). It began when one teen Instagram user gave the stunt a try and tagged the video post #FireSprayChallenge.

The online dare spread rapidly, and now there are over 4,000 posts on Instagram with the #FireSprayChallenge hashtag. The daring feat is an offshoot of the #FireChallenge, another popular and even more dangerous social media craze that involves dousing oneself with a flammable liquid like rubbing alcohol, then lighting your torso or limbs on fire before jumping into a shower or pool. That challenge has resulted in a seemingly endless stream of reports of teens with third- or fourth-degree burns. Last year, an 11-year-old boy in the U.K. underwent a skin graft after the challenge went terribly wrong. A 15-year-old in Buffalo, New York, died from injuries he suffered after taking the dare. Fire safety divisions in several states have issued emergency warnings about the challenge.

Other popular and life-threatening social media challenges have prompted warnings from public health officials. The #CinnamonChallenge, which involves swallowing a tablespoon of the spice without any water, can lead to vomiting, choking and a trip to the ER. That dare became so popular that within the first three months of 2012, poison centers nationwide received 139 calls that involved cinnamon overdoses. A person who accepts the #Eraser-Challenge is required to take a pink eraser and rub it on his or her arm while saying a word for each letter of the alphabet. By the end, some have burns or deep cuts.

The list of the many and varied challenges teens take on from social media reads like a disturbing report from a torture chamber: have a friend douse you with boiling water, eat a Carolina Reaper (the world's hottest chili pepper), pour a bottle of vodka into your open eye, chew and swallow an entire cactus plant.

Attempting to grasp the motives behind the reckless stupidity of teenagers has been a frustrating endeavor for parents since the beginning of time, and many experts believe the Internet has made it even worse. In the good old days, parents typically felt they could maintain control over their misbehaving teen simply by limiting the time spent with peers who were a "bad influence." But thanks to social media, persuasive people with dumb ideas are now omnipresent and a mere click, tap or swipe away. Add in the appeal of 30 seconds of fame, and some teens are willing to try just about anything. In many cases, the more dangerous it is, the better.

Over the years, scientists have tried to better understand the biology behind risk-taking behavior in teens by studying young animals. Early experiments on rodents and nonhuman primates helped pinpoint critical neurochemical and cellular changes in the brain as it matures that may promote novelty- and sensation-seeking behaviors. Then, in the 1980s, magnetic resonance imaging became widely available. Because MRIs are safe to use (they don't expose a person to radiation), researchers were able to use them to scan the brains of healthy kids repeatedly, over a long period of time. Though the resulting data didn't confirm what parents often claim—that their teen has half a brain—it did show that critical neurological development does occur during teen years.

The brain is made up of two types of tissue: gray matter and white matter. White matter is composed mostly of nerve fibers responsible for transmitting the electric signals that ensure communication from one area of the brain to another. Gray matter is made mostly of neuronal cell bodies and dendrites—the thread-like segments of neurons that receive and send signals from other neurons—and is involved in thought processing and memory. By the age of 6, a person's brain is approximately 95 percent of its eventual adult size, but brain scans have indicated that in the following years, gray matter continues to grow in volume, with the most growth occurring during early adolescence.

As gray matter grows, so do the number of brain cells and connections between these cells, which shoot like rapid fire. This constant firing of synapses—the electric impulses that jump from neuron to neuron—is critical to learning and development. In the first few years of life, the brain acquires an abundance of these connections—more than it needs. Then, through learning, it begins to eliminate the weaker connections, a process known as synaptic pruning. Puberty marks the start of "specialization," says Dr. Jay Giedd, chairman of child and adolescent psychiatry at the University of California, San Diego. This is the point when the brain turns to weeding out its weakest remaining connections. At the same time, good and useful connections are strengthened. This process continues well beyond the college years.

Synaptic pruning is the reason young people have a much easier time learning new things, such as languages and driving. The problem, though, is that all of this is happening in the prefrontal cortex, the part of the brain sometimes referred to as the brain's CEO because it is responsible for big decisions, impulse control and the ability to reason (like a rational adult). "The part of the brain that wants to think things through, think of the consequences and think long term is still under construction well until their 20s," Giedd says.

The teen brain is compelled to seek out new experiences that help the brain learn, but teens don't yet have the tools to make rational choices. That's why accidents, drug use, unprotected sex, and other risky behaviors are much more common in young people, some experts say. According the National Institutes of Health, accidental deaths increase dramatically during early and late adolescence. Death by injury occurs at rates six times higher among teens 15 to 19, when compared with those 10 to 14.

Meanwhile, something else is also occurring around this time that makes young people more likely to get into trouble: puberty. As the body gears up for the changes that come with sexual maturity, it ramps up production of hormones—including

dopamine, the "feel good" neurotransmitter that increases when the brain's reward system is triggered. Whether the reward is food, sex, money, drugs, retweets, followers or Instagram likes, dopamine functions pretty much the same way. The biological need to feel good compels a person to behave in a way that will provide stimulus and reward. Research has shown that in order for the brain to commit something to memory, dopamine must be present, which essentially means it is needed for the brain to process important information such as *don't light yourself on fire or you might get burned.*

Because it's flooded with dopamine, the teen brain is driven to seek out constant stimuli and reward, says Laurence Steinberg, a professor of psychology at Temple University. "Things that feel good feel even better when you're a teenager," he says. So although a tablespoon of cinnamon in a teen's esophagus might be a miserable experience, the page views, likes and favorites that trigger a rush of dopamine after the teen posts the video mean the person may not care about the physical pain. "This combination of an easily aroused reward center and still slow to mature self-regulation system is what contributes to a lot of this risky behavior," Steinberg says.

Worse, social media use peaks just when sensation-seeking behavior starts. According to the American Academy of Child and Adolescent Psychiatry, over 60 percent of 13- to 17-year-olds have at least one social media network profile. In 2015, the Pew Research Center found that 92 percent of teens go online daily and that 24 percent are on "almost constantly." Teens reach "social maturity" by age 14 to 16, which is academic-speak for "this kid is on every single social media network"—including ones grown-ups probably don't even know about.

This greatly expands the opportunity for influence—Steinberg's research shows that when it comes to sensation-seeking behavior, teens are equally swayed by unknown peers (such as Instagram influencers) and IRL friends. In one study, published in *Developmental Science* in 2014, Steinberg and a research team divided 64 teens into two groups. The researchers asked all 64 the same questions regarding money rewards, such as "Would you rather have $500 today or $1,000 six months from now?"

However, Half of the participants also were tricked into thinking a peer of the same gender and similar background was watching them on a closed-circuit computer system. Steinberg's team found that people in the fake peer-observed group were consistently willing to accept 15 percent less money than those who were alone. "But we don't see that pattern for adults," Steinberg says.

Amanda Lenhart, a 16-year veteran at Pew, has found one-upmanship is a central part of online behavior for teens. In a 2014 survey that Lenhart helped run, 40 percent of teens said they feel pressure to post content on social media that will get lots of likes and comments. But Lenhart also argues that teenage bad behavior isn't unique to the digital age.

"In my high school, one of the Spirit Week challenges was called the Chubby Bunny challenge, where you were supposed to see how many marshmallows you could stick in your mouth," she says. Everyone did it, even though it was clearly unwise. "And I went to high school before the Internet, before social media was widely available."

Critical Thinking

1. Suggest three ways to make the Internet a safer place for adolescents.

2. Imagine that you had an adolescent son or daughter—how would you address Internet challenges such as #FireSprayChallenge?

Internet References

Danger Ahead: Social Media Dare Games
https://netsanity.net/danger-ahead-social-media-dare-games/

Here's How the "Blue Whale" Suicide Game Is Killing Teens on Social Media
http://iheartintelligence.com/2017/02/22/blue-whale-suicide-game-social-media/

Know! The Dangers of Digital Dares
https://www.revereschools.org/cms/lib/OH01001097/Centricity/Domain/1/digital%20dares.pdf

Viral Internet Trends: A Parent's Guide
http://parentinfo.org/article/viral-internet-trends-a-parents-guide

Why Teenagers Get Suckered in by Social Media Dares
http://www.newsweek.com/2016/05/27/teens-social-media-dares-459419.html

Article   Prepared by: Claire N. Rubman, *Suffolk County Community College*

Pharming: Pill Parties Can Be Deadly for Teens

Adolescents today are playing a dangerous game of pill roulette with prescription painkillers and over-the-counter drugs. Here's how pediatricians can recognize this risky behavior and what they can do to stem a growing national epidemic.

SUSAN SOLECKI AND RENEE TURCHI

Learning Outcomes

After reading this article, you will be able to:

- Explain the concept of "pharming" or "skittling."
- Describe what "robo tripping" involves.

How can something that is prescribed by a doctor, or available for purchase without a prescription at Wal-Mart and Walgreens, be so bad or cause such devastating problems for teenagers? Unfortunately, Corey Suazo, a 17-year-old high school student had been to a "pharm" party before he died. Cocaine and the painkiller OxyContin were found in his system. A pharm party is similar to a bring-your-own-bottle party, except kids substitute pills for bottles. Kids bring whatever they can get their hands on and they may not be sure about what they have. The pills are thrown into a communal bowl and the participants grab handfuls to consume, often washing them down with alcohol. They wait for what's next, which may be death. One could call it prescription roulette.[1]

Introduction

Unauthorized use of pharmaceutical and over-the-counter (OTC) drugs by teenagers is a growing national problem.[2] This latest trend in drug abuse by adolescents is called *pharming*, or the nonmedical use of prescription and OTC cough and cold medications.[3] It is a concerning risky behavior that allows for the ability to get high with disregard for the type of drug that is being ingested, often along with alcohol.[4]

Pharming parties may also be referred to as "Skittles parties" or "skittling" by comparing the pill-popping behavior with the small hard candies that come in multiple colors and flavors.[4] "Robo-tripping," referencing the cough suppressant Robitussin, is the abuse of cough medications containing dextromethorphan, in which the cough syrup, often left over from earlier illnesses, is drunk alone or in combination with other substances to obtain a high.

The purpose of this article is to explore the risk-taking behaviors of adolescents who engage in pharming parties; the effects that pharming parties, with indiscriminate use of prescription and nonprescription drugs, have on children and teenagers; and the approaches that healthcare providers (HCPs) can employ to guide young persons and their families to prevent negative outcomes from this growing epidemic.

Surge in Prescription and Nonprescription Drug Use

Nearly 50 percent of all Americans take at least 1 prescription medication.[5] The quantity of prescription painkillers sold to pharmacies, hospitals, and doctors' offices quadrupled in a little over a decade, from 1999 to 2010.[6] In 2010, enough prescription analgesics were prescribed to medicate every American adult around the clock for one month. The federal Substance Abuse and Mental Health Services Administration

(SAMHSA) reports that after marijuana, prescription medications are the drugs most commonly abused by the adolescent population with the biggest growth of abuse among persons aged 12 to 24 years.[5] Alarmingly, the abuse of prescription and OTC medications has surpassed the use of illegal drugs such as crack, cocaine, ecstasy, and heroin. An estimated 14 percent of high school seniors have used prescription drugs for nonmedical reasons at least once.

Students report that prescription pills often can be bought for less than other drugs such as marijuana and cocaine. However, costs can increase when these medications are in high demand, such as when students use them to cram before midterm and final exams.[5] One study of intentional drug abuse in teenagers and children aged 6 to 19 years revealed that 38 percent of intentional drug abuse involved nonprescription drugs, with dextromethorphan, caffeine, antihistamines, and nonprescription stimulants identified as the most commonly abused nonprescription drugs (Table 1[6]).[7] The Partnership for Drug-Free Kids estimates that 15 percent of teenagers have abused nonprescription cough or cold medications to get high.[8]

Teenaged girls, in particular, see prescription pills as "cleaner" than other drugs and equal their male counterparts in prescription drug use, but girls are less likely to use marijuana or cocaine compared with boys.[5] Student athletes may see pills as a way to enhance sports performance or may self-medicate with opiates for pain related to sports injuries. Seventy percent of all persons who abused prescription pain relievers obtained them from friends or relatives, often without permission.[8] Parents are advised to watch out for their own children as well as for their children's friends who may be searching through the medicine cabinets when visiting the home.[9]

A national effort to reduce illicit drugs such as heroin and cocaine has seen a slight decline in overall drug use among young adults in recent years.[5] However, as prescription drug sales continue to soar, pharming or prescription drug abuse is on the rise, with adolescents now dubbed the "Ritalin generation." Pills are available to sell or share more than ever before, with more prescriptions written every year for antianxiety drugs, sleeping pills, and stimulants such as Ritalin, which is used to treat attention-deficit/hyperactivity disorder.

Table 1   Commonly Abused Medicines

Opioids
Derived from the opium poppy (or synthetic versions of it) and used for pain relief.
- Hydrocodone (Vicodin)
- Oxycodone (OxyContin, Percocet)
- Fentanyl (Duragesic, Fentora)
- Methadone
- Codeine

Benzodiazepines
Central nervous system depressants used as sedatives, to induce sleep, prevent seizures, and relieve anxiety.
- Alprazolam (Xanax)
- Diazepam (Valium)
- Lorazepam (Ativan)

Amphetamine-Like Drugs
Central nervous stimulants used to treat attention-deficit/hyperactivity disorder.
- Dextroamphetamine/amphetamine (Adderall, Adderall XR)
- Methylphenidate (Ritalin, Concerta)

Centers for Disease Control and Prevention[6]

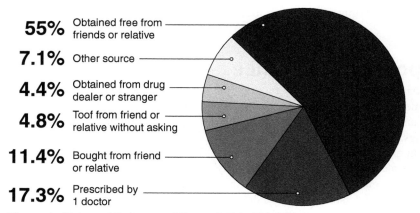

55% Obtained free from friends or relative
7.1% Other source
4.4% Obtained from drug dealer or stranger
4.8% Toof from friend or relative without asking
11.4% Bought from friend or relative
17.3% Prescribed by 1 doctor

Figure 1. Abusers' Sources of Prescription Painkillers
Centers for Disease Control and Prevention.[6]

Skittling or pharming is a party game in which teenagers indiscriminately mix drugs together, putting themselves at risk for stroke, heart attack, or irreversible brain damage.[8] Children have easy access to medications from medicine cabinets in their own homes and homes of their families and friends (Figure[6]). Gathering unused or expired medications often goes unnoticed by family members and does not cost the child anything. Emergency departments (EDs) may have difficulty discerning the combination of medications that an individual has ingested, resulting in delay and uncertainty of treatment.[7] Experts report that it is difficult to identify a teenager who abuses prescription drugs because these medications are odorless and can be easily hidden, and the abuser may not manifest with unusual behavior such as stumbling or slurred speech.[10]

Raising Awareness of Pharming Parties

Under federal law, it is illegal to possess controlled substances without a prescriptiion.[5] However, prosecutions for possession are rare, especially when minors are involved. Although many schools ban students from carrying medications without a prescription, rules can be difficult to enforce.

There has been limited response from state and federal governments, as well as from pharmaceutical companies.[5] The Bush administration introduced an effort to control prescription drug abuse, however, most of the plan focuses on the reduction of sales of narcotic medications online or by HCPs who write pain prescriptions indiscriminately.

The US Food and Drug Administration and SAMHSA have instituted media ad campaigns that highlight the dangers of prescription drug abuse among young persons, and the manufacturer of OxyContin introduced a public campaign about the dangers of abusing the drug after reports of misuse. However, some fear that antidrug television ads can add to the problem by telling kids that they can find illicit drugs in their own medicine cabinets![8]

Parental Support and Guidance

The 2008 Office of National Drug Control Policy reported the disturbing statistic that more than 1 in 4 parents (27 percent) believe that prescription and OTC medications are much safer to abuse than street drugs.[11] Research shows that teenagers whose parents discuss and express strong disapproval of drug use are less likely to abuse alcohol and drugs. Unfortunately, many adolescents report that parents do not discuss the dangers of such drugs.[10] Parents need to understand that legal does not equal safe when it comes to OTC and prescription medications. Providers' instructions should encourage families to routinely

---

Pharming Fact Sheet for Healthcare Providers

Pharming parties are the latest risky trend in which kids pool together a supply of prescription and nonprescription drugs that are placed into a bowl for anyone to sample, often along with alcohol, in order to get high with disregard for the type of drug that is being ingested.'

Provide anticipatory guidance with every patient encounter:

- Educate families to keep medicine cabinets locked and prescription drugs out of reach of their children and their children's friends who may be visiting.

- Clean out medicine cabinets in the home of all unwanted, unused, and expired medications.

- O Emphasize the importance of the parent-child relationship as a protective factor in keeping children safe, and educate on the skills necessary to detect drug abuse and ways in which parents can engage their children in open communication.

- O Instruct on proper disposal of medications and participation in prescription medication take-back programs.

1. Do you ever hear your child talk about a skittles party. Narconon website. Available at: http://www.narconon. org/blog/narconon/do-you-ever-hear-your-child-talk-about-a-skittles-party/. Published August 22,2012. Accessed October 23, 2014.

---

assess the content of their medicine cabinets and "if you don't need it, get rid of it."[8] Anticipatory guidance stressing that parents talk to their kids, watch for behavioral changes, and be vigilant is necessary to counteract this epidemic problem.[12]

The HCPs' Role

Significant morbidity and mortality result from the recreational abuse of prescription medications, nutritional supplements, and nonprescription products that go undetected in the younger population, in the absence of regular interaction with HCPs.[6] Routine office screening must incorporate prescription drug, pharming, and skittling screening in all risk-taking behavior assessments. Providers should discuss recreational drug use with young patients as part of standard pediatric care, in response to the challenge in recognition, detection, and management of nonprescription drug abuse in children and adolescents.[9]

HCPs can play a key role in providing anticipatory guidance regarding pharming parties and in emphasizing the importance of the parent-child relationship as a protective factor in keeping children safe. They can educate parents about the skills necessary to detect drug abuse and discuss ways in which parents can engage their children in open communication. Also, they need to educate families to keep medicine cabinets locked and keep prescription drugs out of reach or out of range for both their children and friends who may be visiting. It is important to educate families on how to prevent accidental ingestion by children, pets, or anyone else, and that certain expired, unwanted, or unused medicines have specific disposal instructions that indicate if they should be flushed down the sink or toilet as soon as they are no longer needed, or when they should be disposed of through a medicine take-back program.[13]

HCPs should remain vigilant and question frequent refills or multiple prescriptions for commonly abused medications.[2] They need to be cognizant of patients who "doctor shop" or "ED hop." Supporting the placement of dextromethorphan-containing products behind counters in pharmacies or the prohibition of the sale to minors could also reduce abuse. Finally, HCPs share a responsibility to support legislation that might curb access to nonregulated Internet pharmacies and the sale of medications without prescriptions.

References

1. Hone-McMahan K. When kids raid the medicine cabinet. *Chicago Tribune*. Available at: http://www.chicagotribune.com/sns-health-kids-raiding-medicine-cabinet-story.html. Published December 3, 2009. Accessed October 28, 2014.
2. White House. Office of National Drug Control Policy. Prescription drug abuse. Available at: http://www.whitehouse.gov/ondcp/prescription-drug-abuse. Accessed October 28, 2014.
3. Levine DA. "Pharming": The abuse of prescription and over-the-counter drugs in teens. *Curr Opin Pediatr*. 2007;19(3):270–274.
4. Narconon. Do you ever hear your child talk about a skittles party. Available at: http://www.narconon.org/blog/narconon/do-you-ever-hear-your-child-talk-about-a-skittles-party/. Published August 22, 2012. Accessed October 28, 2014.
5. Costello D. Their drugs of choice: Teens are turning to Vicodin, Ritalin, and other easily obtained prescription pills. *Los Angeles Times*. Available at: http://www.prescriptionsuicide.com/relnews7.html. Published February 7, 2005. Accessed October 28, 2014.
6. Centers for Disease Control and Prevention (CDC). Policy impact: prescription painkiller overdoses. Available at: http://www.cdc.gov/homeandrecreationalsafety/rxbrief/. Updated July 2, 2013. Accessed October 23, 2014.
7. Partnership for Drug-Free Kids. The Partnership Attitude Tracking Study: Teens and Parents 2013. Available at: http://www.drugfree.org/newsroom/pats-2013-full-report-key-findings. Published July 22, 2014. Accessed October 23, 2014.
8. Stannard E. Problem's as close as medicine cabinet. McClatchy–Tribune Business News. Available at: http://search.proquest.com/docview/462382237?accountid=10559. Published February 17, 2008.
9. Conca AJ, Worthen DR. Nonprescription drug abuse. *J Pharm Pract*. 2012;25(1):13–21.
10. DiConsiglio J. Substance abuse: problem pill. *Scholastic Choices*. 2011;26(4):14–17. Available at: http://search.proquest.com/docview/820583188?accountid=10559.
11. Laughlin M. "Pharming" endangers teens. *J Okla State Med Assoc*. 2008;101(6–7):164.
12. Kisken T. People can fight drug abuse by disposing old pills. McClatchy–Tribune Business News. Available from: http://search.proquest.com/docview/864039097?accountid=10559. Published April 29, 2011.
13. US Food and Drug Administration. Disposal of unused medicines: what you should know. Available at: http://www.fda.gov/drugs/resourcesforyou/consumers/buyingusingmedicinesafely/ensuringsafeuseofmedicine/safedisposalofmedicines/ucm186187.htm. Updated April 28, 2014. Accessed October 28, 2014.

Critical Thinking

1. Suggest three ways to reduce prescription medication abuse.
2. What advice would you give to adolescents who are considering participating in a "pill party"?

Internet References

Not Just Robotripping: 5 Risky Things Kids Do
   http://abcnews.go.com/Health/Parenting/robotripping-telltale-signs-parents/story?id=11657722

Phar-Fetched "Pharm Parties" Real or a Media Invention?
   http://www.slate.com/articles/news_and_politics/press_box/2006/06/pharfetched_pharm_parties.html

"Robo-Tripping": Dextromethorphan Abuse and Its Anesthetic Implications
   https://www.ncbi.nlm.nih.gov/pmc/articles/PMC4358333/

Skittles Party by Teens Is Not What It Seems
   http://www.narconon.org/blog/narconon/skittles-party-by-teens-is-not-what-it-seems/

The Dangers of Pharm Parties
   http://www.lockthecabinet.com/news/pharm-parties/

Susan Solecki is an assistant clinical professor of nursing, Drexel University, College of Nursing and Health Professions, Philadelphia, Pennsylvania.

Renee Turchi is a medical director, Center for Children With Special Needs, St. Christopher's Hospital for Children, Drexel University School of Public Health, Philadelphia.

Article   Prepared by: Claire N. Rubman, *Suffolk County Community College*

What are They Looking For?

There are no simple answers when working with young people at risk of radicalization.

CATHERINE JACKSON

Learning Outcomes

After reading this article, you will be able to:

- Explain the term "problematizing" with regard to adolescent behavior and radicalism.

- Describe the ideal environment and mind-set for radicalization to thrive.

- Explain the concept of "positive socialization."

The ease with which three Asian Muslim girls were able to leave their homes in East London, fly to Turkey and cross the border to join the Islamic State (Isis) forces in Syria has reignited public and political concern about the dangers of radicalization. What, policy makers are asking, makes young people—and young Muslims in particular—vulnerable to following the siren call of extremist groups? Even more important, how do we stop it?

The Government is currently consulting on new duties that the Counter-Terrorism and Security Act, currently going through Parliament, would place on all public sector organisations to contribute to the national strategy to prevent terrorism and extremist violence. The strategy, Prevent, is overtly not about criminalization; rather, through its multiagency Channel programme, it uses existing health and social care safeguarding procedures for children, young people and vulnerable adults to identify and support those at risk. The language is of risk and vulnerability, support and advice, not crime and punishment.

Many counsellors will be working with the age group at highest risk: young people in their teens and early 20s. Counsellors in secondary schools and further and higher education settings may already have been involved in their organization's training programmes and be familiar with the procedures

they should follow if they identify a client who maybe at risk of radicalization. Their statutory duty in relation to reporting concerns is clear: BACP's ethical guidance reminds its members that any legal requirement to disclose information, with and without their client's knowledge or consent, overrides any professional ethical guidelines on client confidentiality. This is absolutely the case with regard to terrorism.[1]

Kalsoom Bashir is the Co-Director of Inspire, the Muslim women's antiextremism campaign group. She sees the vulnerability factors for young women as a combination of the personal—trauma, family upset, family breakup, or relationship breakup—and external issues—a sense of grievance, injustice, experience of racism, difficulties getting a job. They may also be searching for an identity or struggling with their Muslim identity in British society, she says: "There isn't one factor. But we need to recognize that the earlier you can help someone with whatever vulnerability they have, the better chance you have of mitigating that risk of crossing the line into radicalization."

Young girls in particular are vulnerable to a form of grooming, she says. They may be well educated but they may still have had a very conservative upbringing and restricted social lives. "It can be quite lonely. They may be looking for romance, for affection, for that sense of someone wanting you, particularly if it isn't available from their family. Extremist movements exploit that in the same way that pedophiles hook onto vulnerable young women. They tell them they will have a hero husband waiting for them and they will play an important role in establishing a new country. Young women are drawn towards that."

Teachers and others working with these young people need to give out a clear and consistent message, she says: "It's like stranger danger—you need to talk with young women about the risks and consequences."

Kam Bhui, Professor of Cultural Psychiatry and Epidemiology at St Mary University of London, has researched the psychosocial factors that may "push" and "pull" young people from the UK's Muslim communities into supporting violent protest and terrorism.[2] Surprisingly, he found no correlation between extremist sympathies and adverse life events: in fact, in his research wealthier people emerged as marginally more sympathetic to terrorism, as did people in full-time education. "That was a surprise as one of the dominant discourses is that poverty, discrimination and social exclusion are driving these movements," he says.

But perhaps what emerged most strongly is the need to resist simplification: "The Government is in search of certainty but there are so many factors." He is clear that counsellors and psychotherapists need to be alert. "They are privy to all sorts of fantasies and material. If they come across this phenomenon, they have to be very clear about their duties with regard to safeguarding."

What Works?

Professor Bhui's research also uncovered factors that echo Kalsoom Bashir's description of young women brought up in boundaried, close-knit communities. Those in his survey most likely to have extremist sympathies were not the most socially isolated; in fact they tended to enjoy richer social capital in terms of family and friendship networks. But their networks were more likely to be tight-knit, rather than spread across a wide social spectrum. This also gives a clue to what may work to prevent radicalization. "Positive socialization is such an important intervention," Professor Bhui believes. "Young people are in a phase of huge transition. It only takes one charismatic figure to give us a sense of identity and coherence and make us feel better in the world. It's ordinary human vulnerability." We need to be offering young people positive identities and positive alternatives, using proven successful interventions such as those aimed at reducing gun crime. "You don't focus on the guns and the crime. You offer them employment, music, dance, a group identity with a T-shirt and badge."

This is certainly the experience in mainland Europe, where countries like Germany and Holland are further advanced in devising preventive approaches to all extremism—far right as well as religious. Harald Weilnböck, Co-Chair of RAN-Derad, the Radicalization Awareness Network, based in Germany, has extensively researched and evaluated antiradicalization and hate crime programmes across Europe.[3]

His research suggests group approaches are more effective than one-to-one, although they can operate well together. Groupwork offers social contact and socialization. "Most of the people using the programmes we researched came from broken families and were raised by single parents. They are very expert on how to manipulate the one-to-one relationship. In a group you have witnesses; you can't play those tricks. Also the learning effect is multiplied. Once you have managed to trust that group, it has a much greater and more lasting impact."

A trained (but not practicing) psychotherapist himself, Weilnböck says the keys to opening doors to alternatives for young people at risk of extremism are fundamentally the same as those that counsellors and psychotherapists use to help clients choose healthier ways of being in the world: relationship, trust and narrative. "Whether the practitioners are social workers or police officers, they are basically able to do what psychotherapists do—use themselves as a relational counterpoint to the other; establish a relationship that is personal but not intimate and be present so that the young person can mirror that and express what they see for themselves," he says. How you communicate with the young people is also vital: don't teach or preach or instruct or argue with them; instead get them to tell the story of their life. "Narrative is inherently therapeutic," he says. "It's what psychoanalytic therapist Roy Schafer says about psychoanalysis it's nothing more than telling the same story over and over again for two years, only in the end you tell it much better."

Interventions are also much more effective when they are led by practitioners with no statutory powers or remit—third sector, nongovernmental organisations, rather than social workers or police or probation officers, he says. Risk assessment is not helpful. "We should be spotting challenges and then engaging with our young people. We should be supporting their development."

But these are precisely the projects that have suffered under the UK Government's austerity cuts, says Vicki Coppock, Professor in Social Sciences at Edge Hill University in Lancashire. She questions the emphasis on "psychological vulnerability" in the Prevent strategy, arguing that it risks problematizing normal adolescent developmental behaviours.[4] Safeguarding might seem a better arena than the criminal justice system in which to manage these vulnerable young people but "it is no less implicated in issues of power and control, and it's more insidious because it's disguised as benevolent," she argues.

"Young people have a right to be political. Isn't that idealism precisely what we cherish about youth? For me, the way forward is supporting third sector projects that are able to engage locally with young people on the ground and provide safe places for them to express dissent and work through these things."

References

1. BACP. Breaches in confidentiality. G2 information sheet. BACP: Lutterworth; 2014.
2. Bhui K, Everitt B, Jones E. Might depression, psychosocial adversity and limited social assets explain vulnerability to and resistance against violent radicalization? PLOS One 2014; 9(9): e105918.
3. See, for example, www.cultures-interactive.de
4. Coppock V, McGovern M. 'Dangerous minds?' Deconstructing counter-terrorism discourse, radicalisation and the 'psychological vulnerability' of Muslim children and young people in Britain. Children & Society 2014; 28: 242–256.

Critical Thinking

1. What are some of the psychosocial factors that impact adolescent radicalization?

2. How do you encourage adolescents to be "political" while simultaneously shielding them from the threat of radicalization?

3. What type of program could you set up to protect adolescents from the potential of radicalization?

Internet References

Protecting Adolescents from Radicalization, Recruitment
http://www.mdedge.com/clinicalpsychiatrynews/article/89647/mental-health/protecting-adolescents-radicalization-recruitment

Psychological Process and Pathways to Radicalization
https://www.omicsonline.org/psychological-process-and-pathways-to-radicalization-2157-2526.S5-003.pdf

Radicalization of Young Muslims Reasons and Prevention
https://www.psychologytoday.com/blog/stop-the-cycle/201511/radicalization-young-muslims

The Influence of Education and Socialization on Radicalization: An Exploration of Theoretical Presumptions and Empirical Research
https://www.ncbi.nlm.nih.gov/pmc/articles/PMC3337995/

The Social Psychology of Radicalization and Extremism
https://www.psychologytoday.com/blog/naturally-selected/201502/the-social-psychology-radicalization-and-extremism

Article   Prepared by: Claire N. Rubman, *Suffolk County Community College*

How Prison Stints Replaced Study Hall

America's problem with criminalizing kids.

JODY OWENS

Learning Outcomes

After reading this article, you will be able to:

- Explain the development of the concept of "juvenile super-predators."

- Discuss whether "school resource officers" help or hinder with regard to school discipline.

- Explain the "taxi service "in Meridian's public school system.

Police officers in Meridian, MS, were spending so much time hauling handcuffed students from school to the local juvenile jail that they began describing themselves as "just a taxi service." It wasn't because schools were overrun by budding criminals or juvenile superpredators—not by a long shot. Most of the children were arrested and jailed simply for violating school rules, often for trivial offenses.

One 15-year-old girl, for example, was suspended and sent to the Lauderdale County Juvenile Detention Center for a dress code violation. Her jacket was the wrong shade of blue. A boy served a suspension in the juvenile lock-up for passing gas in the classroom. Another landed behind bars because he walked to the alternative school instead of taking the bus.

For many kids, a stint in "juvie" was just the beginning of a never-ending nightmare. Arrests could lead to probation. Subsequent suspensions were then considered probation violations, leading back to jail. And suspensions were a distinct possibility in a district where the NAACP found a suspension rate that was more than 10 times the national average.

In 2012, the U.S. Department of Justice filed suit to stop the "taxi service" in Meridian's public schools, where 86 percent of the students are black. The DOJ suit said children were

being incarcerated so "arbitrarily and severely as to shock the conscience."

We should all be shocked. The reality, though, is that Meridian's taxi service is just one example of what amounts to a civil rights crisis in America: a "school-to-prison pipeline" that sucks vulnerable children out of the classroom at an alarming rate and funnels them into the harsh world of police, courts, and prison cells.

For many children, adolescent misbehavior that once warranted a trip to the principal's office—and perhaps a stint in study hall—now results in jail time and a greater possibility of lifelong involvement with the criminal justice system. The students pushed into this pipeline are disproportionately children of color, mostly impoverished, and those with learning disabilities.

The story of Meridian is more than an example of school discipline run amok. It's a key to understanding how the United States has attained the dubious distinction of imprisoning more people—and a larger share of its population—than any other country. It's one reason why the U.S. today has a quarter of the world's prisoners—roughly 2.2 million people—while representing just 5 percent of its total population. And it helps explain an unprecedented incarceration rate that is far and away the highest on the planet, some five to 10 times higher than other Western democracies.

As the managing attorney for the Southern Poverty Law Center's (SPLC) Mississippi office, I've seen firsthand the devastation wrought by the school-to-prison pipeline, and the senselessness of it all.

When SPLC advocates began interviewing children at the juvenile detention center in Meridian in 2009, we were investigating children being pepper-sprayed by guards when they were in their cells and posing no threat. But we kept hearing stories from students who were pushed out of school and into cells for noncriminal, minor school infractions. These stories would eventually spark the DOJ lawsuit and a thorough examination of how the "pipeline" operated.

A settlement agreement was reached in the SPLC lawsuit over these abusive conditions, but the facility was ultimately shuttered because it simply could not comply with the agreement.

The "taxi service" to the detention center was put out of business.

Origins of the Pipeline

The origins of the school-to-prison pipeline can be traced to the 1990s when reports of juvenile crime began to stoke fears of "superpredators"—described in the 1996 book *Body Count* as "radically impulsive, brutally remorseless youngsters" with little regard for human life. The superpredator concept, based on what some critics have derided as junk science, is now known to be a complete myth. Former Princeton professor and Bush administration official John DiIulio, the *Body Count* coauthor who coined the term, admitted to *The New York Times* in 2001 that his theory of sharply rising juvenile violence had been wrong.

But the damage had been done. As these fears took root and mass school shootings like the one at Columbine made headlines, not only did states enact laws to increase punishment for juvenile offenders, schools began to adopt "zerotolerance" policies that imposed automatic, predetermined punishments for rule breakers.

At the same time, states across America were adopting harsh criminal laws, including long mandatory prison sentences for certain crimes and "three strikes" laws that led to life sentences for repeat offenders. The term "zero tolerance" was adopted from policing practices and criminal laws that focused on locking up minor offenders as a way to stem more serious crime.

Somewhere along the way, as local police departments began supplying on-duty "school resource officers" to patrol hallways, educators began to confuse typical adolescent misbehavior with criminality. Schools became, more or less, a part of the criminal justice system. With police officers stalking the halls and playgrounds, teachers and principals found it easy to outsource discipline. Almost overnight, a schoolyard scuffle could now land a kid in a jail cell.

The results have been disastrous. In some school districts, as in many African-American communities, police seem to view students as the enemy, or at least as potential criminals.

Criminalizing Kids

Contrary to tough talk about scaring bad students straight, criminalizing kids does not make communities safer. A growing body of research suggests that the current approach to juvenile justice does exactly the opposite.

Studies show that the brain does not fully develop until a person reaches his or her mid-20s. In fact, the part of the brain that governs rational decision-making is the last to develop. This means a child may engage in dangerous behavior without fully realizing the risks and consequences for themselves and others. But that child also has a unique propensity for rehabilitation as well.

In other words, we shouldn't give up on kids who get into trouble. But that's what we're doing.

Research shows that an arrest doubles the odds that a student will drop out. The odds quadruple with a first-time court appearance, according to *Justice Quarterly*. And dropping out, in turn, increases the likelihood of prison. In fact, African-American men under 35 who failed to finish high school are now more likely to be incarcerated than working.

Criminalizing students comes at a steep cost to taxpayers. Confining a single young person can cost as much as $148,767 a year, according to a recent survey by the Justice Policy Institute.

This costly "pipeline" disproportionately harms children of color and causes immeasurable harm to their communities, where many of them live in poverty.

Black students are suspended and expelled at three times the rate of white students, according to the U.S. Department of Education's Office for Civil Rights. Even at the preschool level, there's a gaping racial disparity: The department found that black preschool students—a group that represents 18 percent of preschool enrollment—make up 48 percent of preschool children suspended more than once.

When there is such a disparity in discipline at 4 and 5 years old, it shouldn't be a surprise that African Americans are incarcerated at about six times the rate of non-Hispanic whites, according to the National Academy of Sciences. Or that they are three to five times more likely to be arrested for drug offenses than whites, despite using drugs at roughly the same rates.

A New Way

The court victories against harsh school discipline and brutal detention conditions are vitally important to reforming this system. But the school-to-prison pipeline has not yet been destroyed. It is still harming young lives.

We need a new way.

One that does not treat ordinary children like criminals that does not equate bad behavior with criminality.

One that does not target African-American children for incarceration at an early age.

One that does not place children in brutal, filthy jails, and prisons where their needs are neglected and they are subjected to violence, sexual abuse, and psychological torture.

One that does not erode trust in law enforcement among communities of color.

One that believes in the ability of children to change and invests in their futures.

One that provides hope, not despair.

The simple fact is that most children who act up in school or even commit minor crimes will grow out of their bad behavior—if we let them.

This is not to say that children should not be held accountable or punished for committing crimes, particularly violent crimes. But most of the children now being pushed out of school and into detention need a helping hand, not a pair of handcuffs.

We must spend less on prisons and more on education, counseling, therapy, and other rehabilitative services. Such an investment will save taxpayer money, enhance opportunities for communities mired in poverty, and, importantly, lead to less crime in the future.

While it is encouraging that people across this nation are finally asking why we imprison so many people, we will miss the bigger picture by only looking at adult prisons. We must look at the schools and the entire justice system if we hope to truly address the mass incarceration crisis. The path to prison starts at an early age. And as long as we continue to needlessly criminalize children in the name of school discipline, our prisons will continue to overflow.

Critical Thinking

1. Are schools "out-sourcing" discipline?

2. Describe a nonpunitive policy to maintain discipline in our nation's schools.

3. How can parents and teachers work together to maintain higher standards of cooperation among students and teachers?

Internet References

Conduct and Behavior Problems: Intervention and Resources for School Aged Youth
http://smhp.psych.ucla.edu/pdfdocs/conduct/conduct.pdf

Discipline Strategies for Teenagers
http://raisingchildren.net.au/articles/discipline_teenagers.html

Fair and Effective Discipline for All Students: Best Practice Strategies for Educators
http://www.naspcenter.org/factsheets/effdiscip_fs.html

For More Teens, Arrests by Police Replace School Discipline
https://www.wsj.com/articles/for-more-teens-arrests-by-police-replace-school-discipline-1413858602

Racial, Ethnic, and Gender Differences in School Discipline among U.S. High School Students: 1991–2005
https://www.ncbi.nlm.nih.gov/pmc/articles/PMC2678799/

JUDY OWENS is the managing attorney for the Southern Poverty Law Center's Mississippi office.

Unit 8

UNIT

Prepared by: Claire N. Rubman, *Suffolk County Community College*

Psychological Well-being

The multifaceted psychological well-being of our adolescent population is extremely important. David Flack (2016) addresses the concept of "stuckness"—when adolescents don't perceive that they have a mental health issue that needs to be addressed and they are "stuck" in their present mode of thinking and behavior. Read about his "5Rs" method to help motivate adolescents to identify problems and resolve their psychological issues. Learn about the role of "connectedness" in relation to good mental health.

Not all adolescents are willing to seek out or accept help. Griffiths (2015) addresses some of the issues related to why adolescents sometimes fail to seek out help. He focuses specifically on "problematic technology use" that negatively impacts many other domains in a teenager's life including education, fitness, family or personal relationships, and psychological well-being.

It is possibly due to the uniqueness of adolescent thought that teens do not seek out help. Their feelings of invincibility and invulnerability can mistakenly lead them to believe that they can resolve their own issues.

Griffiths also explores the possibility that there really is no technology problem at all! Read the article, "Problematic Technology Use During Adolescence: Why don't teenagers seek treatment?" and decide for yourself . . .

Technology aside, adolescents have other issues that they don't seek out help to resolve. Another such problem is nightmares. While children commonly report difficulty sleeping because of nightmares, adolescents tend not to. A recent study by researchers at the University of Warwick in England suggests that these adolescent nightmares might be the forbearers of psychosis. Wolke (2014) found a possible link between these nightmares and schizophrenia. The article, "Can't Turn Off the Night" explores this relationship by looking at the similarities between dreams and hallucinations or psychotic episodes.

Some adolescent dysfunction is covert—we cannot see what they are dreaming, but some dysfunctional behavior is "hidden" in plain sight. We can, for example, observe when our teens are harming themselves. Although 95 percent of adolescents do not intend to kill themselves, self-harming is, none the less, a serious problem. They cut, burn or hurt themselves in an attempt to block out painful circumstances such as shame, guilt or fear. They also self-harm to fill an emotional void or to regain control over their environment. Read about the "hows and whys" of self-harm and the pediatrician's role in finding a solution to this counterproductive behavior in "Self-Injury: Why teens do it and how to help" by Brickell and Jellinek (2014).

Thinking about therapeutic interventions that were designed for adolescents based on what we know today about their developing brains, Sanders (2015) uses this research develop a more finely tuned intervention. Knowing that adolescents respond differently than both children and adults, she attempts to capitalize on this "unique and different" stage of development. Read about her approach to cognitive therapies that use fear triggers and other strategies in her article "Adolescent Brains Open to Change."

Article   Prepared by: Claire N. Rubman, *Suffolk County Community College*

Getting Unstuck

By keeping a developmental perspective in mind and following five suggested strategies, counselors can help foster change in teenagers with co-occurring disorders.

DAVID FLACK

Learning Outcomes

After reading this article, you will be able to:

- Explain the term "developmental debt."

- Describe the steps involved in recognizing a problem before the onset of treatment.

- Identify and discuss the "5R's" involved in motivation.

Andrew never knew his father. At age 4, he witnessed the death of his mother from an overdose. She was heroin dependent, and they were living in a car at the time. After her death, Andrew entered the foster care system. Between the ages of 4 and 15, he experienced more than a dozen different placements. Not surprisingly, with each move, his behavior became increasingly problematic.

At age 9, Andrew started drinking alcohol. By age 11, he was using alcohol and marijuana regularly. He discovered meth as a 13-year-old and went to inpatient care for the first time. He ran away after four days. When he was 15, he ran from the group home where he was living.

When Andrew entered treatment at age 16, he was on probation and had just moved into a transitional living program after several months on the streets. When he started treatment, he met the criteria for multiple substance use disorders. He also had pre-existing mental health diagnoses that included post-traumatic stress disorder (PTSD), attention-deficit/hyperactivity disorder, conduct disorder and major depressive disorder. At that time, Andrew said he had no interest in stopping his substance use because "that's not a problem for me."

In his treatment journal, Andrew wrote, "Lots of times I feel like I'm living in some kind of black hole. I'm alone, but not really, because everything's there, because I just can't escape it no matter what I try. It's black there, because that's what black holes are, right? But black is really all the colors at once, every single one of them. And that's too many damned colors if you ask me."

Understanding the Stuckness

Very few teenagers enter substance abuse treatment by choice. They show up due to legal mandates, school requirements, family pressure or other external reasons. Often they see treatment as the least bad choice—only slightly better than detention, suspension, or homelessness. Like Andrew, these teens often appear unwilling or unable to do things differently, even though their current behaviors are clearly causing problems. In other words, they're stuck.

I propose that our primary task as counselors is to help these teens get unstuck—not behave better, fulfill mandates or even stop using substances. We can hope those other things happen. I certainly do. However, it seems to me that those changes can occur only when an individual gets unstuck.

When helping teens get unstuck, we need to maintain a developmental perspective as counselors. Various developmental models exist, with most including a progression of stages that individuals move through, and each stage featuring specific tasks to be accomplished. The primary stage-specific tasks for adolescence are generally considered to be developing identity and establishing autonomy. As part of establishing autonomy, it is normal for adolescents to question, rebel against and ultimately reject the plans of authority figures, including the most well-intended plans of professional helpers.

Sometimes, those well-intended plans lead to reactance, which is a tendency to resist influences perceived as a threat to one's autonomy. Many adolescent treatment programs are designed in ways likely to exacerbate reactance. We tell adolescents what, when, why and how. In residential programs, we restrict personal items. In wilderness programs, we often take away everything. Then we wonder why participants are unsuccessful. Worse, we blame them—declaring them in denial, resistant to treatment, unwilling to engage or simply noncompliant. Instead of helping, we've increased their stuckness.

Reactance can be exacerbated by what I think of as *developmental debt*. Most developmental theories state that if a person doesn't successfully complete the tasks for a specific stage, then he or she remains in that stage. It seems to me that this might not be accurate. Instead, sociocultural and biological factors keep pushing individuals forward, even when tasks at another stage are unresolved or only partially completed.

With every push forward, an individual becomes less likely to complete the next stage. This leads to an ever-growing developmental debt. Much like with a credit card that's never fully paid off, the person not only will always have a balance due, but he or she will get further behind each month.

With this developmental perspective in mind, I propose five strategies for fostering change with teenagers who have co-occurring disorders. Inspired by motivational interviewing, stages of change, narrative approaches, and existential psychotherapy, I have found these strategies useful for helping this population to overcome rigid thinking, get unstuck, and start moving forward.

Slow Down

Traditionally, drug treatment programs have assumed that anyone entering services is ready to get and stay clean. This simply isn't true. Change is a process, not an event. When we slow down, we're able to help participants move through that process. Developed by James Prochaska, John Norcross and Carlo DiClemente, the stages of change is an evidence-based transtheoretical model that identifies five steps in the process of change:

- **Precontemplation:** The person doesn't believe he or she has any problems related to the target behavior, so the person sees no reason to make changes. To help participants in this stage, we can focus on building a therapeutic alliance, validate the participant's lack of desire to change, and provide objective information.
- **Contemplation:** The person is considering the possibility that a problem might exist but hasn't yet decided if change is necessary. To help participants in this stage, we can explore the pros and cons of continuing to use substances, gently identify

contradictions, help make links between substance use and mental health challenges, and provide opportunities to imagine or experience alternatives.

- **Preparation:** The person has identified a problem related to the target behavior and is deciding what to do next. To help participants in this stage, we can encourage small initial steps or experiments, continue to explore and solidify motivation for change, and help eliminate obstacles to change.
- **Action:** The person has decided to change the target behavior, has developed a plan, and is now putting that plan into action. To help participants in this stage, we can explore ways to implement change, provide support, build self-efficacy, and remain solution focused.
- **Maintenance:** When the new behavior has become habit, the person has entered this stage. I propose that six months of sobriety is a good milestone for this. To help participants in this stage, we can provide ongoing support, continue to explore real or perceived obstacles, and foster resiliency.

In addition to these five stages, there's *Recycle*, which occurs when a participant reverts to behaviors from an earlier stage. When a participant recycles, many helpers blame the person's lack of skills, situational factors, or unwillingness to change. Extenuating circumstances may certainly be present, but it seems to me that recycles occur because we push participants into the action stage too quickly. As such, recycles are potent reminders that we should slow down and revisit earlier stages, looking for unfinished or overlooked business.

Identify Their Motivators

Teens often enter services believing that they're free of problems or that their only problem is something external. It may not seem like success to some, but the change process has begun when teens report treatment as the least bad option, state that their only problem is that others think there's a problem or make similar comments. These may not be the motivators we desire for participants, but change requires meeting them where they are at, not where we want them to be.

We can help clients discover and deepen their motivators by using the "Five R's" from William Miller and Stephen Rollnick's motivational interviewing:

- **Relevance:** Why is change important?
- **Risks:** What are the risks of changing? What are the risks of not changing?
- **Rewards:** What will you gain from change?
- **Roadblocks:** What are the obstacles to change?
- **Repetition:** Review these elements at each session.

Sometimes, to help participants solidify their motivators for change, we need to assist them in developing problem-recognition skills. We can do this by exploring what defines a problem; nurturing mindfulness; and creating an inclusive, nonjudgmental treatment environment.

Approaches from narrative therapy can also be helpful. Teens with co-occurring disorders typically enter treatment with problem-saturated stories. These tales of stuckness have become the defining stories for their lives. Help them discover new stories and further increase problem-recognition skills by:

- **Externalizing the problem:** Instead of "having" a problem or "being" a problem, assist participants to view problems as existing outside themselves. This helps remove pressures rooted in blame, shame, and defensiveness. Take this even further by encouraging participants to think of problems as characters in their stories.
- **Seeking exceptions:** We build and sustain problem-saturated stories by ignoring times when the problem wasn't in control. Seeking exceptions involves assisting participants to discover those ignored times. These exceptions hold the keys to change, so explore them in great detail.
- **Reauthoring stories:** Once exceptions have been discovered, participants can start reauthoring their problem-saturated stories. Reauthoring gives them the opportunity to create new, more empowering stories with plots that focus on moving forward.

Some teenagers are so stuck that they're unable to identify any exceptions to their problem-saturated stories. In these cases, it can be useful for counselors to add a fourth approach to those cited previously: *creating exceptions*. One way for these teens to break the cycle of stuckness is to try something new. I've had participants explore belly dancing, glass blowing, rock climbing, rugby, hand drumming, and much more.

Expect Ambivalence

As I've noted, the change process has begun when a teen's thinking moves from "I don't have a problem" to "My only problem is that other people think there's a problem." When this occurs, the participant has moved into the contemplation stage of change. This stage is about ambivalence, which can be defined as simultaneously believing two seemingly contradictory ideas.

Ambivalence is common for all teenagers, who desire the privileges of adulthood while retaining the comforts of childhood. In the case of substance-using teens, there is often another, more complex layer—wanting to fix their problem while continuing to use. Andrew described this ambivalence well: "Using has really messed up my life, but I don't think I'll ever stop. When I'm high, the bad feelings go away. I don't think about the past, and I don't care about the future. For a little while, my brain shuts up and I can pretend everything's OK."

Some professional helpers focus solely on the reasons to stop using, perhaps believing that any discussion about the possible benefits of drug use will be seen as an endorsement. This simply isn't true. Helping youth such as Andrew get unstuck requires a sincere, nonjudgmental exploration of both the pros and the cons of substance use. Here are a few other ideas for resolving ambivalence:

- **Normalize the process.** Change is hard. It conflicts with deeply ingrained behavioral patterns and neural pathways. It requires us to ignore the stories we tell about who and what we are. It requires us to face the unknown. Because change is hard, we'd rather stick to the known, even when it is not effective or useful anymore. Helping participants realize that ambivalence is common can be essential to helping them get unstuck.
- **Explore the risks of changing.** High-risk behavior is common in the lives of many teens with co-occurring disorders. Paradoxically, these teens are often risk avoidant. As Prochaska, Norcross and DiClemente noted in 1994, change "threatens our very identity and asks us to relinquish our way of being." This is dangerous stuff for anyone, but for stuck teens, it can feel especially risky. Helping them make lasting change requires exploring the risks involved.
- **Foster self-efficacy.** Albert Bandura wrote that self-efficacy is "the belief in one's capabilities to organize and execute the courses of action required to manage prospective situations." In other words, it is a person's belief in his or her ability to succeed. Teens with low self-efficacy avoid challenging tasks, focus on negative outcomes and quickly lose confidence in their ability to be successful. They have very little interest in attempting to change.
- **Disrupt rigid thinking habits.** Teens with co-occurring disorders typically exhibit all-or-nothing thinking, catastrophize, deny having problems and blame others. These rigid thinking patterns reinforce their ambivalence. Resolving ambivalence requires them to think between the extremes. Traditional cognitive behavioral approaches identify these thinking patterns as irrational, erroneous and maladaptive. I prefer the term *thinking habits*, because habits can be changed.

- **Address existential concerns.** Irvin Yalom identified four "givens" that define an existential perspective to psychotherapy: death, meaninglessness, freedom and isolation. Professional helpers sometimes shy away from these existential concerns, especially when working with adolescents. However, these givens are very much present in the lives of teens and can contribute significantly to both stuckness and ambivalence. Acknowledge these givens and explore them with participants.

Become Trauma-informed

The Substance Abuse and Mental Health Services Administration defines trauma-informed care as "an approach to engaging people with histories of trauma that recognizes the presence of trauma symptoms and acknowledges the role that trauma has played in their lives." Trauma-informed care includes the use of carefully developed approaches that reduce the likelihood of retraumatizing participants while integrating safety, trustworthiness, choice, collaboration, and connection into all interactions.

Studies show that as many as 75 percent of teens in treatment for substance use disorders have experienced some form of traumatic stress. This occurs when an individual is exposed to a potentially traumatizing event or situation that overwhelms his or her ability to cope. Traumatic stress can be caused by a one-time experience or complex trauma, which can be defined as the experience of multiple traumatic events. Traumatic stress can lead to PTSD, a severe anxiety disorder that develops after exposure to traumatic stress. PTSD is a clinical diagnosis that requires the presence of specific symptoms, such as nightmares about the traumatic event, avoidance of stimuli associated with the event, increased arousal and hypervigilance. Regardless of whether they meet the diagnostic threshold for PTSD, teen trauma survivors often exhibit the following:

- **Hyperarousal:** Survivors can become extremely vigilant about their surroundings and often experience high levels of anxiety, which leads to sleep problems, trouble concentrating, feeling constantly on guard or being easily startled.
- **Intrusion:** Memories, flashbacks, and nightmares can continue long after the original traumatic exposure. Additionally, survivors sometimes unintentionally reenact aspects of the trauma. For example, teen survivors often engage in highly risky behaviors.

- **Constriction:** Attempts to avoid intrusion frequently result in survivors withdrawing from the world both physically and emotionally. Agoraphobia, substance use, limited social interactions and dissociation are a few examples of constriction.

When an individual has both a substance use disorder and traumatic stress, we usually assume that the trauma led to using the substance. However, substance use often leads to trauma exposure—or further exposure. In addition, pre-existing mental health challenges and a variety of other factors can increase the likelihood of trauma exposure. Whether trauma leads to drug use, drug use leads to trauma or a more complex scenario is present, substance-abusing survivors often find themselves perpetually stuck.

Even though risky behavior is evident in the lives of most substance-abusing teens, and especially those with trauma histories, these youth are frequently risk adverse, with their risky behaviors serving as ineffective attempts to avoid risk or distractions from their past trauma. Some adolescent survivors are so obsessed with safety that they resort to substances and other maladaptive methods in an effort to find it. Still other teens lead lives so constricted that they barely participate in life. According to Judith Herman, in all these cases, trauma has "cast the victim into a state of existential crisis" in which all choices likely lead to even further stuckness.

Create Connectedness

Edward Hallowell wrote that connectedness "is a sense of being a part of something larger than oneself. It is a sense of belonging, or a sense of accompaniment. It is that feeling in your bones that you are not alone. . . . Connectedness is my word for the force that urges us to ally, to affiliate, to enter into mutual relationships, to take strength and to grow through cooperative behavior."

For teens with co-occurring disorders, this sense of connectedness is typically missing. I believe that isolation exacerbates all life problems, so I strongly propose that the first step toward ensuring a valuable therapeutic experience is helping participants move toward increased connectedness. In clinical settings, we can focus on two types of connectedness: group cohesion and therapeutic alliance.

Group Cohesion: It seems to me that groups should be part of the treatment plan for any teen with co-occurring disorders. That said, for change to happen in groups, a strong sense of cohesion is essential. We can help achieve group cohesion by remembering this simple formula: *Cohesion = Shared Fun + Safety.*

When working in groups, it is essential that we create safe spaces. This includes physical, emotional and social safety. We can create a sense of safety by modeling what we expect. That means being consistent and reliable, treating participants and co-facilitators in a welcoming manner and ensuring that groups are fully inclusive.

Some treatment approaches seem to assume that participants are fragile, hopelessly damaged or completely dysregulated. Fun activities and laughter have no place is such approaches. That's a shame. Shared fun activities build connectedness between group members and provide valuable opportunities to practice interpersonal skills. In addition, the use of fun and games helps alter negative preconceived notions of treatment, provides entry points for less verbal participants and helps teens reauthor their stories to include a world where laughter is the norm.

Therapeutic Alliance: Numerous studies show that a strong therapeutic alliance is the most important indicator of positive outcomes when working with teens. When we take time to foster a strong alliance by genuinely embracing our participants' real motivators, we stop being an adversary and become an ally. This allows us to gently challenge the ambivalence, thinking habits and other roadblocks that keep participants stuck.

Edward Bordin wrote that a strong therapeutic alliance is composed of three elements: a positive bond between the therapist and participant, agreement regarding the tasks of treatment and agreement about the goals of treatment. In other words, there is congruence between the participant and the therapist. It seems to me that there also exists a need for transparency. Here are a few ideas for this:

- **Explain what you're doing as a counselor.** Take time to explain the theory behind your therapeutic approaches. In addition, explain to the teen what you hope to achieve by asking a particular question or assigning a specific homework task. This not only increases transparency but also improves buy-in.

- **Remember that relationships are reciprocal.** We expect participants to be honest. They should get the same from us. Don't disclose excessive amounts of personal information, but do answer questions that have been sincerely asked. Be genuine and model openness.

- **Use concurrent documentation.** Before ending individual sessions, write your progress note. Then have the participant read the progress note and write his or her own summary of the session. This may seem a bit clumsy at first, but in my experience, most participants quickly embrace the process.

Addiction as an Attachment Disorder

Substance abuse specialists familiar with attachment theory invariably report an inverse relationship between substance use disorders and healthy interpersonal attachments. In traditional treatment, unhealthy interpersonal attachments are generally considered the result of addiction. There is no doubt that heavy substance abuse is likely to exert a negative influence on relationships. However, there is mounting evidence that insecure attachment styles are risk factors for problematic substance use.

There are two basic concepts that are important for us to consider. First, if we don't have opportunities to observe caregivers engaging in effective emotional regulation, we may resort to substances in an effort to manage uncomfortable feelings. Second, if we don't connect to other people in meaningful, emotionally satisfying ways, we will find something else to fill that void.

Andrew referred to this void as a black hole made of all colors and tried to fill it with alcohol, drugs and significant acting-out behaviors. Other teens try to fill their voids with gangs, gambling, food, sex or video games. When we slow down and meet participants where they are at, we are able to help them get unstuck and start the change process so that they can see all the colors, not just black.

Critical Thinking

1. How has our approach to mental health changed in the last 10–15 years?

2. How can we promote "connectedness" among more of our adolescent population, those with and those without diagnosed disorders?

Internet References

Adolescents Coping with Stress: Development and Diversity

https://www.pdx.edu/sites/www.pdx.edu.psy/files/15-4-Zimmer-Gembeck-E.pdf

Adolescent Mental Health Disorders

https://www.hhs.gov/ash/oah/adolescent-development/mental-health/mental-health-disorders/index.html

Mental Disorders in Children and Adolescents

https://www.austinchildguidance.org/for-parents/parenting-articles-tips/mental-disorders-in-children-and-adolescents/

Mental Health in Adolescents

https://www.hhs.gov/ash/oah/adolescent-development/mental-health/index.html

New Perspectives on Adolescent Motivated Behavior: Attention and Conditioning

https://www.ncbi.nlm.nih.gov/pmc/articles/PMC3184422/

DAVID FLACK is a licensed mental health counselor, chemical dependency professional, and child mental health specialist. He lives in the Seattle area and has worked for the past dozen years exclusively with teenagers who have co-occurring disorders. He has special interests in the comorbidity of substance use and trauma in adolescents, the use of experiential learning in clinical settings and the unique challenges faced by LGBTQ teens.

Article   Prepared by: Claire N. Rubman, *Suffolk County Community College*

Problematic Technology Use During Adolescence: Why Don't Teenagers Seek Treatment?

MARK D. GRIFFITHS

Learning Outcomes

After reading this article, you will be able to:

- Describe four ways that peers affect the potential treatment for a technology addiction.

- Explain the difficulties associated with providing treatment to adolescents for technology addictions.

- Describe five issues associated with research related to this troubling addiction.

In recent issues of *Education and Health*, I have briefly reviewed the empirical evidence relating to problematic use of technology by adolescents including online video gaming (Griffiths, 2014), social networking (Griffiths, 2013a; Kuss & Griffiths, 2011), and mobile phone use (Griffiths, 2013b). Most of the research studies that have examined 'technological addictions' during adolescence have indicated that a small but significant minority experience severe problems resulting in detriments to education, physical fitness, psychological wellbeing, and family and personal relationships (Griffiths, 2010; Kuss, Griffiths, Karila, & Billieux, 2014). Given these findings, why is it that so few teenagers seek treatment? This article briefly outlines a number of reasons why this might be the case by examining other literature on adolescent drug use and adolescent gambling (e.g., Chevalier & Griffiths, 2005; 2005; Griffiths, 2001). Three different types of explanation are discussed: (i) treatment-specific explanations, (ii) research-related explanations, and (iii) developmental and peer group explanations.

Treatment-specific Explanations

This first set of explanations directly concern aspects of treatment-seeking behaviour that may impact on whether adolescents would seek treatment for problematic technology use.

Adolescents do not seek treatment in general: Griffiths and Chevalier (2005) noted that teenage males rarely contemplate seeking treatment for anything (apart from life-threatening traumas and extremely severe acne). Female adolescents are a little more likely than young males to consult health professionals (especially for gynaecological reasons). The reasons why adolescents in general do not consult health professionals are their perceived invincibility, invulnerability, and immortality. In addition, adolescents are constantly learning and appear to want to resolve their own problems rather than seek help from a third party. Who better than themselves knows what to do with their lives and whatever problem they are facing? They might experience more denial then adults, but come to the conclusion that others (usually adults) do not understand them. Ultimately, if adolescents rarely present themselves for any kind of treatment, it would be surprising to see them turn up for very specific treatments related to problematic technology use.

Adolescents may acknowledge they have a problem concerning their use of technology but do not want to seek treatment: Again, this explanation is plausible, but there is little empirical evidence to support the claim. However, it has been noted that families of adolescent problem gamblers are often protective—if not overprotective—and try to keep the problem within the family (Griffiths, 2002). Therefore, it may be speculated that seeking formal help for problems with technology use may be a last resort option for most adolescents and their families.

There are few or no treatment programmes available for adolescents: It is true that specialized treatment programmes for problematic technology use are almost nonexistent in the UK. Although there are a few private addiction clinics that treat gaming addicts, services specifically for adolescents with problematic technology use appear to be few and far between. It could be argued that this is a "Catch 22" situation. If only a few adolescents turn up for treatment, treatment programmes will not be able to provide specialized services, and adolescents with problematic technology use do not turn up for treatment if it does not exist.

Available treatment programmes are not appropriate and/or suitable for adolescents: To some extent, this explanation is interlinked with the previous reason, but is different. The explanation here is that there may be treatment programmes available, but that most are adult-oriented (e.g., group therapy in private and/or residential addiction treatment clinics). Adolescents may not want to be integrated into what they perceive to be an adult environment.

Attending treatment programmes may be stigmatizing for adolescents: Adolescents might not seek treatment for problematic technology use because of the stigma attached to such a course of action. Seeking treatment may signify that they can no longer participate in the activities by which they and their group define themselves. Furthermore, it may draw attention to what they perceive as a "failure" in their lives.

Adolescents may seek other forms of treatment, but problematic technology use are less likely to be seen as requiring intervention: Adolescent problematic technology use is associated with other comorbid behaviors such as substance abuse (van Rooij et al., 2014) and problem gambling (Wood, Gupta, Derevensky, & Griffiths, 2004). Adolescents may engage in all of these behaviors for the same reasons (to feel part of their peer group, to modify their mood state, to escape other problems in their lives, etc.). Therefore, the few adolescents who do seek treatment may do so for a comorbid behaviour rather than for problematic technology use itself. In most Western societies, problematic technology use is not perceived as a real problem, especially when compared with problems related to alcohol or substance abuse.

Treating other underlying problems may help adolescent problematic technology use: Problematic technology use could be (and quite often is) symptomatic of an underlying problem such as depression, dysfunctional family life, physical disability, lack of direction, or purpose of life (Király, Nagygyörgy, Griffiths, & Demetrovics, 2014; Kuss et al., 2014). Therefore, if these other problems are treated, the symptomatic behaviour (i.e., problematic technology use) should disappear, negating the need for specific problematic technology use-specific treatment.

Research-related Explanations

Another set of explanations may relate to the fact that the empirical research that has been carried out into problematic technology use is overinflating the prevalence rates because of many different factors. The implication here is that adolescents are not turning up for treatment because there is no real problem in the first place.

Adolescents with problematic technology use may lie or distort the truth when they fill out research surveys: This is a reasonable enough assumption to make and can be made against anyone who participates in self-report research—not just adolescents. All researchers who utilize self-report methods put as much faith as they can into their data but are only too aware that other factors may come into play (e.g., social desirability, motivational distortion, etc.) that can either underscore or overplay the situation. In these particular circumstances, it may be that adolescents are more likely to lie than adults. However, it seems unlikely that any differences would be due to this factor alone.

Screening instruments for assessing problematic gambling may not be valid for adolescents: Although there are many debates about the effectiveness of screening instruments for assessing problematic technology use (King, Haagsma, Delfabbro, Gradisar, & Griffiths, 2013), it could be the case that many of these question-based screening instruments are not applicable, appropriate and/or valid for assessing adolescent technology use. For instance, King et al. (2013) reviewed 18 different instruments that assess problematic video gaming but only one had specifically been developed for adolescents.

Screening instruments for adolescent problematic technology use are being used incorrectly: With measures developed for adolescents, as with those for adults, there may be incorrect use of screening instruments. For instance, there may be a lack of consistency in methodology, definitions, measurement, cut scores, and diagnostic criteria across studies, and particularly in the use of lenient diagnostic criteria for problematic technology use youth in some studies (King et al., 2013).

Adolescents may not understand what they are asked in research surveys: Another reason that the prevalence rates of adolescent problematic technology use may be elevated is because of measurement error. If adult instruments are administered to youth (which some researchers including myself have done) adolescents may endorse items they should not, doing so because they do not fully understand the item. For instance, in research on adolescent problem gambling, Ladouceur, Bouchard, Rhéaume, et al. (2000) showed that many of the items on the adolescent version of the South Oaks Gambling Screen were misunderstood, with only 31 percent of youth understanding all of the items correctly.

Researchers consciously or unconsciously exaggerate the problem of adolescent technology use to serve their own careers: This explanation is somewhat controversial but cannot be ruled out without at least examining the possibility. If this explanation is examined on a logical and practical level, it can be argued that those of us who have careers in the field of problematic technology use (like myself) could potentially have a lot to lose if there were no problems. Therefore, it could be argued that it is in the researcher's interest for problems to be exaggerated. However, there is no empirical evidence that this is the case, and all researchers are aware that their findings will be rigorously scrutinized. In short, it is not in researchers' best long-term interest to make unsubstantiated claims.

Developmental and Peer Group Explanations

Finally, there may be some explanations of why adolescents do not seek treatment for problematic technology use as being due to some aspects associated with adolescent development and peer group influence.

Adolescents with problematic technology use may undergo spontaneous remission and/or mature out of gambling problems, and therefore, may not seek treatment: There are many accounts in the literature of spontaneous remission of problematic behavior (e.g., alcohol abuse, heroin abuse, cigarette smoking, problem gambling), and problematic technology use is no exception. Because levels of problematic technology use appear to be much higher in adolescents than in adults (Kuss et al., 2014), and fewer adolescents receive treatment for their problematic technology use, it is reasonable to assume that spontaneous remission occurs in most adolescents at some point, or that there is some kind of "maturing out" process. There is a lot of case-study evidence highlighting the fact that spontaneous remission occurs in problem adolescent gamblers and that gambling often ceases because of some kind of new major responsibility such as getting one's first job, getting married, or birth of a child (Griffiths, 2002).

Adolescent excesses may change too quickly to warrant treatment: Adolescence is sometimes about excess and many addictions peak in youth (Griffiths, 1996). It could be that transfer of excess is a simpler matter for adolescents. They might have an excess "flavour of the month" syndrome, where one month it is binge alcohol drinking, one month it is joyriding, and one month it is video gaming. Adolescents may not seek treatment not because of spontaneous remission in the classical sense, but because of some sort of transfer of excess.

The negative consequences of adolescent problem gambling are not necessarily unique to problematic technology

use and may be attributed either consciously or unconsciously to other behaviors: Some adolescents may attribute their undesirable behaviour or negative consequences to other potentially addictive behaviors that co-occur during adolescent development, such as alcohol abuse or using illicit drugs (Griffiths & Chevalier, 2005).

Adolescent problematic technology use may be socially constructed to be nonproblematic: Problems, whether they are medical or otherwise, are socially constructed (Castellani, 2000). For example, denial may not be experienced because there is no perception of a problem. For instance, if the peer group, or school class of the adolescent is pro-technology use, actively engaged in technology use, and shows signs of problems, it may appear to the adolescent that problems go with the territory. Playing the guitar is hard on the fingers, playing football is hard on the shins, and playing video games is hard on sleep, and schoolwork. Therefore, it may not be perceived as a medical, psychological, and/or personal problem, but merely a fact of adolescent life.

Conclusions

Although this list may not be exhaustive, it does give the main reasons why adolescents with problematic technology use may be underreported in turning up for treatment. It is likely that no single reason provides more of an explanation than another. The reasons provided also raise many questions that require answers. Why do adolescents appear to be reluctant to seek help for problems related to technology use? What is the true prevalence of problematic technology use among youth? Are the available statistics on problematic technology use inflated by a lack of understanding of the survey questionnaire items? Where does problematic technology use fit among the many difficulties young people face during the developmental process? Are the heightened rates of problematic technology use among youth the result of having grown up during times of such extensive availability (i.e., a cohort effect) or are they merely a reflection of adolescent experimentation that they will grow out of (or a combination of the two)?

Research needs to address directions and magnitudes of causality among problematic technology use behaviors and other health and psychosocial problems. What is clear is that there is no single assertion made in this article provides a definitive answer to the treatment paradox in relation to adolescent problematic technology use. It is most likely the case that many of the plausible explanations interlink to produce the obvious disparities between prevalence rates of adolescent problematic technology use and adolescents not enrolling in treatment programmes.

References

Griffiths, M.D. (2002). *Gambling and Gaming Addictions in Adolescence*. Leicester: British Psychological Society/ Blackwells.

Griffiths, M.D. (2001). Why don't adolescent gamblers seek treatment? *Journal of Gambling Issues*, 5, Located at: http://jgi. camh.net/doi/full/10.4309/jgi.2001.5.6

Griffiths, M.D. (2010). Trends in technological advance: Implications for sedentary behaviour and obesity in screenagers. *Education and Health*, 28, 35–38. Located at: http://sheu.org.uk/x/ eh282mg.pdf

Griffiths, M.D. (2013a). Adolescent gambling via social networking sites: A brief overview. *Education and Health*, 31, 84–87. Located at: http://sheu.org.uk/x/eh314mg.pdf

Griffiths, M.D. (2013b). Adolescent mobile phone addiction: A cause for concern? *Education and Health*, 31, 76–78. Located at: http://sheu.org.uk/x/eh313mg.pdf

Griffiths, M.D. & Chevalier, S. (2005). Addiction in adolescence: Why don't adolescent addicts turn up for treatment? *Psyke & Logos (Journal of the Danish Psychological Society)*, 26, 27–31.

King, D.L., Haagsma, M.C., Delfabbro, P.H., Gradisar, M.S., Griffiths, M.D. (2013). Toward a consensus definition of pathological video-gaming: A systematic review of psychometric assessment tools. *Clinical Psychology Review*, 33, 331–342.

Királyi, O., Nagygyörgy, K., Griffiths, M.D. & Demetrovics, Z. (2014). Problematic online gaming. In K. Rosenberg & L. Feder (Eds.), *Behavioral Addictions: Criteria, Evidence and Treatment* (pp.61–95). New York: Elsevier.

Kuss, D.J. & Griffiths, M.D. (2011). Excessive online social networking: Can adolescents become addicted to *Facebook*? *Education and Health*, 29. 63–66. Located at: http://sheu.org.uk/ sites/sheu.org.uk/files/imagepicker/1/eh294mg.pdf

Kuss, D.J., Griffiths, M.D., Karila, L. & Billieux, J. (2014). Internet addiction: A systematic review of epidemiological research for the last decade. *Current Pharmaceutical Design*, 20, 4026–4052.

Ladouceur, R., Bouchard, C., Rhéaume, N., Jacques, C., Ferland, F., Leblond, J., et al. (2000). Is the SOGS an accurate measure of pathological gambling among children, adolescents and adults? *Journal of Gambling Studies*, 16, 1–24

van Rooij, A.J., Kuss, D.J., Griffiths, M.D., Shorter, G.S., Schoenmakers, T.M. & van de Mheen, D. (2014). The (co) ocurrence of video game addiction, substance use, and psychosocial problems in adolescents. *Journal of Behavioral Addiction*, 3(3), 157–165.

Wood, R.T.A., Gupta, R., Derevensky, J. & Griffiths, M.D. (2004). Video game playing and gambling in adolescents: Common risk factors. *Journal of Child and Adolescent Substance Abuse* 14, 77–100.

Critical Thinking

1. Is a technology addiction a real and persistent problem?
2. How could peers be used to positively impact a teen's use or overuse of technology?

Internet References

Are Teenagers Replacing Drugs with Smartphones?

https://www.nytimes.com/2017/03/13/health/teenagers-drugs-smartphones.html

Screen Addiction Is Taking a Toll on Children

https://well.blogs.nytimes.com/2015/07/06/screen-addiction-is-taking-a-toll-on-children/

Technology Addiction

http://parentingteenagersacademy.com/technology-addiction/

Teens Say They're Addicted to Technology. Here's How Parents Can Help

https://www.washingtonpost.com/news/parenting/wp/2016/05/03/teens-say-theyre-addicted-to-technology-heres-how-parents-can-help/?utm_term=.2ca30c6d4518

Why Adolescents Overuse Technology, and What We Can Do about It

https://www.psychologytoday.com/blog/apologies-freud/201201/why-adolescents-overuse-technology-and-what-we-can-do-about-it

---

Dr. Mark D. Griffiths is a professor of Gambling Studies and the director of the International Gaming Research Unit, Nottingham Trent University.

Article   Prepared by: Claire N. Rubman, *Suffolk County Community College*

Can't Turn Off the Night

Nightmares during Adolescence May Be a Warning Sign for Psychosis

RONI JACOBSON

Learning Outcomes

After reading this article, you will be able to:

- Explain what is meant by a psychotic episode.

- Explain the term "transliminality."

Chuck has had vivid nightmares his whole life. When he was a kid, he dreamed about being attacked on a battlefield, with the dead bodies of family members strewn around him. Once every few months, he would dream that he was drowning. "I'd wake up sweating, with my heart pounding," he says.

Nightmares are common in preschool and elementary-school children. Kids often dream about being chased or falling from great heights and then are startled awake just before being caught or hitting the ground. Most children outgrow their nightmares, however, and the latest research suggests that if nightmares persist, they could be evidence of a deeper problem.

Chuck, now 20, was still having regular nightmares by the time he was a teenager, but instead of facing down monsters, he was confronted by social rejection. In one familiar scenario, he was naked at a party that his academic adviser happened to be attending, and he remembers feeling "very exposed and vulnerable." Now, a college student in Memphis, Tenn., Chuck (who asked to remain anonymous) still has nightmares. He was also recently diagnosed with schizophrenia.

It turns out that nightmares and psychosis may be connected. A team of researchers led by Dieter Wolke, a psychology professor at the University of Warwick in the U.K., recently found that children who had frequent nightmares between the ages of two and nine were about one and a half times more likely to have a psychotic experience in early adolescence.

Psychotic experiences, which include delusional thoughts and auditory and visual hallucinations, are usually nothing to worry about in young children, who often have trouble distinguishing between reality and make-believe. During adolescence, however, such experiences are more unusual and may be a sign of burgeoning mental illness.

Chuck's first clinically significant schizophrenia symptoms came out at 18, when he began to suspect that his friends were informing on him to school administrators. He also started thinking he was being watched 24/7 by cameras in his dorm room, and by the time he was 19, he was "hearing voices all the time."

But while his diagnosis didn't come until college, he remembers having delusional beliefs early on. When Chuck was 11, he thought he had caused his aunt to have a miscarriage with his mind. "I would sometimes get very strange ideas," he says. "Like, I would spend days reading and watching shows about life on other planets." Between the ages of 15 and 17, his strongest hope was to be contacted by aliens. His friends found his obsession with extraterrestrial life a little weird, he says, but most dismissed it as a mild eccentricity.

At the same time, he was having nightmares about once every two to three months—a high frequency for a teenager. They mostly involved themes of "losing control, being in chaotic situations," he says. The dreams were distressing, but his parents generally shrugged them off.

The potential link between nightmares and psychosis has intrigued researchers for decades. It's easy to see why: One of the most noticeable characteristics of schizophrenia—hallucinations, or seeing or hearing things that aren't there—could be interpreted as "dreaming while awake,'" says Nirit Soffer-Dudek, a psychologist at Ben-Gurion University of the Negev in Israel. One early hypothesis was that people who develop schizophrenia and other psychotic disorders are higher in a personality measure known as "transliminality," meaning that their border between sleeping and waking states is more fluid than that of other people.

Indeed, a significant body of research has indicated that people with schizophrenia tend to have more nightmares than the general population. In a 2009 study, for example, young adults with schizophrenia reported more frequent nightmares than control subjects.

Building off of this work, Wolke and his team sought to find out if it is possible to trace schizophrenia back to childhood nightmares. They followed almost 6,800 children born in the U.K. between 1991 and 1992 until they reached the age of 12. About 75 percent of them had at least one bout of regular nightmares at some point during their first nine years, according to their parents. But by the time the children turned 12, only about 25 percent reported having recent nightmares.

The children in that last group were three and a half times more likely to have had a recent psychotic experience. "It's pretty well established that these things overlap. I think the big question now is why," says Erin Koffel, a clinical psychologist at the U.S Department of Veterans Affairs. The study, she says, helps "get at kind of the chicken-and-egg problem. Which came first: the sleep problem or these daytime symptoms?"

The answer may be neither. Recent research suggests that, rather than one causing the other, nightmares and psychotic experiences in adolescents may be linked by a third factor: stress.

"Nightmares occur more frequently when you have been exposed to trauma. They also occur more frequently if you are anxious or have had something highly stimulating happen during the day," says Wolke. And chronic nightmares are directly connected to stress: Studies show that they commonly follow experiences with war and violence, and frequently with childhood sexual abuse. Recurring nightmares also are among the diagnostic criteria for post-traumatic stress disorder.

Likewise, psychotic experiences may originate in anxiety and stress. For example, people (even those without a mental health disorder) are more likely to hear voices after suffering a loss or a trauma, such as the death of a loved one. And psychosis-inducing stressors can also often be traced back to childhood. In a study from 2012, individuals who had auditory and visual hallucinations were more likely to have experienced emotional and sexual abuse in childhood, compared with a control group with no hallucinations. Other research, including an upcoming study by Wolke, indicates that many children who have psychotic experiences in adolescence were bullied in school.

Some psychologists hypothesize that trauma causes people to experience a loss of agency and disassociate, stepping outside of oneself into a fantasy world. "One of the main symptoms of post-traumatic stress disorder is this kind of reliving of the event and seeing it play out in front of you, as well as having quite severe nightmares," says Helen Fisher, an anthropologist at Rutgers University who co-authored the paper. "That often happens when someone has experienced a stressor and doesn't process it properly."

Chuck's female swim instructor molested him when he was 5, he says, and he was constantly bullied until around his freshman year of high school. As an open atheist in an all-boys Catholic school, he felt ostracized and was targeted for being different. "I just lost my will to fight back," he says.

The combination of being bullied at school and maltreated at home leaves children with 24-hour days filled with fear and uncertainty, says Wolke. "How can you deal with a world that is so stressful?" he asks. "So you perhaps create your own world, or you become hypersensitive—you see problems everywhere, and you feel persecuted even though these experiences are not real."

Chuck is doing well now. He made the dean's list last semester, has many good friends, and stays active—he recently started power lifting and will compete in a tournament later this year. But he was relatively lucky—he got therapy and found an antipsychotic medication that worked for him soon after his diagnosis.

Wolke and others hope that understanding the factors that contribute to psychosis can help clinicians steer children at risk of mental health disorders into early interventions sooner. "We are realizing that once people have developed a mental disorder, then it's pretty tough to do something about it," Fisher says. But providing them with treatment early on can dramatically improve their prognosis, she adds.

It's easy for parents or family members to miss a child's struggles with mental problems like depression or psychotic experiences. After all, children don't know what's "normal" and are unlikely to be able to share experiences that adults might interpret as warning signs. And if troubling signs do come up, doctors must closely monitor them, says Ian Kelleher, a psychiatrist at the Royal College of Surgeons in Ireland.

Nightmares, on the other hand, are easy to spot.

Of course, "having nightmares doesn't mean that your child is mentally unwell, and it doesn't mean they are having psychotic experiences," says Kelleher. "But it does highlight the fact that when they are having persistent nightmares, you need to ask what's going on in their life." In addition, while the link between nightmares and psychotic experiences is clear, the vast majority of adolescents who experience psychotic symptoms won't develop schizophrenia. Most will go on to have another, nonpsychotic disorder, however, such as depression, ADHD, or anxiety.

And it's too early in the game to think about diagnosis-specific interventions, Fisher says. But fairly noninvasive treatments—such as bolstering coping strategies and self-esteem, and making sure people have strong support networks (things that are probably generally useful for teenagers anyway)—could help adolescents deal with underlying stress.

The terror of nightmares is usually fleeting, but in some cases, it's better to investigate than sit back and hope for the best.

Critical Thinking

1. How would you react if your adolescent reported frequent and vivid nightmares?

2. Discuss some of the potential issues associated with correlational studies that report a relationship between nightmares and a psychosis diagnosis.

Internet References

Childhood Sleep Disturbance and Risk of Psychotic Experiences at 18: UK Birth Cohort
https://www.ncbi.nlm.nih.gov/pmc/articles/PMC4486818/

Development of Disturbing Dreams during Adolescence and Their Relation to Anxiety Symptoms
http://dreamscience.ca/en/documents/publications/_2000_Nielsen_Laberge_S_23_727-736_NM_ado.pdf

Frequent Childhood Nightmares May Indicate an Increased Risk of Psychotic Traits
http://www2.warwick.ac.uk/newsandevents/pressreleases/frequent_childhood_nightmares/

How to Cure Nightmares in Teenagers
http://oureverydaylife.com/cure-nightmares-teenagers-9713.html

Nightmares
https://my.clevelandclinic.org/health/articles/pediatric-nighttime-fears/nightmares

Nightmares Predict Adolescent Mental Illness
http://guardianlv.com/2014/02/nightmares-predict-adolescent-mental-illness/

Article   Prepared by: Claire N. Rubman, *Suffolk County Community College*

Self-injury: Why Teens Do It and How to Help

Pediatricians are most likely the first clinicians to discover that a teenager is engaging in self-harming behavior, and it's their initial evaluation of the context and severity of the self-injury as well as their empathetic relationship with the patient that sets the stage for treatment.

CLAIRE M. BRICKELL AND MICHAEL S. JELLINEK

Learning Outcomes

After reading this article, you will be able to:

- Explain some of the reasons behind adolescent self-injury.

- Identify the most "at risk" population for self-harm.

- Better understand self-injury through three case studies.

Every year, pediatricians care for adolescents who hurt themselves deliberately, in ways that include cutting, burning, abrading, and hitting. Roughly, one in six teenagers has tried self-harm at least once.[1] The majority of teenagers do so only mildly or occasionally, but approximately 5 percent hurt themselves in serious and persistent ways.[2,3] Collectively, these actions are referred to as self-injurious behavior (SIB), which is defined as the deliberate, direct destruction of body tissues. Notably, most teenagers who engage in SIB do so without the intent to kill themselves. Clinicians and researchers thus often speak of nonsuicidal self-injury (NSSI), the focus of this article.[4]

A pediatrician is likely the first clinician to discover that a teenager has been self-harming. Wounds or scars may be uncovered during a routine physical examination, or a panicked parent may call for an urgent evaluation of a son or daughter. The first clinical encounter can be difficult for everyone: Parents often experience guilt, betrayal, or outrage; the adolescent may feel exposed and ashamed; the pediatrician might respond with frustration or just incomprehension. The first clinical encounter

is also critical for setting the stage for successful treatment. As a 15-year-old patient with a history of self-injury stated during a therapy session, "I hate it when people freak out. It makes me feel disgusting, and then I don't want to talk."

The goal of this article is to introduce the phenomenon of NSSI, including information on who self-injures and why. In terms of treatment, a variety of effective and evidence-based interventions for self-injury are available, but most require specific training and are implemented over a lengthy period of time, usually by psychiatrists.[5] Therefore, this discussion focuses on the preliminary evaluation of NSSI, with an emphasis for primary care physicians on how to present a supportive and nonjudgmental stance that can facilitate further assessment.

Why Self-injure?

It is intuitive to classify self-injury as a problem and to assume that once the behavior has stopped the patient will feel better. However, studies show that the most common function of self-injury is to manage a range of negative emotions or to create feeling where there is only numbness or emptiness.[6] In other words, the *problem* for the patient is feeling unbearably sad, anxious, ashamed, or lonely—or not feeling anything at all. Self-injury is a *solution* that, in the short term, can be incredibly effective at easing intolerable emotions.

In this type of situation, NSSI provides relief immediately and independently of any response from the outside world. Adolescents do not start self-injuring "just to get attention." In fact, many teenagers self-injure in secret for months or years before they are discovered, and rather than seeking attention will take active steps to hide their behavior. Once discovered, the behavior can take on a whole new dimension. Depending on the reaction they get from those around them, teenagers who have few emotional skills may quickly learn to use NSSI as a way to affect others.

For example, if a teenager starts cutting herself because she feels lonely and cannot bear it, and her family responds by rushing to express love and support, it is likely that she will start hurting herself every time she needs affection. Or, if a teenager is miserable at school and is allowed to stay home every time he starts hitting himself, he may continue hitting himself whenever things get particularly tense at school. Not surprisingly, then, adolescents in community samples report using NSSI as a means of influencing people and of communicating distress.[3]

As these examples suggest, NSSI can work to avoid something unpleasant or to provoke a reaction, even if it is a negative one. Therefore, many practitioners may dismiss adolescents who self-injure as manipulative. However, it is normal to want attention. Everyone tries to minimize suffering and to maximize pleasure. The problem is that the self-harming adolescent may not know how to ask for help in a direct or effective way. Self-injury is a temporary and blundering solution to a failure to communicate or to have critical needs met.

Far from being the master manipulators that some may make them out to be, teenagers who cut or hit themselves are often trying to manage their emotions and their relationships without really knowing how. Simply put, in our experience, many adolescents who self-injure do so because they do not know what else to do. This is an important underpinning of many of the treatments for NSSI, which aim to teach alternative problem-solving methods.

Who Self-injures

Based on the explanations we have offered, young people use NSSI to manage negative or empty feelings and to communicate suffering when they lack the ability to apply more effective solutions. Therefore, it makes sense that rates of self-injury are highest in those with troubling emotions, complex or stormy relationships, and poor coping skills.[5]

The *Diagnostic and Statistical Manual of Mental Disorders*, *DSM-IV-TR*, mentioned NSSI only as a symptom of borderline personality disorder (BPD), which in adults is defined as a pervasive pattern of unstable relationships, self-identity, and emotion, accompanied by impulsivity.[7] Thus, NSSI in adolescence was considered a marker of severe and potentially lifelong illness. However, research suggests that NSSI often occurs independently of BPD; for example, in patients with depression or substance abuse or even in those with no other diagnosable psychopathology.[5,8] Therefore, NSSI is now recognized as a

distinct condition in the DSM-5.[4] Future research will likely define subtypes of NSSI, some of which are more likely to persist into adulthood than others.

Estimates of the prevalence of self-injury vary according to assessment methodology and by whether or not nonfatal suicide attempts are included in the count. However, self-injury is accepted to be especially common in teenagers. Rates in community samples average around 18 percent as compared with 6 percent in the adult population.[1,9] Rates are comparable in North America, Europe, Australia, and Asia, indicating that NSSI is an international phenomenon.[1] Although NSSI has been traditionally associated with girls and women, more recently studies suggest there may not be a gender difference in prevalence.[10]

NSSI and Suicide

By definition, NSSI is self-injury carried out without the wish to die. In the moment, people who engage in this type of self-injury are not exhibiting suicidal behavior. On the contrary, they often use NSSI as a way to make being alive more bearable. Nevertheless, NSSI is a risk factor for later suicide attempts.

As a recent review article highlights, individuals who engage in NSSI are more likely to think about suicide and to actually attempt killing themselves.[11] NSSI that occurs more frequently and in more severe forms is also a strong predictor of suicidal behavior. In a clinical sample of depressed teenagers, NSSI predicted future suicide attempts just as strongly as past suicide attempts.[12] This link between NSSI and suicide held up even when the reviewers controlled for demographic differences, psychosocial conditions, and comorbid psychopathologies.

It remains unclear whether NSSI leads directly to suicidal behavior or if unbearable feelings lead to both. Regardless, adolescents who engage in NSSI should be assessed for immediate suicide risk as part of their clinical evaluation, even if suicide is not necessarily the sole or central focus.

Clinical Examples

Teenagers turn to self-injury as a solution to problems for various reasons, including genetics, temperament, or particular stressors. Thus, self-injury might be the sign of a relatively healthy teenager under extreme duress, or of a generally vulnerable teenager under more mild circumstances. For example:

CASE 1: *Consider a teenager whose boyfriend breaks up with her just two weeks after her best friend moves to another city. She has experienced some mild anxiety for years but is usually able to keep it in check. She does well in school and enjoys her guitar lessons. Today, however, she feels sad and alone, certain that she will never be happy again. With her boyfriend and her* *best friend gone, there is no one who will understand how she is feeling. She knows of a friend who cuts herself. While in the shower after school, she superficially cuts her wrist with the blade from her shaving razor. The pain helps her "snap out of it," and by the time her mother comes home from work she is able to tell her that she is feeling sad.*

CASE 2: *More concerning is the teenager who has been in treatment for attention deficit disorder since elementary school. He used to be able to keep up with his schoolwork, thanks to medication and help from teachers, but now that high school has started he is overwhelmed. He is afraid that his new friends will make fun of him if they find out that he has a learning disability, and he is ashamed to ask for more support. He stops turning in his homework on time and daydreams and doodles in class. He feels dumb, pathetic, and anxious about all the work that he has not done. He and his parents have started fighting about his slipping grades. He spends more and more time alone in his room playing video games. He is not sleeping well. He starts thinking that it would be better if he just did not wake up in the morning. While sitting in class, he rubs the skin of his forearm hard with an eraser until it blisters and bleeds. This calms him down enough so that he can get through the hour without running out of class or yelling at the teacher.*

CASE 3: *At the most severe end of the spectrum is the teenager who has been cutting and burning herself almost every day for months. It feels as if everyone in the world is against her. She used to have friends, but they are frustrated that she is not getting better. They are sick of her sending text messages in the middle of the night asking for help. She just cannot seem to get a handle on her mood, which swings from angry to sad and back again for reasons she cannot explain. Cutting herself is like hitting a "reset" button and helps her stay calm, but it only lasts until her next text message goes unanswered. Her parents are at their wits' end, and she is fairly sure that if they could get rid of her, they would. She feels terribly guilty about being such a mess and also furious when they will not let her go out with the new guy she met. The next time her mother takes away the car keys, she walks into the kitchen and puts her hand on the stove. The pain feels like appropriate punishment for being such a bad person, but her mother still does not seem to understand just how bad she makes her feel. Later that night she sneaks out of the house, calls her new "boyfriend," and has sex with him. She comes home before anyone is awake, thinks about killing herself, and looks for her razor.*

As these vignettes illustrate, teenagers have different problems that they are trying to solve, and some are more or less well equipped to do so. It is the pediatrician's job to evaluate the context and severity of self-injury to set the stage for successful further treatment.

Evaluating NSSI

When evaluating a teenager who engages in NSSI, it is important to first establish a general relationship with the patient by asking about school, home life, friendships, and activities. Then, a pediatrician can ease into asking about NSSI (Table 1). A good first question is "What does your self-injury help you with?" This is the same as simply asking "Why do you self-injure?" but the former question is less likely to be perceived as accusatory. Phrased in this way, the question demonstrates an understanding of the use of NSSI as a solution or self-treatment. Thus, it can open the door to a more specific discussion of psychiatric symptoms (depression, anger, anxiety) and interpersonal stressors (strained relationships with parents, breakups, loss of friendships).

Another approach is to ask the patient to remember a specific instance of self-injury. Helpful questions can include: "Do you remember how you were feeling before you injured yourself? How did that change after you injured yourself? How do you feel about it now?" Try to create a place that is nonjudgmental and safe.

Next, a pediatrician should try to gain information on the patient's mood and the logistics of self-injury: "How do you do it? What instrument do you use? How often do you do it? What part of your body is involved?" The doctor should also provide factual medical information that can help minimize complications and additional injury. For example, physicians can counsel patients about the risks of blood-borne illnesses and ensure tetanus vaccinations are up to date.

Self-injury is a sign that a teenager is both experiencing uncomfortable feelings and is ill equipped to manage them. Therefore, the general practitioner should ask about other dangerous behaviors that, like self-injury, tend to be used to cope with stress. Disordered eating, substance abuse, and risky sexual activity are all associated with self-injury and can have independent medical consequences that warrant evaluation.[5] Normalizing the experience can help teenagers talk about behaviors that they believe might get them into trouble. Try asking "Do you do anything else to make yourself feel better that might be risky in the long run?" or "Has your stress gotten so bad that you have turned to drugs or alcohol to try to escape?"

Of note, although many practitioners used to take for granted that teenagers who engage in NSSI had experienced childhood abuse, recent research has indicated that the relationship is much more modest.[13] Many who have been abused do not go on to self-injure and many who self-injure have never been abused. Nevertheless, abuse does happen, both inside and outside the home, and the office of a trusted physician may be a good place to talk about it. A helpful first way to inquire is to ask "Has anyone hurt you—physically or mentally—in a way that is still affecting you?" In addition to screening for abuse by

Table 1 Assessing Self-injury.

What to Assess	Sample Questions
The function of self-injury	• What does your self-injury help you with? • Do you remember how you were feeling before you injured yourself? How did that change afterward?
The method of self-injury	• How do you do it? • What instrument do you use? • How often do you do it? • What part of your body is involved?
The potential for medical complications	• Have you required medical attention (e.g., stitches)? • Do you use a clean blade or have you shared a blade with anyone? • When was your last tetanus shot?
Other dangerous behaviors	• Do you do anything else to make yourself feel better that might be risky in the long run? • Have you used drugs or alcohol to make yourself feel better? • Do you find yourself restricting your food or purging after meals? • Are you sexually active? Do you feel comfortable with your level of sexual activity?
Abuse or bullying	• Has anyone hurt you—physically or mentally—in a way that is still affecting you? • Do you feel safe at home? • Do you feel safe at school?
The risk of suicide	• Have things ever gotten so bad that you thought you might be better off dead? Have you thought about killing yourself? • Are you thinking of killing yourself now? • Do you have a plan for how you might do it? What is the relationship between your self-injury and thoughts of suicide?
Areas of strength	• What is going well in your life? • Who are the people you can count on? • Who or what do you turn to for comfort?

adults, the practitioner should specifically ask about bullying, which is often overlooked and can be severe.

Finally, although we have shown that NSSI should not be confounded with suicidal behavior, it is critical to evaluate for suicide risk. This is an area where it is helpful to be matter-of-fact, with progression from the general to the specific: "Have things ever gotten so bad that you thought you might be better off dead? Have you thought about killing yourself? Are you thinking of killing yourself now? Do you have a plan for how you might do it?" The word "kill," although jarring, is chosen to be distinct from the word "hurt."

For the sake of building an alliance, and of doing a complete evaluation, it is essential to also ask about what is going well for the patient. Is there a friend who is particularly supportive? Is there a class at which the patient excels? Does the patient have an artistic or musical talent? These relationships and skills are the basis for some level of self-esteem. They can be drawn on in therapy to help the teenager to get better and also to provide a picture of someone who is more than just a "self-injurer."

Confidentiality

Many teenagers will ask if what they reveal can be kept secret. Although conversations between physicians and their patients are generally confidential, when safety is at stake a patient's parents will need to be informed. In the case of NSSI, this means the answer to that question is often "no." It is important to explain to teenagers that their safety is your primary concern and that you will do what it takes to preserve it.

You can offer to help them tell their parents about the problem, and to mediate what is likely to be an emotionally charged conversation. You can also assure them that you will not talk to their parents without their knowledge. It is important that parents or legal guardians be informed so that they can support and participate in treatment. Most teenagers who are talking about NSSI for the first time are embarking on a lengthy road involving many encounters with healthcare professionals. It may be expedient in the short term, but it is most certainly damaging in the long term to promise confidentiality that you cannot or should not deliver.

Table 2 Management of Nonsuicidal Self-injury.

Intervention	Details
Create a safe, trusting environment to further ongoing communication	• Assess for strengths as well as weaknesses • Look at self-injury from the patient's point of view
Perform a thorough evaluation	
Involve parents and other appropriate adults	• Legal guardians need to know about dangerous activities
Make a referral to a mental health practitioner	• Adolescents with high risk for suicide should receive emergent psychiatric care • There are specialized treatments for BPD but none yet for NSSI

Abbreviations: BPD, borderline personality disorder; NSSI, nonsuicidal self-injury.

Psychopharmacologic Treatment

Currently, the US Food and Drug Administration has not approved any medication for the specific treatment of self-injury. Patients who additionally suffer from depression and/or anxiety may benefit from the pharmacologic treatments of those conditions. Researchers have also suggested that NSSI works to control negative emotions via the endogenous opioid system.[14] This raises the possibility that the opioid antagonist naltrexone (ReVia) might be effective in the treatment of NSSI, perhaps by blocking reward pathways and preventing positive reinforcement. Although helpful to treat associated disorders such as depression, medication is not a treatment for NSSI.

Psychotherapy

Different types of therapy for the treatment of NSSI have in common the necessity for consistent therapeutic contact for a relatively long time. Practically speaking, a teenager who self-injures warrants a referral to a mental health professional (Table 2). How and with what urgency the referral is made depends on the risk to the particular patient in question. Teenagers who are more fragile, more isolated, less successful, and who have families with fewer resources will require referral more urgently to a mental health clinician than others who are not at such high risk.

Any patient who is at imminent risk for suicide should be evaluated immediately by a crisis team or in an emergency department. He or she may require inpatient hospitalization to ensure safety in the short term. The inpatient team should then assist the pediatrician and the family in establishing longer term outpatient mental health care.

Thus far, treatment for self-injury has been considered only in the context of treatment for BPD. Perhaps with the development of the *DSM-5*'s new diagnosis, trials of treatments specifically designed for NSSI will come. The good news is that there are several empirically validated psychosocial treatments for BPD and its symptoms, including NSSI. These include transference-focused psychotherapy, mentalization-based psychotherapy, and dialectical behavior therapy, as well as manual-assisted cognitive-behavioral therapy.[5] These therapies differ in theoretical underpinnings, method of application, and emphasis of treatment, but all provide the patient with the opportunity to acquire new skills for the management of ways to solve the problems of emotional distress and interpersonal conflict.

Conclusion

The goal of the pediatrician's care is to establish a safe doctor-patient relationship, which will help the patient accept services and participate actively in treatment. Given the disturbing nature of self-injury and the frequent assumption that those who self-injure are "just manipulating" those around them, it can be difficult for the pediatrician to reach the respectful and nonjudgmental stance that is most effective in building a safe, trusting relationship. A better understanding of why teenagers self-injure and what can be done to help them get better is a first step in creating a comfortable, empathetic relationship. This work is difficult—but rewarding.

References

1. Muehlenkamp JJ, Claes L, Havertape L, Plener PL. International prevalence of adolescent non-suicidal self-injury and deliberate self-harm. *Child Adolesc Psychiatry Mental Health.* 2012;6:10.

2. Manca M, Presaghi F, Cerutti R. Clinical specificity of acute versus chronic self-injury: measurement and evaluation of repetitive non-suicidal self-injury. *Psychiatry Res.* 2014;215(1):111–119.

3. Zetterqvist M, Lundh LG, Dahlström O, Svedin CG. Prevalence and function of non-suicidal self-injury (NSSI) in a community sample of adolescents, using suggested *DSM-5* criteria for a potential NSSI disorder. *J Abnorm Child Psychol.* 2013;41(5):759–773.

4. American Psychiatric Association. *Diagnostic and Statistical Manual of Mental Disorders, DSM-5. 5th ed.* Arlington, VA: American Psychiatric Publishing; 2013.

5. Kerr PL, Muehlenkamp JJ, Turner JM. Nonsuicidal self-injury: a review of current research for family medicine and primary care physicians. *J Am Board Fam Med.* 2010;23(2):240–259.

6. Klonsky ED. The functions of deliberate self-injury: a review of the evidence. *Clin Psychol Rev.* 2007;27(2):226–239.

7. American Psychiatric Association. *Diagnostic and Statistical Manual of Mental Disorders, DSM-IV-TR.* 4th ed text rev. Washington, DC: American Psychiatric Association; 2000.

8. Wilkinson P. Non-suicidal self-injury. *Eur Child Adolesc Psychiatry.* 2013;22(suppl 1):S75–S79.

9. Klonsky ED. Non-suicidal self-injury in United States adults: prevalence, sociodemographics, topography and functions. *Psychol Med.* 2011;41(9):1981–1986.

10. Rodham K, Hawton K. Epidemiology and phenomenology of nonsuicidal self-injury. In: Nock MK, ed. *Understanding Nonsuicidal Self-Injury: Origins, Assessment, and Treatment.* Washington, DC: American Psychological Association; 2009;9–18.

11. Hamza CA, Stewart SL, Willoughby T. Examining the link between non-suicidal self-injury and suicidal behavior: A review of the literature and an integrated model. *Clin Psychol Rev.* 2012;32(6):482–495.

12. Wilkinson P, Kelvin R, Roberts C, Dubicka B, Goodyer I. Clinical and psychosocial predictors of suicide attempts and nonsuicidal self-injury in the Adolescent Depression Antidepressants and Psychotherapy Trial (ADAPT). *Am J Psychiatry.* 2011;168(5):495–501.

13. Klonsky ED, Moyer A. Childhood sexual abuse and non-suicidal self-injury: meta-analysis. *Br J Psychiatry.* 2008;192(3):166–170.

14. Bresin K, Gordon KH. Endogenous opioids and nonsuicidal self-injury: a mechanism of affect regulation. *Neurosci Biobehav Rev.* 2013;37(3):374–383.

Critical Thinking

1. What would you do if you noticed that your friend had scars that seemed to be from self-harming?

2. Describe two ways to help adolescents cope with new or difficult situations.

Internet References

Adolescent Self-Harm

http://www.aamft.org/iMIS15/AAMFT/Content/consumer_updates/adolescent_self_harm.aspx

Deliberate Self-harm in Adolescents

https://www.ncbi.nlm.nih.gov/pmc/articles/PMC4469847/

We Help Understand, Detect, Treat, and Prevent Self-injury

http://www.selfinjury.bctr.cornell.edu/

Self-injury/cutting Symptoms and Causes

http://www.mayoclinic.org/diseases-conditions/self-injury/symptoms-causes/dxc-20165427

The Adolescent Self Injury Foundation, Inc. (ASIF)

http://www.adolescentselfinjuryfoundation.com/

CLAIRE M. BRICKELL is a resident in child and adolescent psychiatry, Massachusetts General Hospital/McLean Hospital, Boston.

MICHAEL S. JELLINEK is professor of psychiatry and pediatrics, Harvard Medical School, and chief clinical officer, Partners HealthCare System, Boston, Massachusetts. He is also an editorial advisory board member for *Contemporary Pediatrics.* The authors have nothing to disclose in regard to affiliations with or financial interests in any organizations that may have an interest in any part of this article.

Unit 9

UNIT

Prepared by: Claire N. Rubman, *Suffolk County Community College*

Emerging Adulthood

This final unit looks at the skills that we must develop to succeed in the transition from adolescence to adulthood. The first skill is our ability to feel comfortable on our own. This separation from family can be a difficult experience. Luxmoore (2014), a school counselor and psychotherapist, describes the difficulties that some adolescents experience with separation and loneliness. He describes the hostility that sometimes masks the anxiety that many adolescents may experience in high school situations, with the fear of leaving home or with concerns about college acceptances.

Not all adolescents attend college or have employment as their primary concern. Sometimes that transition to adulthood is not so smooth, for example, when pregnancy thrusts teens into the adult role of parenthood. Read about Natasha's personal quest to gain respect as a teenage mother. Learn how she confronted the stigma of being a 17-year-old mother and how she faced the stereotype of being an irresponsible and promiscuous teenager. When society showed disdain for her situation, read about how she channeled her energies in a more positive way in "Bumped Off" by Natasha Vianna (2016).

Continuing to view life from an adolescent's perspective, Jeffrey Arnett (2015) explores how adolescents believe that they are perceived in the workforce. As adolescents struggle to fit in to the adult world, Arnett describes them as "emerging adults" in deference to the fact that teens today take longer to enter adulthood than their cohorts in past decades. Find out why emerging adults may be perceived as lazy or easily distracted in their place of work and why, according to Arnett, they are neither overindulged nor narcissistic—or are they . . .

Article   Prepared by: Claire N. Rubman, *Suffolk County Community College*

Learning to be Together Alone

Learning to be alone is part of growing up. Nick Luxmoore reflects on his role as counsellor in guiding young people through this important stage on the journey to adulthood.

NICK LUXMOORE

Learning Outcomes

After reading this article, you will be able to:

- Explain why Jake wouldn't pick up his sandwich.

- Discuss the concept of "aloneness-togetherness."

- Explain "potential" space.

The theory is relatively straightforward. A baby with an attuned, attentive parent gradually internalizes the presence of that parent, no longer needing them to be physically present to know that she's never forgotten and, in that sense, never alone.[1] With enough of this experience, the baby is likely to grow up comfortable in her own company.

But without enough of the experience, without ever being able to take the attention of other people for granted, a baby/child/young person will grow up feeling nonexistent, terrified of being alone, clinging to other people, shouting for attention and, where necessary, seeking out confrontation as a desperate way to have any kind of relationship.

The fear of aloneness is a constant subtext in the behavior of young people. It's a fear that affects the quality of their relationships because it can make being apart from other people—even temporarily—feel impossible. Whether the aloneness is physical or psychological, young people's anxieties about it seep into everything: unconscious reminders of what they've experienced and don't want to experience again, of an original baby experience when they felt helpless, disconnected from the world, unable to attract anyone's attention, ignored by those around them. Young people dread the prospect of living through anything like that again. They come to counselling expecting to learn how to have happier, loving, more fulfilling relationships.

They don't come to learn how to get better at being alone. And yet the quality of their relationships will always be informed by this ability to be alone.

Jake's dropped his sandwich in the school corridor, where it lies messily. I ask him to pick it up. He looks at me fiercely: "Why should I?" "Because it's going to get trodden on." "So? I don't care," he says, "I don't want it!"

No doubt he worries that being seen by his friends to scoop up a soggy sandwich from the floor will be vaguely humiliating but there's a part of him that simply won't take responsibility for this most mundane of incidents. To pick up the sandwich would be a brief but solitary experience. He'd rather get into trouble, which will give him a prolonged social experience involving arguments with me and possibly with other members of staff.

It's a tiny incident and, of course, there's a lot more to know about Jake's relationship with authority figures. But young people feel alone in all sorts of daily situations and often struggle to deal with the experience. They range from the mundane—getting up in the morning ("Do I have to?"), to doing your homework ("Do I have to?")—to the more dramatic—going to a party can provoke huge anxieties of aloneness: "When I get there, will anyone talk to me? Can I rely on my friends to be there?" These are situations where, however supportive the people around you may be, no one can do it for you: you're on your own, obliged to take responsibility for your own life.

Sensing how much this disturbs young people, parents sometimes use aloneness as a threat and punishment—isolating or sending young people to their rooms, taking away their phones. (Schools and prisons have always used aloneness as a threat.) As a result, there are some young people who grow up to be compliant, desperate to please, doing anything to avoid aloneness being imposed on them. At the other end of the spectrum, there are young people who are never left alone by anxious parents and, as a result, never get the chance to practice being alone. And there are other young people who grow up with aloneness as their modus vivendi, avoiding eye contact, staying on the margins, keeping quiet. No one has ever taken any notice of them; they become so accustomed to being alone that the thought of company is terrifying. For them, relationships involving trust and intimacy are threatening rather than comforting or reassuring.

Merger and Separation

From the moment we're born, we're negotiating a pathway between merger and separation. Initially, that negotiation is with a mother or parent figure: we want to be close to her, to be intimate and trusting, but at the same time, we want to be independent, in need of no one, autonomous, solitary, proud. Gradually, we start learning where she ends and we begin and, in so doing, we start making sense of the world, making meaning. Ogden writes that " . . . meaning requires difference, a dynamic relationship between an idea and that which it is not."[2] We learn that our mother has her own identity, that she's no longer an extension of us, that she's a person with a will of her own and not just an experience. We can affect her but can't control her. Phillips writes about the developmental importance of frustration: a child who is never frustrated never learns the limits of what can and can't be controlled.[3]

Caught up in all this, young people scorn the extremes of merger and separation: the shy boy still wholly dependent on his mummy and the loner incapable of relationships. Most young people give their parents mixed messages: "I want you with me!" and "I don't want you with me!" They're practicing, discovering how much separation, how much aloneness they can tolerate.

So how do counsellors and psychotherapists help young people get better at being alone? How do they help them learn where one person ends and another begins? How do they help them learn to be intimate and trusting while remaining independent and able to take personal responsibility?

Seventeen-year-old Annie sits with me and howls, tears all over her face. "Why?" she wails. "Why?" Normally articulate, her 17-year-old words have been replaced by noises of bewilderment, fear, frustration: "Why?"

She's asking why people behave toward her as they do. I could say, "Because that's what they're like, Annie. Sometimes they don't understand. Sometimes they don't think. They don't realize that what they're saying affects other people." I could say all this but, right now, it would be pointless. She wouldn't hear. So I say nothing. I sit with her and wait. In effect, she's reminding herself of what she always knew: that there's nothing to be done, that this is how the world is, that we might have

other people with us—in this case, a counsellor—which might feel fine but never takes away the brute fact that we're on our own, in relationships with lots of people while also being alone.

At the moment, it seems as if this normally articulate 17-year-old person has become a 17-day-old, 17-month-old infant, unable to speak, terrified of the world and wanting to be scooped up in a parent's arms and comforted. Other 17-year olds might regress into complete silence or might, as a grandiose defence against aloneness, start hurling things around. Annie simply howls. I could scoop her up with comforting words but I judge that, for now, she can bear this panic with me alongside, implicitly supportive but in the background: part of her life but never able to change it.

Being with young people in counselling is like being a parent with a baby, constantly judging when to intervene and when to let the baby discover things for himself. Newborn babies need a parent to intervene most of the time, taking charge, making all the practical decisions. But there are also times when the parent simply sits with the newborn, reflecting back his sounds and facial expressions, extending them and adding new ones. There are times when the parent judges that the baby can be left for a minute to gaze at the ceiling, while they go to make a cup of coffee. Leave the baby for too long and she'll panic; never leave the baby and she'll only ever recognize the face and voice of the parent. The aim is to hold the baby securely in a relationship while also giving her opportunities to explore for herself. Parents never stop making judgments about when and how much is enough: how much relationship and how much aloneness a baby can tolerate.

Aloneness–Togetherness

Hobson writes about "aloneness–togetherness" where, in a therapeutic relationship, "there is an apprehension of distinction and of mutuality, of autonomy and of reciprocity, of identity and of sharing."[4]

Young people bring to counselling an experience of "aloneness–togetherness" in their lives so far. At the extremes, some will come expecting to get nothing whatsoever back from a counsellor and others will expect the counsellor to do all the work. Annie brings to counselling a perfectly adequate experience of aloneness-togetherness, which will have been developing from the beginning of her life. She can listen and she can talk; she can initiate and she can allow me to initiate. It's just that, from time to time, when life gets tough, she panics, and when she panics she regresses, temporarily like a baby.

"Why?" she asks, glaring. "Why can't they understand? Surely, they know what it's like when people say things about you that aren't true? Surely, they've been through that themselves? So why?"

As a 17-year-old, she knows perfectly well that people can be cruel as well as kind. But as a 17-day-old baby or 17-month-old child, she can't answer her question. Appealing to a 17-day-old baby's rational mind ("Well, it's because people can be cruel as well as kind, Annie . . .") would indeed be pointless. However, she's starting to rediscover her words. It's as if she's growing up again, leaving behind her howling, panic-stricken baby-state. "I suppose there's no answer," she volunteers. "People are just bastards!"

"It's tough," I say. "Tough when people behave badly."

The context is important. In a few weeks' time, Annie will be taking exams, and after that our sessions will finish because she'll be leaving school. For her, the prospect of aloneness is everywhere, from going into the exam hall on her own, her academic life in her hands, to leaving school and (as she says) the "whole weirdness" of that. For most young people, leaving school throws up old anxieties about leaving mother figures.[5] In the weeks and months before leaving, they regress: they feel like giving up; they fall out with their friends; they panic. So it's not surprising that Annie is revisiting anxieties about aloneness at this time in her life. It is as if she's a baby, wondering all over again, "Does anyone notice me, hear me? Does anyone understand me, think about me? Am I worth anything to anyone?"

She wipes her face. "I know there's nothing you can do. I know I have to deal with it . . ." I ask, "What's it like when you're alone, Annie?" "Fine, most of the time," she says, "except when no one's replying to my texts. Or when they've all gone out somewhere and they haven't invited me." "What does it feel like?" "Like no one wants to be with me. Like I'm worthless. Like I don't exist . . ." Again she looks panic-stricken. "Can we not talk about this?" I explain that I'm asking because being alone can feel horrible and we tend to think that we're the only people feeling it. "But it's important to be alone sometimes," I say, "not because it's good to have horrible experiences, but because in lots of ways we are alone and have to get used to it. In our relationship here, in this room, we're together but also alone. Sometimes we might feel very together and very connected and at other times we might feel very alone and disconnected. That's normal. It's a bit like being connected to another person and alone."

Playing Together

Winnicott would describe us as playing together.[6] Like a parent and child, we take turns, sometimes anticipating each other, sometimes frustrating each other. It's what he calls the "potential" or "intermediate" space wherein the counsellor and client try things out, practicing being together and being apart, understanding each other and not understanding each other. If a young person begins a counselling relationship in a baby-state,

the counsellor will—like a parent—need to keep control, initiating the conversations and steering them in certain directions in anticipation of the young person's need. But as the young person grows up within the relationship, the power will increasingly need to be negotiated and shared as the young person learns to bear the ups and downs of the relationship, with all its satisfactions and limitations. In this sense, the young person is learning what it feels like to be alone sometimes (frustrated, relaxed, angry, calm, lost, happy) while still connected. At the end of each session, he or she goes away, physically alone but remembered, as if the counsellor were saying, "See you next week! I'll be thinking of you."

Sometimes young people regress and grow up again within the space of a single counselling session. In response to my comment about being connected and alone, Annie says that she understands. "I worry that I'm not normal, though. I mean, you don't see other people worrying all the time about stupid things, do you?" I suggest to her that they might worry in private. "I doubt it!" she says. "Other people are just better at dealing with stuff." She's tussling, challenging me as an independent 17-year-old. In Winnicott's terms, we're playing together as adults: Annie's no longer my baby and I'm no longer her parent.

I say that I admire her ability to be honest about how scared she feels. "You mean, when I come in here and lose the plot?" "No, I mean when you're being honest about how you feel and about how scary things are." "They are scary," she says. "Especially when bad things happen and there's nothing you can do." Her grandmother died of cancer nine months ago. I ask if that's what she's referring to. "Not just that," she says, "but everything. All the crap . . ."

For babies, the world is a mother who does or doesn't make things safe. But for a sophisticated 17-year-old, the world has become a whole set of variables: some good, some bad; some within the young person's control, some not; some understandable and some that make no sense whatsoever, like people dying. Annie's also aware of an existential aloneness. ". . . All the crap in the world that doesn't make sense, that's pointless . . ."

I say nothing. She's quiet, thinking.

Silence can be disturbing at the start of counselling relationships. For those young people with little or no internalized sense of being connected to other people, the threat of nonexistence is ever present and the need for another person's verbal presence is desperate. An ability to tolerate silence in counselling is an ability to tolerate aloneness. When they feel connected, young people can bear silence. When they don't feel connected, they can't. My silence with Annie feels comfortable at the moment but all that may change. I break the silence myself sometimes, as evidence that our relationship is fluid, mutual, not bound by rigid rules, that we share responsibility for initiating conversation.

I remind her that we have three more meetings before she leaves school. Still she says nothing, still thinking. Then, she starts telling me about an old film she's seen. A teenage girl and her much younger brother are lost in the Australian desert after their father tries to kill them. They get more and more lost until they meet an Aboriginal boy who's on "walkabout," forced to survive by himself as part of his initiation into adulthood. He teaches them to survive before eventually leading them back to the city. I ask what made her think of this film.

"It's quite scary at first," she says, "because they're lost and you think they're going to die. And the girl's trying her best but she hasn't got a clue. And then, at the end of the film, she's grown up and living in the city with a really boring husband and you can see her thinking about the past and what happened when they were alone in the desert and how she misses it. How it was just her and her brother and the Aboriginal boy and they didn't really need anyone else. They were fine on their own."

I ask her if she feels like the girl in the film. She laughs at me. "God," she says, "you're such a counsellor sometimes!"

References

1. Winnicott DW. The maturational processes and the facilitating environment. London: The Hogarth Press; 1965.
2. Ogden TH. The matrix of the mind: Object relations and the psychoanalytic dialogue. Northvale, NJ: Jason Aronson Inc.; 1986.
3. Phillips A. Missing out: In praise of the unlived life. London: Hamish Hamilton; 2012.
4. Hobson RF. Forms of feeling: The heart of psychotherapy. London: Routledge; 1985.
5. Luxmoore N. Feeling like crap: Young people and the meaning of self-esteem. London: Jessica Kingsley Publishers; 2008.
6. Winnicott DW. Playing and reality. London: Routledge; 1971.

Critical Thinking

1. Luxmore suggests that adolescents sometimes worry in "private"—what does worry "look like," private or public?
2. How do you cope with being "alone"?
3. What advice would you give to adolescents who are developing their sense of autonomy?

Internet References

Adolescent Home-leaving and the Transition to Adulthood
https://www.ncbi.nlm.nih.gov/pmc/articles/PMC3785225/

Leaving Home . . . a Teenage Dilemma
http://linguapress.com/intermediate/leaving-home.htm

Letting Go of Your Teen
http://www.focusonthefamily.com/parenting/teens/letting-go-of-yourteen/letting-go-of-your-teen

What Are the Laws on Teenagers Leaving Home
http://teens.lovetoknow.com/What_Are_the_Laws_on_Teenagers_Leaving_Home

Young Adults Delay Leaving Family Home
https://www.theguardian.com/society/2009/apr/15/twentysomethings-staying-at-home-social-trends

---

NICK LUXMOORE is a school counsellor and psychotherapist and author. Annie is a fictionalized character drawn from the many young people he meets in his work.

Article   Prepared by: Claire N. Rubman, *Suffolk County Community College*

Bumped Off

What Will It Take to Destigmatize Teen Motherhood?

Natasha Vianna

Learning Outcomes

After reading this article, you will be able to:

- Describe what contributes to a "culture of shame."

- Explain the function and purpose of "#noteenshame."

When I gave birth to my child in 2005, I was 17-years-old and only a few months into my senior year of high school. After 20 hours of painful labor, I laid in a hospital bed struggling to remember how I got from my school locker to a maternity floor.

I pushed and cried until my daughter was pulled from inside me, untangled from her umbilical cord, and placed gently on my chest. Shaking in fear and pain, I wrapped my arms around her skin and held her close. As the midwife began to tug on the infant's placenta, I wept in panic. Had I just given life to the person who would ruin mine?

Today, I understand that the moment was not one of regret—it was the moment when I began to confront the stigma I would face as a teenage mother. Reproductive-justice advocates routinely criticize conservatives for shaming young women for their reproductive choices, but when these same advocates frame teen pregnancy and parenthood as a universally negative outcome of sex—to be avoided at all costs—they are contributing to a culture of shame.

Well-established organizations, such as the National Campaign to Prevent Teen and Unplanned Pregnancy (NCPTUP), have implicitly participated in the development of stigma for teenage parents. Framing teenage pregnancy as a pathological condition and focusing on the "public costs of teenage childbearing" is degrading for both teen parents and their children.

In 2014, there were 250,000 births to U.S. women ages 15–19. More than 80 percent of these were the result of unintended pregnancies. MTV hits *Teen Mom* and *16 and Pregnant* allow the entertainment industry to profit from vulnerable young women going through stressful, life-changing journeys—with help from the NCPTUP, which consults on both shows. As a result, pregnancy-prevention organizations are able to drive the national conversation about teen pregnancy with these stories, edited for reality-TV ratings, which help reinforce stereotypes of teen moms as immature and unequipped.

Pop culture has rarely used storylines of teen mothers to go against stereotypes. *Gilmore Girls*, which began airing in 2000, might have been the first family-oriented series to focus on a successful woman who was a former teen parent. Despite assumptions about young, unwed mothers and their children, the show portrays Lorelai Gilmore and her daughter, Rory, as incredibly driven and accomplished. Together, they defy expectations and define happiness for themselves. It's one of the only shows I can think of where teen parenting leads to a positive, even enviable future. Granted, that future belongs to a white woman from a wealthy family. Young moms from less privileged backgrounds, as well as teen moms of color like me, are still waiting for positive reflections of ourselves on TV.

Stigma blocked my ability to feel valued as a real person in our society; I felt that people saw me as trashy and my body as damaged goods. Feelings like that are reinforced when society judges teen moms for not marrying or staying with their partners. And too many of us are conditioned to accept a predestined fate of poverty and failure. These are the ways in which stigma creeps into our lives and rarely leaves us.

The pervasive messages about how harmful teen pregnancy is and how promiscuous and irresponsible teen moms are, a characterization rarely used to describe teen fathers, promote discrimination in the very places teen parents should feel safe, like our doctors' offices and our schools. Just two weeks after giving birth to my daughter, I was coerced by a doctor into accepting an injection of Depo-Provera, a controversial provider-administered shot with documented negative side effects. Despite explaining that I had not consented to birth control and was not ready to make a decision, she returned with the injection anyway. To that doctor, my choice did not matter because my young parenthood proved that I was incapable of making responsible choices on my own.

When I returned to school, my guidance counselor refused to help me apply for college. Her assumption was that because, statistically, girls like me are less likely to graduate high school, it would be a waste of her time to help me prepare for college. This wasn't a unique situation. The Bill and Melinda Gates Foundation recently reported that roughly ⅓ of girls who dropped out of high school cited pregnancy or parenthood as the leading reason. However, those same girls reported that they were doing well in school but did not feel like they had the support from their school and educators that they needed to stay. Teen parents are left to flounder on their own in a system that makes assumptions about what we are and aren't capable of doing.

It wasn't until years after my daughter was born that I could objectively look at my own situation, and it finally clicked in that it wasn't my teenage pregnancy that made part of my life harder, it was the disdain from a society that painted moms like me as irresponsible and undeserving of respect. So I decided to do something about it. Through social media, I connected with a national cohort called Strong Families led by Forward Together, a community-focused organization that works on both policy and culture change meant to shift the way people think about and support families like mine. Through genuine allyship with them, I was able to unpack and redefine what it meant to be a teenage mom. In 2013, with their help, I cofounded #NoTeenShame, a project centering the use of new technologies to shift the way our culture frames, talks about, and impacts teenage pregnancy.

#NoTeenShame started as a series of conference calls between seven young mothers and Strong Families, but we saw an opportunity to use it to shift power back into the hands of young mothers. Working with an incredible cohort allowed us to push back against the judgment we faced. We had the opportunity to speak openly and freely about our lives, with support from Strong Families and each other.

Some of us were victims of abuse, some of us faced unintended pregnancies, some of us intentionally became parents, some of us were raised by teen parents ourselves, and many of us had issues that intersected with our lives before we became pregnant. We experienced lack of access to healthcare, obstacles as immigrants, fear of reproductive coercion, inability to afford abortion, and misinformation due to our LGBTQ identities, among other challenges. But all of us were impacted by the stigma of being a teenage mother in the United States. #NoTeenShame allowed us to share our experiences with each other and support each other in the face of shaming messages and cultural assumptions.

#NoTeenShame promotes the idea that teenage mothers are not irresponsible and promiscuous, but rather valuable people in our society who deserve recognition, respect, and support. We want reproductive rights organizations to stop treating teenage pregnancy as a misfortune and framing it as universally negative. Today, we fight for a culture that embraces families of all structures, affordable and safe reproductive services, and access to high-quality, comprehensive, accurate, LGBTQ-inclusive, culturally sensitive, trauma-informed, and stigma-free sexuality education for youth. Teen parenthood is very much a reproductive- justice issue, a matter of access to support, resources, autonomy, agency, and choice—not a pathological condition that needs to be aggressively prevented at any and all costs.

Critical Thinking

1. How can society empower teenage mothers without endorsing teenage pregnancy?
2. Why are teenage mothers stigmatized?
3. How would you respond if your teenage daughter told you that she wanted to become pregnant?

Internet References

Pregnant at 14, Valedictorian at 17, Local Teen Mom Put Herself through College and Law School
http://www.timesfreepress.com/news/life/entertainment/story/2011/jul/05/she-never-said-i-cant/53289/

Success Stories—Teen Outreach Pregnancy
https://www.teenoutreachaz.org/donate/success-stories/

Teen Pregnancy in the United States
https://www.cdc.gov/teenpregnancy/about/

Trends in Teen Pregnancy and Childbearing
https://www.hhs.gov/ash/oah/adolescent-development/reproductive-health-and-teen-pregnancy/teen-pregnancy-and-childbearing/trends/index.html

When Your Teen Is Having a Baby
http://kidshealth.org/en/parents/teen-pregnancy.html

Winning the Campaign to Curb Teen Pregnancy
https://www.nytimes.com/2016/07/19/opinion/winning-the-campaign-to-curb-teen-pregnancy.html

Natasha Vianna is the co-founder of #NoTeenShame. She is a community builder and reproductive justice activist.